FILMMAKERS SERIES
edited by
ANTHONY SLIDE

1. *James Whale*, by James Curtis. 1982
2. *Cinema Stylists*, by John Belton. 1983
3. *Harry Langdon*, by William Schelly. 1982
4. *William A. Wellman*, by Frank Thompson. 1983
5. *Stanley Donen*, by Joseph Casper. 1983
6. *Brian De Palma*, by Michael Bliss. 1983
7. *J. Stuart Blackton*, by Marian Blackton Trimble. 1985
8. *Martin Scorsese and Michael Cimino*, by Michael Bliss. 1985
9. *Franklin J. Schaffner*, by Erwin Kim. 1985
10. *D. W. Griffith and the Biograph Company*, by Cooper C. Graham et al. 1985
11. *Some Day We'll Laugh: An Autobiography*, by Esther Ralston. 1985
12. *The Memoirs of Alice Guy Blaché*, 2nd ed., translated by Roberta and Simone Blaché. 1996
13. *Leni Riefensta*
14. *Robert Florey,*
15. *Henry King's*
16. *Aldous Huxley*
17. *Five American*
18. *Cinematograph* nna Kate Sterling. 198
19. *Stars of the Sil*
20. *Twentieth Cer*
21. *Highlights and* *m*, by Charles G. Clarke. 1989
22. *I Went That-* Harry L. Fraser; edited by Wh 1990
23. *Order in the U* C. Cumbow. 1990 (out of print;
24. *The Films of*
25. *Hollywood Be*
26. *The Charm of* eeler Winston Dixon. 1991
27. *Lionheart in* with Katherine Orrison. 199
28. *William Desm*
29. *The Films of* 91
30. *Hollywood H* *Story Ever Told,"* by Ken Darb
31. *The Films of* hy, by Wheeler Winston Dixon. 1992

Hollywood in Wide Angle

How Directors View Filmmaking

Jack Rothman

Filmmakers Series, No. 115

THE SCARECROW PRESS, INC.
Lanham, Maryland • Toronto • Oxford
2004

SCARECROW PRESS, INC.

Published in the United States of America
by Scarecrow Press, Inc.
A wholly owned subsidiary of
The Rowman & Littlefield Publishing Group, Inc.
4501 Forbes Boulevard, Suite 200, Lanham, Maryland 20706
www.scarecrowpress.com

PO Box 317
Oxford
OX2 9RU, UK

British Library Cataloguing in Publication Information Available

Library of Congress Cataloging-in-Publication Data

Hollywood in wide angle : how directors view filmmaking / Jack Rothman.
    p. cm. — (Filmmakers series ; no. 115)
  Includes bibliographical references and index.
  ISBN 0-8108-5015-X (alk. paper)
  1. Motion picture industry—California—Los Angeles. 2. Motion
pictures—Production and direction. I. Rothman, Jack. II. Series.
PN1993.5.U65H594 2004
384'.8'0979494—dc22

                                                    2004009401

To Judy Rothman,
my wife and undaunted editor in the trenches; her many
supporting roles command my critical acclaim

Contents

~

An Excerpt at the Coffee Table:
Encounter with Director Gil Cates

Jack Rothman: Directors have been telling me that things are different now. Can you describe the current filmmaking environment for me?

Gil Cates: In the last ten years, studios haven't been much attracted to the stories in which I am interested. They seem to be engrossed in violence, sex, buddy pictures, the Mafia and gross-out humor. If you were to open up the movie section of the *L.A. Times* and find forty movies listed there and ask me how many of these movies would I like to see, let alone make, I'd be lucky to say maybe three or four. In the 1960s and '70s, if we tried the same experiment, I probably would have said twenty-five.

JR: What do you think accounts for the change?

GC: We live in a society . . . of unbridled greed, and the studios are a big part of that. Huge conglomerates control film studios, which are only a small part of the corporate empire, and the bottom line is central to their thinking. Back in the 1960s and '70s, if a company made a profit of 5 percent a year, maybe 6 percent, they thought it was great. Now, if a company makes 10 percent one year, they want to make 15 percent the next year. If they make 20 percent, they want to make 30 percent. Nothing is enough now. . . . Where will it end?

JR: That's no bed of roses. So what keeps you going?

GC: All I can say is that directing a movie is unique; it is an experience unlike any other. I'm a proud father of four children and two stepchildren, and a grandfather of five; my family means more to me than anything else. I have also been president of

the Directors Guild of America, dean of the University of California's School of Theater, Film, and Television, and produced eleven Academy Award shows. I've had a lot
of unique experiences in my life. But there's nothing like making a movie. It is a
unique, engrossing, and fulfilling experience. . . . It's a narcotic. Anyone who does it
once, willingly, never wants to stop.

JR: Can you make that narcotic thing clear for an outsider like me?

GC: You are in the *god-like* position of creating your own world. Designing it to your
specifications, peopling it to your choosing, determining what is said and to whom. I
tell you, it's an extraordinary privilege to call "Action" on the set. You are talking to
another human being and then say the magic word, "Action," and in some miracu-
lous sense, that person becomes somebody else. Another being is created. The electricians focus the lights, the operator shifts the camera, the grip moves the dolly, and
everything begins happening at once. It's like a beautiful little ballet, totally imaginary and otherworldly. And then you say "Cut," and everything is ordinary again,
everyone becomes the person they were before the magic happened . . . and you have
a cup of coffee and plan the next shot. It's amazing, utterly amazing. I've never experienced anything like it.

~

Preview: The Ivy Tower Meets the Silver Screen

The system is built on lying. Everyone lies to each other. It's like a poker game. Almost all the lying goes to the studio's benefit, though. If you say a movie will take 60 days to make properly, the studio thinks to itself that that's right, but gives you 50 days. Then the movie goes over budget in production. Now, there's a psychological thing the studio has over you. The fact that you are over budget makes them somehow smarter about the content and ending of the film.

—Walter Hill

Why should a well-set university professor and social researcher like me choose to delve into the workings of Hollywood? Why attempt to put an evasive, perpetually moving target under a microscope using many of the same empirical methodologies akin to a university research study? Was I punch-drunk from staring at too many statistical print-outs? Or were Hollywood directors and the motion picture industry-at-large ripe and fertile for an intensive, invasive look? And if so, would an industry rampant with fear and the strangest of bedfellows be willing to speak openly and unload on a stranger, without the usual fanfare and make-believe, if not spill its collective guts?

But I should tell you first what got me started on this project.

Like many Americans—in actuality, a great many people around the world—I've been fascinated with film and moviemaking all of my life. My very name is mixed up with the movies. My mother adored going to the pictures, and at the time I was born Jackie Coogan was all the rage—America's favorite rascal playing "The Kid" to Charlie Chaplin's doting tramp. Although my birth certificate announced my given names to be "Seymour Jacob," my mother took to calling me "Jackie." And Jack has stuck, always, even on my passport and Navy discharge papers.

I lived across the street from the Glenwood Theater in Ridgewood in Queens, New York, and that became my hideout and refuge. Many a late afternoon, when I was lost for a second go-round in a Western or Fred Astaire flick, my father had to extricate me and lead me home for dinner. The manager and projectionists would come into my father's candy store for a soda or newspaper and I would horse around with them.

That's how I got my first full-time job one summer when I was fifteen. It was at the Alhambra, an old-fashioned ornate palace, where I was usher, ticket taker, and general go-fer and troubleshooter. With a flashlight, I led people down the dark aisles to their seats and had the unenviable assignment of toning down the raucous voices of kids filling the house to see Saturday morning "serials" and cartoons. I often helped open the theater in the morning and clean up and close it after midnight. It was this movie job that led to acquiring my first working papers and applying for my now venerable Social Security card.

Movie dates were where I got my first chance to hold a girl's hand and see what kissing like-on-the-screen feels like. After World War II it was at out-of-the-way art houses that I discovered French and Italian film as the counterpart of treasured novels and museum pieces. Through it all, I was drawn to that faraway, mythical-seeming domain called Hollywood, long regarded as the epicenter of the film industry.

But not until 1984, when I moved to West Los Angeles to take up a professorship at UCLA teaching community organization in what is now the School of Public Policy and Social Research, could I fully indulge my private little interest. Hollywood was now a nearby place, its geographical presence not only furnishing evidence of real-life inhabitants but also exuding a pervasive style and state of mind.

Around virtually any corner or down any boulevard, movie stars often could be spotted in passing limos and Jaguars. Charles Durning and I shared the same local supermarket in Westwood near the university. Occasionally I encountered famous directors lunching in restaurants I frequented. (They're right. The camera does put ten pounds on you.)

Moreover, I had discovered that on the UCLA campus, a little less than the distance from the concession stand to a theater's big screen, was a renowned film school that focused on training professionals for a variety of jobs in the film and television industries. UCLA's Department of Film and Television provides students hands-on involvement that can range from acting and directing, to scriptwriting and film editing; from costume design and set construction, to cinematography and the creation of special effects. This beehive of active learning also contains a wonderful library that specializes in film-connected books, publications, photographs, and archived memorabilia.

A curious researcher, ever in pursuit of that thing called truth, I began hanging out there at times. I also sat in on courses in the film department and UCLA Extension, a division of the university that provides an excellent after-hours outlet for continuing education for industry professionals. The cinema bug bit deeper. Call me a moviestruck university scholar. I fell into working as a production assistant, volunteering my time—between lectures, writing, and research—in the shooting of a film. In all this, I was consciously renewing an old love for the movies by combining it with an intention to apply, somehow, my own brand of scholarly expertise to some particular corner of filmmaking that needed elucidation.

All the while, it struck me that something is missing in the academic solar system. There's a sociology of education, a psychology of medicine, an anthropology of religion, a social psychology of politics; the list is long. Yet in those general fields of study, no specialized discipline has been focused on filmmaking and the movie industry. Perhaps the social sciences haven't come around as yet to taking film seriously because it's historically new as an art, craft, and entertainment form—perhaps also because it's so saturated with hoopla and crassness.

Ironically, however, more than other human institutions studied, this one enterprise has had, and will surely continue to have, vast influence in shaping the fundamental attitudes and worldviews of millions upon millions of people in the United States and around the globe. Yet much of what most people know about filmmaking reaches them through the mainstream mass media—hardly a hotbed of profundity.

L.A. Times—"Shame on the Sham"

Hollywood! It's tough for anyone to get a real handle on the place. Filmmaking is an exercise in creating illusions, and the illusions cut a wide swath. A film director I interviewed for this book spoke of this phenomenon at length. "Hollywood," he said, "is based on lies—lies they call fantasy. For example, time is compressed and manipulated. An actor says, 'I'll see you tomorrow,' and pulls back his chair. Cut! Immediately he's seen getting out of a car and walking up to a house to knock on a door. In a split second, it's tomorrow, or later in the day."

In this director's experience, industry people find it hard to draw a clean line between the contrived and the genuine. "Now, since film basically is a deception, this condition seems to have been internalized on some level by the executives who run Hollywood. They also dwell in deception. They carry the falsification inherent in film into the whole business of making film."

When I began studying the current status of Hollywood in terms of its salient and underlying structures, this was just the type of telling comment I had expected. Curiously, it came from someone who worked in the film industry and presumably loved it, despite its fraudulence, uncertainties, and turbulence. And there *lies* the rub. (No pun.)

Hollywood in Wide Angle: How Directors View Filmmaking takes a look beyond all that Hollywood-style obfuscation to grasp what is real. Sometimes aspects of an uncovered or revealed reality can be disenchanting, even distasteful—like finding ants scurrying in your popcorn just after you've settled into your seat to see the movie. Yet shouldn't we know what's there, especially if our thinking, our feelings, even the lives we live are being affected by this potent reality?

I'm not the only person aware of knowledge gaps concerning the making and marketing of movies. A four-part series carried in the *Los Angeles Times* in February 2001 made clear the need for authentic information. When it hit the stands, the series shook the filmmaking community to its evasive core by documenting the extent to which mendacity pervades the Hollywood scene.

Not that fact-skewing is new in the industry. Anyone with even the most casual contact with show business, or who has dipped into novels like Nathanael West's *The Day of the Locust* or Budd Schulberg's *What Makes Sammy Run?* or seen Robert Altman's picture *The Player* or the TV series *Project Greenlight* is well aware of Hollywood's legendary hypocritical and hyperbolic ways.

The difference here was the detailed evidence put in stark print by *Los Angeles Times* lead media critic David Shaw and a team of investigative aides.[1] And this was current events, not the stuff of history.

I found the usual revelations in the piece: when it serves their agenda du jour, people concoct stories about stars angling for parts, executives finagle the results of test screenings, and everyone gossips about the revolving doors at the executive suites. It's routine to "fudge," "embellish," and "minimize." But for me, the most telling disclosure coming from a newspaper was coverage on how the media, including the *L.A. Times*, are engaged in a symbiotic tango with this industry that regularly spews out disinformation.

The media are obsessed with opening weekend box-office grosses, in part because the studios are. Every studio wants to claim the top movie of the week, hoping that people will then flock to it. Studios exaggerate the number of prints in distribution, the number of screens showing the film, and average revenue per screen. And the media simply regurgitate these figures that are handed to them. Further reading convinced me that an abundance of the statistics in the industry only serve to quantify the ubiquity and magnitude *of the deceit.*

The media also appear to be obsessed with film budgets. To make their movies look profitable, studios habitually scale down reportage of the cost numbers to make revenues look better. Hollywood's notorious "creative accounting" permits this. Yet the media use up large volumes of space with this smoke-and-mirrors information.

Furthermore, the *L.A. Times* observed that since the media are dependent on millions of dollars in advertising revenue from the studios, they are, of course, reluctant to offend their benefactors by unpleasant coverage. Fearful of losing future access, reporters chime in by doing softball interviews of superstars.

Certain events taking place around the time of the *L.A. Times* exposé gave it further credence. Peter Bart, an editor at *Variety*, owned up to pitching a script to a studio, a clear conflict of interest for a media person.[2] Longtime *Hollywood Reporter* columnist George Christy was suspended and later resigned, accused of receiving fraudulent screen-acting credits from a producer crony. He allegedly had wanted those credits to qualify for health and pension benefits, unearned, from the Screen Actors Guild.

Details surfaced on the extent to which studios use press junkets to influence the reviews of movie critics. Throughout any given year, studios invite up to two hundred critics from around the country to New York or Los Angeles for a screening and to interview the stars. These "blurbmeisters" receive free airfare, hotel accommodations, ground transportation, per diems for meals, and even gift bags. After all this special treatment, they aren't obligated to write a positive review—although, when bedazzled, it's likely they're apt to be so inclined. While the jury is still out on whether any publicity, favorable or unfavorable, is good publicity, these entertainment reporters and critics are expected, at the very least, to mention the movie and generate buzz.

Of course, there are solid discussions in books by academics and scholars: historians like Robert Sklar (*Movie-Made America*), social analysts like Neil Gabler (*An Empire of Their Own*), and sociologists like Emanuel Levy (*Small-town America in Film*)—who has also doubled as a movie reviewer for *Variety*. Critical studies departments of film schools add to the output. And you can always count on an Andrew Sarris, J. Hoberman, or Richard Schickel for incisive commentaries.[3]

Insiders have added to the information pool by writing anecdotal books telling all, or a lot, in revealing ways. There's producer Lynda Obst's *Hello, He Lied*; screenwriter William Goldman's *Which Lie Did I Tell?*; and producer Julia Phillips's *You'll Never Eat Lunch in This Town Again*. *Variety* editor Peter Bart has also tried his hand with *The Gross* and, switching to fiction, his collection of short stories, *Dangerous Company: Dark Tales from Tinseltown*.

Still, solid truth telling and analysis is scarce among the billions of words lavished on film every year. The *L.A. Times* series also came to the conclusion that media information is not only faulty, but trivial. Specifically, "coverage of the process of moviemaking, of the culture of Hollywood, and of where movies fit into the larger culture of America has become more narrow and superficial." Critic David Shaw lamented that frequent preoccupation with minutiae and gossip has led to a shift away from "substantive reporting."

It was the challenge, then, of doing some substantive and meaningful reporting on the film culture that brought me to this book.

Putting Hollywood under the Microscope

To be sure, I'm an academic researcher with both a curiosity about what makes communities and institutions tick and a solid background in factfinding research. So I decided to see if I could add a few droplets of objective information to the murky knowledge pool on contemporary filmmaking as both art and industry. But beware: there's a curve in the road ahead and you may hear the tires squealing. Actually, that's the sound of the language of social research, by nature sober, heavy, and discordant to some ears. I will try to make this noise as light and as halcyon as I can. And I invite you, the reader, to accompany me through the Hollywood labyrinth, using the headlights of empirical inquiry to guide us both through the fog.

In the aggregate, I had, arguably, a pretty good background for taking on this sort of work. When I taught at the University of Pittsburgh, I investigated ethnic neighborhoods that pocket the hillsides of that city. At the University of Michigan, I joined in a study of innovation in the automotive industry, that state's prime bread-and-butter enterprise. In London, I examined the workings of social service departments run by local governments. And in Los Angeles, I have studied the county's Mental Health Department and the Department of Children's Services. Over the years, I've published many scholarly papers and more than twenty books on community organization and social welfare.

Since film had been a long-standing avocational interest of mine, it wasn't much of a flip to make it a professional one now that I lived in Los Angeles. I remembered well how in graduate school at Columbia University I had become enthralled with a unique book on filmmaking, *Hollywood: The Dream Factory*, published in 1950, which presented a ground-breaking dissection of the movie industry.[4] Its author, anthropologist Hortense Powdermaker, having previously studied the Stone Age culture of Melanesia in the southwest Pacific, used the tools of social science to dig more deeply into the Hollywood subculture than I had ever seen done before. This academic pioneer systematically applied the research methods of anthropology to reveal and understand the mores of Hollywood. Her book, which gave the denizens of the Old Hollywood quite a jolt, is still considered a classic work.

But I knew that the Hollywood apparatus of filmmaking had changed drastically over time. Powdermaker would no longer be able to recognize the place. Nor would Louis B. Mayer and his mogul cohorts. The "Dream Factory" has a new structure and is under new management.

When I went about planning my foray into the world of contemporary filmmaking, Powdermaker's book served as my field manual. Her method, based in anthropology, was very broad—total immersion into the Hollywood community, looking at everything and talking openly to the people crossing her path. I would build on her work sociologically. I wanted to pinpoint and structure the areas I needed to look into and the questions I wished to ask. So I examined some of her conclusions and then extrapolated backward to identify the kinds of questions she would have had to ask to invoke the responses she gathered. At the very least, this gave me a point of departure.

To make my project manageable—for I would be working alone and with no outside funding—I decided to concentrate on feature-film directors, both commercial and independent, interviewing them at length and in detail.

But why interview movie directors to find out about the real inner workings of Hollywood? I believed that directors could be extremely valuable informants because of where they stand in the filmmaking community. In one direction, they have to communicate with creative people who are actors and crafts professionals; in the other direction, they have to communicate with managers and finance people who are producers and studio executives. They are poised on a fulcrum that tips alternatingly across the full spectrum of filmmaking. Better than any other group, they might be able to provide a panoramic overview of how movies are made. And they did not disappoint me.

Setting the Lens

Let me explain the methodology I used in conducting this survey. I met with a total of thirty-two directors, whose names are listed in the Directors' Credits appendix to this book. They have a very wide range of backgrounds, credits, and identities. My aim was to come up with a "purposive" (hand-selected rather than random) sample that represented diverse voices across the community of directors. I conducted the interviews over a fourteen-month period in 2001 and 2002. I also did supplementary interviews and solicited contextual information from some fifty additional individuals—actors, people at the Directors Guild of America and the Screen Actors Guild, UCLA faculty and staff, film industry professionals, and library consultants—most of whom are listed in the Supplementary Interviews and Information appendix.

From the start, I saw this project falling into the category designated "exploratory research," geared to producing a set of suggestive trends and patterns, as well as possibilities for further research, rather than ultimate generalizable truth. From my experience with past studies, I knew the sample size was sufficient for that purpose. Ethnographic or qualitative research such as this is particularly common in anthropological investigations but is used across the board among social scientists.[5]

The Directors Guild of America was initially helpful, giving me a list of filmmakers to contact. I had asked them for people from diverse backgrounds who were well informed, articulate, thoughtful, and who might find it interesting or challenging to talk about their work and how it has been affected by the current industry. A few persons on the list agreed to talk with me; others declined. Those I did interview passed along other names, which allowed me to use a "snowballing" procedure to build up to the number of participants sufficient for the survey.

In my core directors' group there was a range in age, from Salvador Carrasco in his early thirties to Delbert Mann in his eighties, who started way back with the Philco Television Playhouse and directed such classics as *Marty* and *Desire Under the Elms*. In experience, there is a range from Nandi Bowie, who has directed one short feature and worked as an assistant director with several outstanding filmmakers, to Gilbert Cates, who has directed dozens of distinguished productions for film, the stage, TV movies, and TV special events, notably Academy Awards programs. Among the thirty-two directors are five women, four African Americans, two Latinos, two Asian Americans, and seven individuals who have strong independent-film backgrounds. The group reflects almost every genre and storytelling mode.

The directors I spoke with—in their homes or mine, in offices, cafés, restaurants, studios, editing rooms, and hotel lobbies—were frank and spontaneous in expressing their opinions and providing information. My judgment is based on more than forty years of conducting research with diverse subjects in many different situations. By now I have a sense, not infallible but pretty good, of when people are giving me genuine answers or are ducking. These directors, who so often must give unstinting heed to actors, producers, agents, studio executives, and others, seemed to welcome talking and unburdening themselves to someone truly interested in hearing them out—someone who wasn't trying to hustle them into a deal and who, hopefully, came over as an informed and responsive listener.

It probably helped, too, that I had said during my initial contact—whether by letter or by phone, which varied according to the circumstances—that I wasn't interested in sensationalism or rumor-mongering. I offered them full confidentiality, assuring them that I wasn't on a mission to embarrass or expose anyone to sell my book.

I also told them straight out that I wasn't an industry insider—and considered that both an advantage and disadvantage. It meant, in theory and practice, that I wasn't a captive of ongoing definitions and perceptions and could look at the whole situation with fresh eyes. But at the same time, I would sometimes need, and ask for, rounded and maybe elementary descriptions and explanations.

Always in this kind of project a crucial issue is how to make data-gathering systematic. In the survey of directors, I used what researchers call a *semi-structured, open-ended questionnaire*—one that forgoes a checklist and instead encourages people to talk freely in responding to a predetermined set of prompts. I carried them out conversationally and with give and take. Most lasted between an hour and two hours. I tape-recorded all the interviews and personally transcribed them.

I wanted to know from each of the interviewees what they see as the most pressing problems that directors face, what they consider the attributes of truly gifted directors, and how they think the quality of American film can be raised. I asked the directors for their views and experiences related to crucial issues, such as emerging digital technology, opportunities for women and minorities in directorial roles, whether screenwriters should be on the set, and how directors can optimize their artistic freedom in the absence of final-cut rights. Their cumulative responses, I hoped, would provide a wide-angle view of Hollywood and filmmaking, including the immediate job of directors and the broader social and economic forces that bear down on how they carry out their work. The itemized questions, sometimes in combination, break out to form the remaining chapters of the book.

Some of the questions I asked were derived from the Powdermaker model; others had been suggested by faculty colleagues at the UCLA Department of Film and Television. I also included items based on my own reading and curiosity. A copy of the questionnaire is included at the end of this chapter.

A Single Directors' Voice That Doesn't Always Agree with Itself

The bulk of this book sets down the directors' answers in their own words. I have used an anonymous format because I needed to induce directors to consent to meet with me and to answer questions candidly. Readers will understand how some of the directors' strong language would not go over kindly if repeated in the film industry's executive suites. (The preponderance of social research reports use this same anonymous informant approach, which I have used in all my previous books.) My assurance of anonymity worked against attributing specific ideas and statements to specific directors. Occasionally, though, when certain comments were allowed "on the record," I have identified the person—as in the quotes at the top of each chapter—or I let an obvious connection to a person remain transparent.

Using standard questions for each person allowed me to cumulate, collate, and compare data across individuals. I do not simply reproduce the interviews in sequence and in raw form, so my book is different from the multivolume Projections series, *Film-makers on Film-making*, edited by John Boorman and Walter Donohue,[6] and so many other books reporting interviews with film folks. These books contain a series of back-and-forth questions and answers that make for a fragmented thought pattern and an all-too-often choppy read. The standard interview format asks readers to put together all the disparate responses on different topics gathered from individuals and then make sense of them.

My work instead carries out a narrative synthesis of the ideas, trials, and successes of this group of thirty-two working directors. This approach enabled me to summarize, analyze, and critique the material, which is in keeping with a survey format. There is, overall, a flow of anonymous voices in the directors' comments on a particular subject. Thus, I present the directors' responses as a composite whole, rather than detailing a series of spasmodic person-by-person Q&A comments.

This composite, then, appears as a single "director's voice" or stream of consciousness— a composite that often has opposing opinions. The full commentaries are grouped within the areas discussed by the participants, showing the main tendencies, agreements, and disagreements. My intention was to provide this information free of percentages and statistical encumbrances so that the discussion, often multisided and complex, has a smooth narrative feel. With a relatively small sample, this procedure is considered to be suitable or even preferred. I'll hold to that approach with few exceptions. Collectivizing respondent comments into patterns of thought allows readers to focus on ideas without the confusion of jumping from one person to another or one topic to another.

While I kept faithful to the original meaning and context in the polishing process, some editorial input came from me in making transitions, linking ideas, and clarifying language. In each chapter, after reporting illustrative participants' comments, I analyze them and share the conclusions I have drawn. The directors conversed in their ordinary colorful language, not without a sprinkling, quite light, of words consisting of four letters. I have reported their responses as spoken to present a candid and factual report of these conversations.

I have brought a sociological perspective or "way of seeing" to the task of understanding the filmmaking world, drawing on C. Wright Mills's artful phrase in his book *The Sociological Imagination*.[7] But I also strained mightily to keep technical language and academese under rein, including footnotes and other rites of scholarship.

As I trudged with my tape recorder across the Hollywood landscape, sometimes I felt a bit like Powdermaker poking around on one of her exotic Pacific Islands. But instead of meeting up with natives who were unfamiliar and distant, I got to know natives who were *familiar* but distant. It was a thrill and a revelation to make flesh-and-blood contact with people who, up until my encounters, merely had been names scrolling before my eyes in the screen credits of my neighborhood multiplex. From these men and women (augmented by other interviews and long days at the library), I learned a tremendous amount about the culture of Hollywood and the character of film directors.

Familiarity is supposed to breed contempt, but here it forged admiration and respect. I know a social researcher is supposed to be cool and objective about the subjects of his scrutiny. I've striven to accomplish that, and I think my assessment grows out of my scrutiny. But you will be able to arrive at your own conclusions.

You'll see that while using the following questionnaire I have let the voices of the directors—eloquent, perplexed, angry, inspired—tell their own story. And quite a story they tell.

The Questionnaire: Toward Breaking the Silence

1. What are three big problems of directors in filmmaking?
2. What are the qualities of gifted directors?
3. How are directors of most help to actors? Can you illustrate with specific actions on the set?
4. How have directors responded to the advent of new digital techniques for filmmaking?
5. How would you categorize the main types of directors currently in filmmaking? (Think in terms of background, experience, ability, approach, etc.)
6. How do directors attempt to optimize their artistic freedom (for example, control of final cut)?
7. How widely do women and minorities participate as directors? What can be done to expand the level of participation?
8. Do directors think writers should have more input during shooting? That writers should be given more status in filmmaking?
9. What changes would you recommend to raise the quality of American film?
10. Is there anything else you would like to add?

~

CHAPTER ONE

Troubles in Mind

You face immense pressure in trying to accomplish what you think is good work rather than being a traffic cop who moves through the mechanics of getting a movie made. The authority of directors is being attacked on all sides.

—Martha Coolidge

THE SCENE: EXT. DAY. SUMMER. Not a cloud in the sky. A yellow poppy brightly basks in the noon sun. As the camera widens out, a horse-drawn carriage enters from the right. The carriage pulls up to stop before a "new" prairie home. A hoop-skirted newlywed, circa 1860, is escorted off the carriage and into the arms of her dapper farmer beau. Love is in the air . . . So is thunder! *Wait a minute. Stop. Hold it! Where in the script does it call for thunder? And what's this on my hand—Rain droplets! Who ordered rain? CUT!*

The director faces a staggering number of challenges and decisions in a single working day—such as beginning with a jolting phone call at dawn with news that outdoors it is beginning to pour, together with frantic queries about which scene to shoot first, and "Can a covered wagon do in place of a horse-drawn carriage since the props guy couldn't find one but managed to track down the other?" Oh hell, *let's call the whole thing off . . .*

Problems, Problems: Two Bags Full

Back in 1973, Elia Kazan expounded on the extraordinary repertoire of skills and roles required of a film director: construction-gang foreman, psychoanalyst, poet, animal trainer, hypnotist, PR operative, jewel thief . . . on and on. In "On What Makes a Director," a discourse by Kazan distributed by the Directors Guild of America, the filmmaker elaborated with a suspected note of pain: "Until he escapes into the dark at the end of shooting to face, alone, the next day's problems, [the director] is called upon to answer an unrelenting string of questions."[1] In Kazan's scheme of things, at his or her core a director must be a superhuman jack-of-all-trades problem-solver. Working from this notion, I asked all thirty-two directors on my list to discuss what they regarded as three big problems for directors in filmmaking. It made a good ice breaker as it inadvertently induced them to get things off their chest. Their answers flowed over the dam of reservation that usually bottles up the beginning of an interview.

Reviewing their statements, I see the responses falling into two broad areas. One director's observations uniquely summarized the collective opinions as a yin and yang construct: There are "good problems" that directors regularly come up against—and also "mean, ugly ones." So for a moment, let's get ugly.

The ugly ones, for them, are *structural*: they stem from the broader systemic environment in which their work gets carried out. This backdrop of problems—social, economic, and organizational—restricts what directors can do, the subjects they can tackle, stories they can tell, the techniques they can use.

The "good" ones, on the other hand, are *functional* or *operational*—part and parcel of the work itself. They come from the challenge of the craft, from coping with on-the-job decisions directors must make to fulfill their creative agenda. In the interviews, most of the directors focused on the structural problems, the external hindrances that they felt restricted them, burdened them, and downgraded their work, before the fact, even before any movie got made. The structural impediments carried with them a higher intensity of grievance, and I sensed that in many cases directors had to get them on the table before they could look at the immediate, subjective art and craft of directing, both idealistically and realistically.

I'd like to elaborate on this archetypal dualism from my academic perch: It was sociologist Robert Merton who gave us a classic description of structural and functional attributes of a system in his book *Social Theory and Social Structure*.[2] Structural for him meant how an organization or a community is set up or constituted, and functional indicated the way it operates to achieve its desired ends. This is the framework I am using in my analysis of the responses of the directors. For example, structural aspects concern the formal governance of a studio: *who* makes the decisions—which individuals or groups, like an executive committee, have that authority. Functional or operational aspects signify *how* decisions are made, *how* they are carried out.

In the interviews, I saw that the structural elements kept intruding upon the operational ones. The structural problems centered on the profit-making obsession in the industry and on the frenzied deal-making carousel that directors have to ride to get a movie before a camera. I'll address them first and in order and then segue into operational problems.

Structural Problems—The Bottom Line as the Top Offender

What disturbs Hollywood-based directors the most is the obtrusive dominance of money and the drive for profits deeply embedded in the culture of the film industry. This problem, by far, was mentioned most often.

With the frequency and flurry of press releases surrounding a premiere, again and again my informants stated that the industry is awash in money and that the bottom line drives everything. Their overriding complaint hyper-focused on how the fixation on profits affects the apparatus of the industry.

In their view, this executive mindset, which filters down to lower levels of management, is pervasive and pernicious because it determines a picture's content and quality. The "machinery of mass culture" simply grinds out the preponderance of movies that get made.[3] Although this isn't astonishing news to anyone familiar with the mores of Hollywood, the force and fervor of the directors' sentiments, expressed almost unanimously, registered on my radar.

The McMovie: Or "Would You Like Fries With That Quarterly Report?"
Let's listen to the restive voices of the directors on this theme.

> All the studios are actually only pieces of huge conglomerates that are interested in a smorgasbord of products, not just film. Every company, with the exception of maybe MGM, is a small subdivision of a global business behemoth.
>
> Studios will not make a picture unless they see the potential for home-run profit, almost across the board. They are only interested in a *mega-smash* because a mega-smash shows up in the next quarterly report. You can see it happening with big-ticket films like *Harry Potter* and *The Lord of the Rings*.
>
> I think there will be more pressure to make the McMovie, a consumer good, something you put on the shelf, like a SONY PlayStation.

One director had a pickled herring slant:

> I gave a lecture at the Moscow State University, and they asked me for the title of my talk. They wanted to make a poster announcing it.
>
> I couldn't come up with anything, but finally I called them and said put on the poster, "The Hollywood Myth and Pickled Herring." They were puzzled and they were curious. The amphitheater filled up. Someone told me he thought that I was going to recommend having a restaurant connected with every movie house.
>
> I started by saying that the Hollywood myth is that the industry loves cinema. No. They don't like cinema. Cinema is a means to an end. *It's a way of making a lot of money.* Hollywood is an extension of the most capitalist motives of our country.
>
> I gave an example. A few years ago, a Russian film, *Burnt by the Sun*, wins a Foreign Film Academy Award, and then they only show it in two small theaters in the L.A. area, with only tiny little ads to advertise it. So it plays for only a couple of weeks to practically empty houses. If you love film, is that how you deal with a film by a masterful Russian film director?
>
> Now for pickled herring. Let's say I walked into a studio tomorrow, and I said, "Fellows, I've got some papers here with irrefutable evidence that you can make more money using your facilities to make pickled herring than to make films. *They'd be converting within the week.* Hollywood would rather make pickled herring than movies if that would bring in bigger profits.

Slip-Sliding South
It wasn't just the presence of a perceived offensive corporate tone in the workplace that bothers directors. These creatives are riled by the downward impact of corporate thinking on the content and quality of pictures as well.

Look, during the Victorian times the Penny Dreadful pulp novels were like comic books today, knocked out in massive numbers and read very widely. Those were what was popular, not the good literature that we associate with that time. I think that films are the Penny Dreadfuls of today.

The whole push is to make films that go for the lowest-common-denominator market. Film is becoming more and more strictly a mass-media product.

Directors were less than thrilled with the cinematic fireworks they were expected to set off to thrill their audiences.

The more blow-'em-up action you give, the more and then more action you have to give—because the teenagers demand this if you cater to them. They've already seen explosions. They've already seen cities go up in smoke. They've already seen airplanes dive and disintegrate. They've already seen car chases where twenty cars pile up. *They've seen it.*

Studios go along with this because they perceive of *only one audience*, and the audience is stupid, the audience is kids. So they're dumbing down the audience to get the widest possible exposure for every film. But, look, there are people who are interested in other action—internal action, psychological action, action between people, where you have the dynamic of character against character. There are so few films for them. There is an almost parallel process happening in American theater, where spectacles and musicals abound.

I'm not deluded. I know this is show business, and it's a business, and I'm not against doing commercial movies. But I think this system has basically created a Xerox-machine mentality where creativity is stifled by the desire to repeat last year's hits. So they duplicate the genre, and they *literally* repeat the stories. They blur together, and you don't come away with anything.

Who the Hell Directed It?

To me, the studio films have no personality. You can't tell who the hell directed it, like you could with someone like a Sam Peckinpah, or a Howard Hawks, or a John Ford. Only a few American moviemakers—Scorsese, Woody Allen—have managed through luck and good timing and whatever else to have gotten around that.

The studios are turning all the content into pablum. Instead of the art form being provocative and uplifting and disturbing and insightful in a social context, the way art needs to be for the growth of the society and the civilization, it becomes a palliative, a drug, and an entertainment lacking any other values. But art really has to change the way people think about things.

In the final assessment, directors view executives in general as box-office-obsessed and as an obstacle to meritorious work, and they condemn the heavy reliance on "that tool of the frightened corporate devil"—test marketing.

"A," "B," or "C," or "All of the Above"—The Audience Directs the Movie

There's a movie snooper afoot equipped with an 8½ by 14 inch blue-green card. If you've ever been seized upon by one of those young movie-market research recruiters touting clipboards equipped with instructions detailing a mini-demographic profile of the "average moviegoer" and practically lying in wait on the busiest corners of most major metropolitan cities, then you know the price you pay to attend a *sneak preview screening* of a soon-to-be-released Hollywood film: an extra thirty minutes of your time after the credits roll. It's during that half hour that a team of market researchers distribute detailed questionnaires and tiny pencils, which you're asked to use to fill out little multiple-choice bubbles in the dimmed light of an emptying theater. Directors feel they pay an even higher price.

Directors are seriously put off by the ubiquitous, all-encompassing market testing that is de rigueur in today's Hollywood. This testing can radically alter a film's look, feel, ending. They believe that all this testing caters to petty whims of the audience, and that the heavy reliance of executives on this "crutch" simply reveals that they are out of touch with the audiences they are trying to reach.

> I find great pressure on me to not in any way offend *any portion of the audience*. Everyone in-house may agree that you have put together a great film, and then it goes out for test viewing. Maybe 95 percent of the audience thinks it's wonderful, but 5 percent don't like a particular scene. Executives want you to take the scene out. It's as though you had birthed a beautiful baby and some ignorant man in the audience doesn't like the baby's thumb, and you're expected to take your precious offspring and snip it off.

So who or what is the culprit? In no uncertain terms, one director thinks he knows.

> Money has been thrown at shooting whole new endings, then previewing the movie and going back to the original ending. Executives don't have the sense and film experience to rely on intuition, which is the surest way of knowing if the movie is working. After a screening of a comedy movie I did where the audience was screaming with laughter during the show and applauded in the middle and afterward, I was walking out with the head of the company and said that I thought this was a pretty good screening. He came back with, "Let's see what the numbers say." It's all about the numbers now.

A few directors suggested a sense of mistrust—mistrust of self by the very people green-lighting the pictures.

> In the old studio system you had people who had some faith in their own instincts, the Harry Cohns and the Goldwyns. Those guys didn't see themselves as separate from the audience—they *were* the audience. They didn't feel that they were *elite*. They thought, if I think this is funny, *they're* going to think it's funny. Today, the basic assumption is, we who make the movie, the business people in charge, we require this entire apparatus, called market research, to understand what *they* want and what *they* think of what we've made for them.
>
> A lot of this testing serves to protect the distribution people who make the decisions. Because they can point to some, quote, objective piece of research, unquote, supposedly scientific, and claim that that's why they did what they did, and if it doesn't work, well, "What would you have done, faced with this data?"

Directors say that while test marketing is endemic, the method is riddled with flaws. Rather than a tool to get at "the truth," it's often a club to manipulate directors into manufacturing the kind of movie executives think will be a commercial success. According to some insiders familiar with the practice, since market research firms catering to the movie industry get paid by the test, there is incentive on the part of the testing company to misrepresent the results in hopes that the studio will test the picture again and again and again.[4]

> Testing is inaccurate, no help at all, and usually based on one or two screenings. An audience coming on a Tuesday night is in a different frame of mind than one coming on a Saturday night. And they are not people, like in a typical audience, who laid out cash to go to a movie they wanted to see. All those kinds of variables are brushed aside.
>
> Supposedly, the audiences are scientifically recruited, but it's rigged. Without a question *it's rigged*. I counted the number of black females over the age of thirty-five in an audience at a preview for a film of mine, and my count was way off from the studio's paperwork summary. There's been a lot of stuff written about marketing employees being asked to change cards and totals. In any other business this would all have been thrown out for being inaccurate. If 85 percent of the time movies lose money—the target audience doesn't turn out to see the movie—the system is flawed.

Are the studio market researchers testing films or the directors? One director sensed that the target is them.

> When you probe, as I have, and try to find out how objective this is, and why are we doing it this way, I get to understand that it serves the studio's need to have some ammunition to use against the filmmaker. Usually it has to do with shortening the movie, making the pace go faster at the beginning, and shooting a new ending. Invariably, they try to intimidate with the use of this extremely questionable so-called research. I think if you ask directors what is the thing you hate most, test screening will be right up there near the top.

But It Can Save Your Hide, Mr. Big Shot

One director felt that there are times when testing is a good vehicle for keeping the creative vision in check, particularly in those few cases where directors have almost complete control over their work. In these instances, test marketing can be a useful reality check on their judgment.

> Once you've proven yourself and you're one of a handful of elite filmmakers, you can suffer a tremendous loss of objectivity. You can develop what a director friend of mine called a "Citizen Kane complex."
>
> These directors begin believing their own press. They come to think they can do no wrong, they become self-indulgent, while everyone else stands back saying, "He's a genius and his movie has got to be great." The right people need to be there to say, "Hey, wait a minute, the emperor isn't wearing any clothes."
>
> For a long time Steven Spielberg has refused to put his movies before preview audiences, which I think can be a valuable tool for a filmmaker to signal what is going right and what is not. Take *AI*. If Steven had screened it in front of an audience or two, he

would have made some changes before it came out. But he was so much by himself and there was no pressure on him to do that, and the movie suffered as a result. It had the potential of being better.

Test marketing is an instrument. Like any other, it can serve the devil or heavenly spirits. It all depends on who controls and uses the instrument and for what purposes. A hammer can be wielded by a carpenter to build a house or by the brat next door to annihilate his kid brother.

Blasting the "Suits": Dry Clean, or Hang Out to Dry

When directors named executives as the main culprits for the sorry condition of film today, they often unfavorably compared the current crop of executives with the moguls of yesteryear. They take the same view as that expressed by Thomas Schatz in *The Genius of the System*: that the old studio heads were a "vigorous, dynamic breed" who applied "discipline, efficiency, and quality control" to the making of films.[5] I was surprised by how many directors, regardless of their own age, centered their criticism on young executives with law and business degrees who are charged with making crucial decisions about filmmaking but have little or no film or show business experience.

Producers came off looking better in this stage of the interview, although they engage in securing financing and keeping directors to the budget. Directors also view some producers as creative partners, tough older brothers and older sisters, because they are deeply involved in developing the script and also sometimes fight for the director's final version of the film against the studio heavyweights.

You see, there was a time when the studios were owned by the people who started them, and owners had self-regard about the films they produced. I remember taking walks through Warner Brothers with Jack Warner and hearing him say, "Every year we want to make some pictures here where we go for an Academy Award, films that make us proud of the product." You know, pictures like *Emile Zola*, *The Good Earth*, *Pasteur*. He said that those are pictures that he takes pride in, where the studio *name* is important. *Listen to that.* Who today is at the head of a studio and would say this? *Who?*

Sure, those guys wanted to make money, but they also made films that they *liked*.

The Choice between Wall Street and Hollywood? Easy. Better Girls

A big problem is all the young, fresh-out-of-business-school executives who don't have a clue about film. There they were with their fresh MBAs or law degrees, and a full-blown corporate consciousness. They didn't know whether to head for Wall Street or Hollywood, and they figured there are better-looking girls in Hollywood. *They could be selling shoes or autos.* It's a product, a tool of profit, not a product they have a longing to make. When I have to deal with them, I don't know where these younger execs are coming from.

They have absolutely no show business background or interest. What they all have is a sense of omnipotence. But there's an element of fear in this for these guys, a feeling of being lost at sea, because they are required, in some intangible, non-numerate way, to help to fulfill someone else's dream.

There's something else that bothers me about this executive group. In the current atmosphere, you are judged so much by your last project. The body of your work and its trajectory is important and needs to be regarded, but that's ignored. It may be a twenty-five-year-old kid executive who makes the decision, and he may not even know about your previous work—even if was exceptional. The truth of the matter is that *most* Hollywood executives *aren't very good at what they do.* The success of American film is a tribute to two things: the American audience and its insatiable demand for entertainment—for more and more movies—and the craft level of the American film worker who's shown the whole world how to make movies.

Hardly any of the credit falls on the executive side. Fuck it, no matter how bad a movie you make, over the long run *audiences flock in.* The audience comes and demands to be entertained, at both a low and high plane, mainly low. The American film is an outrageously successful commercial product, very little of which is attributable to managerial talent. It's mainly due to the fact that there is a market that is utterly insatiable and the craft level of the American film community is superb, including writers, cinematographers—the whole gamut.

Directors regarded the contemporary corps of executives as so infatuated with the status of the bottom line that they are utterly indifferent to the condition of film as creative expression. The directors' vehement disdain for young corporate-minded executives surely affects the morale and efficacy of these filmmakers. The powers-that-be at the pinnacle of the industry, whoever they are, would be well advised to address this issue through retraining, recruitment, or replacement. How about some mandatory evening brush-up courses at the UCLA Extension program for the worst offenders?

The Invisible Man (and Woman): Or Working with Vanishing Authority

Like Alice in Wonderland, as directors feel themselves surprisingly becoming smaller and smaller, they ponder over whether they are going to disappear. They are finding it a struggle to maintain control of their films against the intrusion of studio executives. They feel that pressures are on the rise to force them to share the director's chair with executives.

Whatever romance America may ever have had with the auteur theory, where the director is the master of his or her film, that ardor is passing. In his book *Easy Riders, Raging Bulls*, Peter Biskind writes that in the 1970s directors were kings and had great leeway in making movies.[6] The directors I spoke to agree and feel that now they are more like hired hands, grappling with an erosion of their creative control.

The level of interference is increasing. Those same executives who meddle in scriptwriting don't leave you alone once the movie is made. Studio people are commenting on everything. Everybody sees dailies. The bigger the studios, the more people see the dailies . . . and everybody has something to say. Because everyone has to justify their jobs, they think they have to say *something.* You can't just say *nothing.* So you get bombarded ad nauseam with all kinds of notes and suggestions.

This whole notion of the director as the author of the film is just a myth. You get suggestions about cinematography: "I can't see faces," "I don't like the way my female star looks," to performance, to art direction, to costumes . . . everything that it's possible to get suggestions on. Many films don't make it out alive.

And the invasion doesn't stop with the script auditing. Now, say some of the informants, it has invaded the audition.

Casting is an area where studios have been eating away constantly at the influence of directors. About 90 percent of the director's vision, I would say, comes through in casting the parts. Studio execs want to approve more and more of the casting decisions, not just the stars and a few main characters. Now they sometimes go right down to one-line parts, including the waitress and the doorman.

Some directors feel under the gun from a younger generation of filmmakers who grew up in the video and computer age and have a flair for the instant-by-instant emerging technologies. Not a few established directors are looking for exit doors.

A new thing is that instead of trying to steer the directors, studios are hiring a new breed—we call them "shooters"—who will do their bidding. Shooters are young people who they can pay less and control more. They come out of doing music videos or commercials. Their films look terrific and sound good and have a great sheen and a bounce to them, but not much soulfulness.

They don't help develop the script; they don't even know much about story or character. The studio, the producer, they develop the script, with five, six, eight, ten writers on it. You hand them the script and shooters just gather you the footage to choose from. The idea of a shooter is indicative of where the business has gone in its perception of what they need from a director. Even some big directors are becoming fed up and looking to get out of the business.

In chapter 9, I will lay out the sociostructural components of Hollywood that account for its greenback fixation.

Structural Problems—Making the Deal

The gyrations of deal making has become crucial for getting projects mounted and for finding or creating a job. This seems to be a continual, nerve-jangling, exhausting element in the life of almost all directors. Money carries over as a prominent factor in deal making, because it's critical to putting together a package. Getting a high-priced name actor to sign on is a part of the ordeal. Directors describe the money issue in a different way when they discuss concocting the deal, but money and profit were an overriding theme throughout my interviews.

The first-order problem for us directors is getting work. Most people become directors because they, for whatever reasons, want to create their own world, a world in which they can tell a story. We are basically storytellers at heart.

But, different from when a singer tells a story or a writer tells a story, we create the world in which the story can unfold, even if it's a synthetic world. To do that, you need to find the story, to find the sizable resources with which to tell that story, and to carry out the directorial work of telling the story. All of that involves setting up a deal.

When the studio system broke down and contracts were thrown out, everyone became an independent operator who is constantly involved in the grind of making deals, except for the few people who have multiple deals. There is no system in place. We work in a vacuum, constantly trying to put together one-shot packages. Only a few ideas for a film will catch on, and the process stretches out for three, four years. There are ups and downs, inside and outside of studios. It can happen in any which way; there's no clear and easy path.

I think it was a bad thing, the taking away the theater chains, that anti-monopoly thing that broke up the studio system. If you were a director under contract to a studio, *look what you had.* You had at your disposal, and under contract, writers (good ones), actors (the best), production designers, cameramen. When you finished your film, the studio said, "Here's some new scripts; which one do you like?" And you said, "I'll take that one," and you immediately started working on the next film. You did three, four films a year. Think about how good you get if you *keep working,* keep your skills honed. Those people went from one film to another without in-between dead time.

Stars and Sharks Together

Directors say that to make a deal they need a star. A-List performers are few in number, in terrific demand, hard to get to, and drive up the cost of the film enormously. Stars also exert pressure for changes in the script.

Let's face it, it's stars that determine what films get made, not the studio, not the director. It's grueling work to get the top actors you want, and you may have to give up some of your story and how it's played out to get the person. There's a constant tension between a good story you love, the financing, and the star talent that's necessary to make the project come to life. You get Harrison Ford, you have your film in the can. You don't get the star and immediately you are down on a lower rung and you've got to start all over in trying to get the money.

You sometimes start with marginal, somewhat raw material, and you have to move it ahead. An example: I worked with a writer, going through several drafts of the script. It wasn't catchy enough for the high-level actors we approached. They usually aren't focused only on the story. They want roles that have a *meat and potatoes* quality, something that lets them emote.

So I engaged another writer to juice up the main parts. He's an old-time Hollywood writer who *stars just love* because he has the knack of creating very interesting characters. He worked on the whole script but concentrated on the two or three lead roles. The original writer doesn't know about this going on, but if we get to do the film he'll receive a fat paycheck, and I'm sure he won't stay angry all the way to the bank.

Getting high-profile actors can be a Catch-22. The studio wants a sexy performer involved before they will invest in the film; otherwise they may not make money. Actors want a studio to OK the film before they sign on; otherwise they could lose face, you know, become wallflowers who are not invited to dance by the studio. Nobody wants to *go first.*

After interviewing more than thirty film directors, I get the impression that even though directors and agents may be connected by the same picture, they swim in entirely different waters. Directors say they count on agents to negotiate deals and find work, but that work often isn't the kind of work directors want to do. The real interests of directors can get relegated to second place. Hollywood is a sea of combat, and for many directors, agents are the biggest sharks.

Agents aren't much of a help in getting me connected to the kind of movies I want to make. Generally speaking, agents don't give a shit. An agent gets 10 percent of what a director makes, regardless of the quality of the movie. In a sense, the agents have control over you because of their *ties to stars*. I have submitted pictures to stars through their agents, scripts I cared about, and I found out later that the stars never even saw them. The agent stopped it. "That's not commercial enough. *Out!*" That's the system today.

If a studio offers a director $10 million to make a movie, do you think the agent is sitting there in deep thought about the piece of material, whether it's in the director's best interests as a creative person? The agent certainly doesn't want the movie to be a turkey, so he won't be able to sell the director next time. Other than that, agents will take anything with good money attached.

What do directors want? Do they want a hit movie? What you'll find, in varying degrees, is directors will say that they want to make a *good movie* that's also *a hit*. Agents just want a hit movie, whether it's good or not, if it rings up cash. Quality is very important to the director, the writer, the producer. Those are the kinds of projects most directors are trying to set up. Agents operate on a different wavelength.

Let's Elope to Canada

Another problem bearing on the corporate mentality that my respondents mentioned, but less frequently, was runaway production and how that dries up their access to jobs.[7] It means that deal making more and more has to include a reach across borders. Directors decry the ills of runaway production, a cost-saving initiative actually brought on by many factors, like the federal government eliminating 200 percent write-offs for people investing in film, the exploding costs of superstars, and tough union rules. The consequences fall not only on directors, but heavily also on working actors and crafts and technical people who are left little of the remaining budget pie for job opportunities and decent salaries. Executives, naturally, stretch out a long arm for the sweet tax benefits offered in distant climes.

Directors had strong objections to the trend to shoot films in other countries for budgetary purposes.

More and more executives have been insisting on shooting in overseas locations to save money when the story is set in America. Of course, the incredible costs of making and marketing movies drives this, so you have British, Australian, and Canadian actors taking American parts, and the accents are not convincing. The backdrops look phony.

A film that is supposed to take place in New York is shot in Toronto and looks like it is taking place on Mars. Cutting costs overrides the need to have a setting that is authentic for the story. The studios are making more money than they ever did, but they're crying poverty and forcing this disconnect. This is beginning to devastate the film business in the United States. It's taking directors away to do their work on foreign soil, without the high level of talent they usually can call on, in artificial locations and with equipment that's inferior or unfamiliar.

Runaway production is clearly a source of insecurity for film folk. Los Angeles is one place in the world where the topography and the people are intimately intertwined. The ground is always shaking, and so are people's lives. Directors mentioned ageism, sexism, and racial and ethnic bias as other sources of insecurity and frustration. One of my questions in the interview asked specifically about women and minority issues in filmmaking, and I'll address that in a separate chapter. But the subject surfaced before then to a more limited extent as a general problem in the industry.

The (112-Page) Paper Chase

Making a deal and shooting the kind of movie you would like to do, and that you would respect yourself for doing, is potentially paradoxical. Directors say that the art and commerce tug of war that they mentioned more generally plays out in the specifics during the process of putting together these package deals.

> In looking for a story to start your project, I think you should aim for something that you want to live with for at least a year or two, something that has enough resonance and depth to keep you interested during that period of time, and that other people will find interesting when they see it. But it isn't that easy to find a story that you can get onto film.
>
> So to try in every which way to find a story that you want to make, one you can give something of yourself to, and that someone else is willing to support to the tune of 5, 10, 30, 50 million dollars, *that's some trick*. The personal pictures I want to package and shoot aren't home-run movies. Every once in a while there's a *Kramer vs. Kramer*, or an *American Beauty*, but that's very rare.
>
> This is a really tough business for keeping your values intact; thousands of other people will do the work for less money than you and will do anything the studios tell them. You can get in trouble sometimes by going beyond manipulating the mechanics of putting pictures on celluloid.

Operational Problems—The Vision Thing

Shifting over now to *operational* problems in the more bounded arena of the job itself, two types come to the fore. These are mentioned less frequently than the structural ones. One of them concerns the dual challenge of knowing your vision and keeping it intact in the face of competing views and intrusions from executives. The other involves contending with the always-present pressures of budget and time in doing the shoot. Of the operational problems, the directors are most distressed about the rising invasion of their artistic control by executives.

Despite these difficulties, directors seem animated and intrigued by the professional problems of shooting movies. There's an analogy lurking here to my friends who are attracted to theology and a need for God in their lives but can't stand the church and organized religion. Directors love filmmaking, but they often hate the studios and organized filmmaking.

Although some may relish the adventure of that game, working up to the point of getting a project ready to shoot can be an ordeal for any director There is extraordinary relief and exhilaration in getting through all the hurdles blocking the pathway to the goal they were chasing, and having finally an opportunity to practice their craft. With the deal now wrapped, another entire array of problems surfaces related to the core job of the director—*actually shooting films on the set.*

A major difficulty directors confront is double-sided: to keep their vision clear and to uphold the integrity of that vision in the face of the drumbeat of voices and interests that want to push the movie in different directions. As we've seen, directors are particularly agitated by the encroachment of executives into directorial decisions. At its heart, the directors agreed, filmmaking is a collaborative process, a multifaceted one, which involves conflict and compromise, sometimes resulting in the downfall of the project and sometimes in its taking full flight. Let's look first at the problems of having a vision and holding to it.

> In shooting a film, you've got to try to be specific about your vision, know what you want to say, and be able to translate that vision into cinematic form, and that isn't easy. In order to do any fine work, you have to *know who you are*, and that's a lifelong struggle. Finding a piece of material that comports with who you are, material that you can fill with truth and put on the screen in that way, is a challenge. When I look back on the films I made, and that's twenty-two movies now, the ones I have pride and satisfaction in are those where *a piece of me* is tied in to the film in some way.

To find those pieces, one teacher of film suggests grabbing scissors.

> A faculty member in the film program at UCLA who I know works with students along those lines from the beginning. He starts out right on the first day of class trying to help students get a sense of themselves personally. He asks them to go home and cut out a hundred pictures from newspapers and magazines. When they come back, he tells them to take two minutes to get rid of half of them. Then he has them cut the number down again through three more passes, until they distill out all but ten that they are left with.
>
> Now he walks around the class, and what does he see? *Lo and behold*, he sees that one student has only black and white pictures, another primarily landscapes, or people, or animals. Some have photos that are mainly horizontal; others have vertical ones. Each student is *amazed*. They didn't know that about themselves, that they had an affinity for certain kinds of photographs and themes. It's a discovery, and they gain a certain level of respect for their uniqueness in how they see the world, and what they may want to do with a camera in telling a story.
>
> For me, what is appealing and gets me in the gut is the theme of the human condition. For me, the biggest battlefield is between a couple, between a father and son, between two sisters. Those are the real battlefields. Other people may want to tell stories of a more visual bent, or science fiction, or travel, or self-absorption by an individual peering inward. Films where I've veered away from my own particular vision, I think, were less successful.

Directors understand very well that this is a collaborative art and other voices have to be brought into play during this fluid and ultra-complex process. Nevertheless, they habitually acknowledged the struggle to protect their own vision in the face of so many competing influences.

> Control in life is an illusion, and control as a director is also an illusion. But you need to have a reasonable amount of say. Sure, this is a collaborative enterprise that needs many talents to carry it through, but the director is the only person who understands the mystery, knows how the jigsaw puzzle is to be pieced together. Successful cinema ultimately is one person's vision, always. The script is just one element among the pieces, and not the grand one—there is also design, acting, music, editing.
>
> My experience has been that the fight to carry out your vision is intense and ever present. There are so many people, technical processes, and other filters to get through in bringing your vision to the celluloid, like producers who have a different idea of things, the screenwriter, and mega-stars, that you can easily lose control of the concept that was driving you. Any project can start one way and end up at an altogether different place. If you find yourself cut out of post-production, the wrong music can convert your drama into a soupy melodrama.
>
> It takes a lot to be able to come to the final screening and say to yourself, "God, that's a film I would have gone out to see." Instead, directors often think, "That movie I made is a bummer, and the actors put their trust in my hands." That's not easy.
>
> I try to balance things out by making one movie for Caesar—my corporate bosses— and one movie for God—my own artistic impulses. It's as though artistic weeds come out, no matter how much market-driven DDT they put on them.

Flying Solo

A growing number of directors are trying to get around the artistic stranglehold of the studio edifice and bring their vision to the screen by going the independent route. But as we'll see, this decision is fraught with real pitfalls and perils.

> The other venue we have is making independent films, which means finding individuals with money who will finance films, smaller and more adventurous ones. The upside of that is that there is less compromise in aiming for a small niche market that goes for intelligent films. With the Indies, you can't do *Something About Mary* and bring it to a film festival; you've got to have some creativity in your story or in the way you tell the story. *Boys Don't Cry* was a film where the subject matter was very controversial and wouldn't be given the go ahead in the usual circles. *Memento* was a different animal in its form, too risky stylistically for the studios. As an independent filmmaker you are almost forced to the edges, because if you try something mainstream you're going to lose.
>
> In my experience, even to get an *independent film* made and distributed it's essential to get a piece of talent that is known. For a beginning-level director like me, investors have to take a huge risk, so it makes it hard to get started. You could do your film digitally, low-budget, and without a high-profile star, and take it to festivals, but the chances of picking up a distributor are so small.

While the conventional wisdom holds that you're only as good as your last picture, for the Indie filmmaker, your first picture could easily be your last picture.

A problem here is that most of the independent films are one-shot, stand-alone deals, so there's no continuity. Most of the films don't make money, meaning that people come in and invest for *whatever* reasons. It's an anomaly. It happens once and then they're *gone*. You have to find someone else. There's no continuing relationship you can build on to move ahead as a filmmaker. And you make an offbeat film and it sucks. Your career is over.

Operational Problems—The Wallet and the Clock

Directors pointed to the enormous budget and time pressures surrounding the shoot while trying to guard their personal vision of the film. When everything is in motion, there is never enough time or money, or the luxury to ponder on what is really happening. As director Kazan revealed, directors have to make a constant stream of creative decisions about the production—acting, photography, sound, backdrop, special effects, and the invariable mishaps and surprises that crop up minute by minute—in getting a movie made. All of these things cost money, one way or another, as well as consume time.

We have an obligation to keep to the budget. There are always choices to be made. If you are a young person starting out with limited funds, less than a million dollars, or if you are backed by a large studio, you make choices every moment of the day. The budget you have intertwines with the time you have. But you always want more.

It's a crucial problem for everyone, even for the 80 million dollar picture. Because if you're spending 80, you can easily spend 90, and you're under the gun not to. It can cost one to two hundred thousand dollars a day during the shoot. All kinds of things arise that can hold you up. You're supposed to have a clear day in the script and it's raining and you have to figure out how to deal with it. A generator blows up and you need to get another generator right away. Or an actor refuses to come out of his trailer.

Let me tell you a story. I was shooting on location, and my wife accompanied me. One day I worked late into the night, and very early the next morning the phone rang in our bedroom and woke my wife and me out of a deep sleep. When I picked it up, there was a voice asking what color horses I wanted in the scene—white, tan, black, palomino, or whatever. From that time on, whenever the topic comes up of what is the job of a director, my wife says that it's to decide what color the horses should be.

From Trotting to Ticking

The biggest enemy in filmmaking is the clock. It's always there. You never have enough time to prep a movie, to shoot a movie, never enough time for the day, for the scene. The sun is going down, you're losing light, the clock is ticking, you're behind schedule. Then, when you finish the movie, nearly exhausted, you've got to get the first cut ready in nine or ten weeks. It's always the clock: the clock, the clock, the clock.

This is really bone-wearying hard work, with long hours and a colossal amount of stress. But those are good problems, really; they have to do with thinking quickly on your feet and finding a way to go ahead with the movie. Those are problems I actually enjoy.

The problems I don't enjoy have to do with money and producer-induced problems. They tell you they want you to put a little more tit in there, and if you don't do *this* we won't give you money to do *that*. It's a complete waste of time and those are the annoying problems. In filmmaking, 95 percent is pure bullshit and 5 percent is pure gold. And it's the bullshit I'm talking about. You really have to be strong and Machiavellian to get around it.

This whole thing is like painting a picture in a little area of a canvas at a time, with no chance to step back and see what the whole thing looks like. There's a constant tension between getting the work done and getting it done right.

A Shoestring Can Lift an Oscar

Some directors, interestingly, thought the fiscal squeeze isn't all bad. It forces you to make inventive decisions that can be intriguing and result in a more distinctive movie. Proverbially speaking, it takes pressure to make diamonds. Apparently, sometimes in the midst of time and budget pressures, lucky breaks materialize serendipitously, bringing beauty.

I believe this budget tyranny has an upside. Orson Welles once observed that "The enemy of art is the absence of limitation." If you embrace your limitations, you are able to create art. If you have a plenitude of money and time, you create technical solutions, like special effects, but not creative ones, not ones that are as artistically exciting. Let's face it, in every artistic endeavor there are constraints. I try to relate to them as a challenge, because they force me to reach beyond where I thought I would go, to think in new ways. You start spinning straw and getting gold. You know, if there were no bounds, you could spend an enormous amount of time on a project and never get it finished.

A case for accidental creativity or, as some directors consider it, creative carpe diem on a per diem.

In doing the shoot you have to keep an eye out for what I've heard one director call "happy accidents." A happy accident is an incandescent moment that occasionally happens in a movie, but no one plans it, and it just comes out of the blue. Like you're outside and taking a low shot, and you're in the middle of a scene, and they're doing it beautifully, and at that instant a bird flies by in the background. That's great!

Or you get up to shoot a scene in the morning and the weather has taken a turn and there's some bewitching mist hovering that you had no idea would be there. Part of the craft of directing is to be able to take advantage of these accidents. You've got to know the craft well enough to be able to recognize and use them, not be thrown by them. It's absolutely thrilling when they pop up at you out of nowhere.

Savoir Faire and Victimhood

As someone informed about film but not an industry insider, I took on this project with a backlog of questions about directors and their work. Scanning the movie pages in the newspapers and sampling a fair share of the offerings, I wondered how, year after year, directors could go about foisting on the public so many crude films, artistically and otherwise, films having no weight whatsoever. Not that there's anything new about this. After all, many years ago now, novelists like Nathanael West, social critics like Carey McWilliams, and academics like Hortense Powdermaker tagged Hollywood a "wasteland" and a "dream factory."[8]

Simple entertainment has a legitimate and necessary place in the cinematic scheme of things. Think of *American Pie* (1999) or *Freddy Got Fingered* (2001) or *Dude, Where's My Car?* (2000). Of course, these films will and should be made. But directors dish them out by the bushel, endlessly. What drives them to do that? Don't they know any better?

I found out that many *do* know better. Those I talked with were painfully in touch with the kind of "products" they are creating. As we talked, these men and women reflected intelligence, sophistication, taste, eloquence, sensitivity, responsibility, competence: all the attributes of estimable artists and cultural workers. So they weren't the mindless purveyors of banality, and worse, that most of the pictures in the movie houses I frequented insinuated they would be.

This group of directors was clearly conscious of the strictures that the Hollywood production machine imposes on its drones. They obviously long to do good work—much better work than they have been allowed to accomplish. And, from what they say, they struggle, in what can only be small ways, to breach the structural restraints pressed on them by a global industry that is overwhelmingly fixated on profit accumulation.

Los Angeles Times film critic Kenneth Turan argues that directors go along with manufacturing feeble movies because of large paychecks and the sense of power and enthrallment they get from commanding the set.[9] Maybe I am letting them off the hook too easily, but I estimate that their collective talents and more lofty aspirations, by and large, far exceed what they or anybody have been permitted to bring into being by their corporate overlords.

I detected an underlying ennui almost across the board, a sense of alienation from their work and their work environment. There was discomfort about corporate norms of avarice that creep ubiquitously into every corner of filmmaking. There was anguish about the rat race of deal making that turned all of them into salespeople, negotiators, and con artists for long periods of time between episodes of practicing the craft of directing films. Most were distressed about the shallow quality of films that make it past the corporate gatekeeping power elite.

What I heard in the interviews sounded more like an epidemic of discontent than the complaints of a few disgruntled and atypical souls. Their comments of dissatisfaction, however, didn't include spoken concern about their personal incomes. The money situation appears good for the work that they do. For Directors Guild of America members, as I write this, the *minimum* salary for typically budgeted films is $12,106 a week, with a guaranteed ten-week shooting period and two-week preparation period. But there is a cloud of insecurity about making the next deal and getting the next job, insecurity that focuses on paying the mortgage on the Bel Air home tomorrow and keeping the career in flight over the long term. With all the competition, unpredictability, and deception that swarms around filmmaking, anxiety is pervasive—for everyone. To many industry aficionados, you can't spell Hollywood without

I.N.S.E.C.U.R.I.T.Y. Perhaps that is why Los Angeles boasts as many therapists as it does palm trees.

During the time I was conducting these interviews, I attended a forum on filmmaking that took place at the 2001 annual *Los Angeles Times* Festival of Books conducted at UCLA. A panel was composed of Peter Bart, editor of *Variety*; Lynda Obst, the producer of *Sleepless in Seattle* and *Contact*; Rachael Abramowitz, film reporter for the *Los Angeles Times*; John Ridley, screenwriter; and Peter Biskind, film critic and author.

This sundry collection of industry mavens, without exception, knocked Hollyworld and felt dispirited in the same way as the directors I interviewed. But they added a few flourishes. Because of the dominance of the multinationals, few organizational loyalties exist nowadays among film industry denizens. Independent film, once a great white hope, is quickly becoming Hollywoodized. Peter Bart pronounced that the Indie system, such as it is, is not working artistically or economically because a lot of trash is being produced by inexperienced filmmakers, and the cost of distribution dooms the showing of all but a tiny portion of the films made. But, as he said in his usual blunt fashion, the film industry has only changed under dire conditions—"when things are fucked up." These views are entirely consistent with my interview data and serve to validate what the directors said.

Consider that William Goldman chose to subtitle one of his recent books *Who Killed Hollywood?* University scholar Jon Lewis named his book on contemporary filmmaking *The End of Cinema as We Know It*. And a PBS program giving an update on the industry was dubbed "The Monster That Ate Hollywood."[10] For people who cherish film, there is mortal consternation about Hollywood these days. More so than in the past.

The waste of the remarkable abilities still in evidence in today's filmmaking community is an appalling loss for these talented individuals personally, and even more so for audiences all over the world who could be so much more astonished, delighted, and uplifted—yes uplifted, an OK goal for film—by what they have to offer.

I was struck by the discontent manifested, to a lesser or greater degree, in the whole group of directors that I interviewed. An ever-vicious circle, this negative feeling can't help but contaminate both their work relations with studios and the film products they create.

I should add, though, that the general tone of the interviews wasn't at all as sour as the impression you might get from reading this chapter. Remember, in my interviews of every director, my first request had been to name the major problems they all face; so invited, they naturally zeroed in on their dominant troubles with the new Hollywood system. Instead, had I asked them to tell me what they relished about filmmaking, they would have enumerated their joys in the work itself—and, as future chapters will demonstrate, this they did. And did with abundance.

A folksong I've liked begins, "*Trouble in mind . . . I'm blue / but I won't be blue always.*" These filmmakers are not blue always. The saving grace for them—I saw—is clearly the satisfaction they derive from the hands-on experience of directing films: telling a story in a totally novel way, making an imaginary world come alive, having exhilarating interactions with gifted actors, solving a string of fascinating problems on the set, and orchestrating an extraordinarily complex human and technical enterprise— all to hopefully create something new and breathtaking. Also, while speaking about these matters in the chapters and conversations to come, the directors weigh in on how problems they described might be remedied.

CHAPTER TWO

~

Directors in Close-Up

There are films I want to make. I've got the scripts in hand, and the studios won't make them. They say, "You do this film for us and then we'll let you do your film," and it's always a lie. Always a lie. You just keep trying, taking another shot at it.

—Irvin Kershner

Anecdote from an anonymous Director: "I was once sitting at a table in the famous Buena Vista restaurant near San Francisco's Fisherman's Wharf, an institution self-credited for the invention of the Irish Coffee. At the 'B.V.' as the locals call it, customers sit together at long park-style picnic tables. In the course of conversation with the patron to my left, he challenged me to guess his profession. 'Do you run a florist shop or maybe you're an interior designer?' I offered. (After all, this was San Francisco.) 'Interior designer?' he marveled. 'Close. I'm a psychotherapist.'"

We have just taken a wide-angle look across the landscape of present-day film-making. Now, pressing forward from my far-fetched anecdote (after all, this is Los Angeles), I will zoom in on directors themselves and their *interior* world. I want to look at two kinds of personal issues for directors. One is the question of what motivates them to continue in this work, a work that is inundated with obstacles that agitate and dishearten them—obstacles they abundantly revealed in the previous chapter. The other issue deals with the special traits and talents directors must possess or acquire to perform at a high level of excellence.

Means of Survival

Orson Welles was rumored to have commented, both sardonically and sagely, that directors should have *strong feet*, because directors stand and are moving around so much of the time. (Forget the vaunted director's chair!) When I asked filmmakers what they believed were the attributes of gifted directors, they perambulated well beyond what Welles proposed. I'll get to their responses shortly.

I should say at the start of this chapter that when I began my survey, a how-you-persevere query was not an item in the original questionnaire. But the litany of lamentations expressed by the directors I'd interviewed started to pile up, as if demanding that I take note of them. My informants were telling me that the artistic and creative elements of their work were ever receding. The studios, by and large, had abandoned the quality film business and were now producing only one or two films a year of substance. At the time, the majors had cannibalized important independent distributors like Miramax and New Line, choking off the classic Indie pathway to making good movies at low cost.

These are conspicuously intelligent, capable, well-connected people qualified to succeed in any number of pursuits. I couldn't help but be curious about why, and how, they endure these frustrations and indignities. So when I saw that this discouraging news kept coming up, after a time I began informally to ask my interviewees, "What keeps you going?" or "How do you manage to keep plugging away at this work?"

This line of questioning generated some introspective and surprising responses. But because it was a late-arriving question, I could only ask it of nine directors in all, and each of the points to follow generally was made by only one or two respondents.

Money/Luck/Control

First of all, there is the bread-and-butter dimension. Directors have to eat, and filmmaking is their meal ticket. There are expensive mortgage payments and private school fees to meet, and high-flying friends and colleagues to keep pace with. This work is what they know how to do to garner an income commensurate with a Hollywood lifestyle.

> What keeps people going? You're *stuck*. You spend a lifetime building up a craft and a capability in what you're doing. I've had to support a family, my kids. And I'm carried along by the love of my crew and by how they back me up. So I feel obligated to them, too. You know, you begin to compromise and to get sucked in.

A person always hopes that success, or bigger success, will be just around the corner. In a Dream Factory environment, everybody fantasizes that better luck is within reach. This brand of luck is of the high-stakes money and fame variety. It can also propel directors to a place where they can have more artistic leverage over the films they direct.

> The truth is that this is a very desirable job in a very desirable profession and there are *thousands* of talented, capable people willing to do this job. And what really distinguishes some people who make it from other people is *a lot of luck*. I'm not saying there isn't a lot of talent involved, because there is. But why some people get to the top of the food chain and get to call the shots—to pick their movies and control their movies—and others don't, it comes down to luck.

The way of raising your chances of being lucky is through creating more opportunities for yourself, and persistence is one way of doing that. It's like the more lottery tickets you've bought, and the more tickets you have, the more likely you are to win the lottery. This is lotto. I say, being in filmmaking is *playing lotto with your life*. If you happen to get in the right place at the right time, then success breeds success.

People also count on the luck of some good films managing to see the light of day, at least every so often. The hope is that just possibly you can get to direct one of those worthy movies.

There's still high ground in this work. There is, finally, through the independents, through the foreign movies, through one that slips through the studio system, through movies that get made to excuse the other movies being made by the studios—there is still the high ground. Truly, there's nothing better in the world than a feature film that really works. You can get very cynical, but sometimes a movie of yours gets made for all the wrong and stupid reasons, purely commercial reasons, and turns out to be quite good.

The Lure of the Set

In their comments, there's almost a sense of ecstasy about the challenges of working on the set, and about the close, comradely relationships that grow from joining together with other people in a common creative quest. This work seems to have a palpable addictive quality.

A few years back, I went into a kind of retirement. I felt tired of fighting the battles of drumming up deals. I was emotionally and physically exhausted and just didn't want to face the rat race and the frustration that goes with being a filmmaker nowadays. Then I came to realize that I had this deep yearning to be tackling those problems on the set. I like the day—going to the job, getting the set ready, dealing with the problems that come up. You know, the sun is going down and the rain is coming and you have to break and be at another location tomorrow. It's like taking a voyage, with all those twists and turns and uncertainties along the way that you have to find a way to overcome. That stimulates you and gets the juices going. I *had* to experience that again.

I absolutely and totally love this work; it makes me happy. I really love working with actors, and also other creative people. It's like being a symphony conductor. This is not an art that a single individual can carry off alone, like putting paint on a canvas. You've got to collaborate with other people and create something new involving everyone's contributions. There's almost a feeling of family. Without question, making movies is a high, a real addiction. Directors are adrenaline-rush people and will do anything to make movies. I'm dead serious—it's totally true that it's addictive. I have a lot of psychologist and psychiatrist friends who work with film folk, and they are all in accord on this.

Directors gather in an enormous sense of accomplishment from creating an illusionary world on the set from their own imaginations. It is a world that, although contrived, once registered on celluloid becomes enduring, almost immortal in character. And the director's self is part of that immortality.

I get a bigger charge from shooting a movie than directing a play, and I've done both. They both involve storytelling, but the satisfactions are different. The thing about a film that's ultimately wonderful is that at the end you have a living, indelible embodiment of what you've done. I've directed so many plays, and do you know what they are? They're *posters* on my wall. There's nothing left. It's ephemeral. Part of the joy and excitement of film is that it's alive long after you've finished your job of creating it.

Artfulness and Craziness

Some directors yearn to convey something of meaning that dwells within them, something that they are impelled to say to an audience. And there is tremendous satisfaction in moving an audience deeply in response to what the director has created.

I'm from an academic family and one that has always been involved in public service. I was raised to be an artist and I was raised to contribute to society. *That's what my ideals are.* I feel I have important things to say to people, to the public, and to share the insights I have gained in my life. I try to pick projects that allow me, always in an entertaining way, to put out there the things I know are true about life. I have that kind of personal moral goal that I impose on myself and that dictates what projects I take on or cast off. I want to entertain audiences and speak to them about things that matter in people's lives. Film gives me a means to carry through on those strivings within me.

It's really very special to have five hundred, a thousand people, sitting together in the dark for two hours paying unconditional attention to what you are telling them through the brain or through the heart. It's like gathering in the temple, the lights go out, and you are all embarking on a journey together. And I can't think of any other media form that accomplishes that. TV—that's more detached. The viewer is clicking the remote, standing up, going to the kitchen.

There's also the zaniness of it, the show business high jinks that some people find hard to resist. You can keep putting on your high school class play for the rest of your life.

You get into it and it's fun. It's a lot of fun, actually working on a film. The characters you meet are a hoot. There's a kind of silliness to it that's very visceral. It's hard to break away from. There's the agony and the ecstasy—very low lows and very high highs. It's like being in the Army or the circus, where there finally *aren't good reasons to be there.* Yet, not to be there is unthinkable. What's that old joke about the guy who cleans up the elephant shit at the circus? Someone tells him that he ought to get another job and he says, "*What,* and leave show business?" There's a lot of that to it.

The experience of running the show is a real dividend for some. Some directors thrive on being in control of a complex mélange of people and equipment, and they luxuriate in the status that adheres to the directorial mantle.

There are all the perks. The going all over the world, to the most interesting places, in style. It's great being king of the city on the shoot. You know, I had Park Avenue closed off and I was in charge of that whole part of Manhattan, with the police and traffic people at my call, until the filming closed down.

There are all the psychological appurtenances—the drives, compulsions, yearnings, neurotic quirks, obsessions, and personal agendas. For some, these elusive factors are what attracted them to this job in the first place and hold them to it.

> You don't have to be crazy to keep to this work, but it helps. Craziness and megalomania help you make it. I was connected with *Back to the Future* and it took four years to break through, including fifty to sixty rejections by studios and production companies, sometimes two or three by the same company. I kept saying to myself, "I want to see this picture. If I want to see it, maybe 20 or 30 million other people will want to see it." That thought led me through the bleak times.
>
> I know some directors don't stick with it. They quit the business or turn to producing or teaching at a film school. Some do the same thing by taking a long time—four or five years—between movies. That's another way of opting out because things are so tough. But I think a lot of us go forward because, in art, people do what they do because they have no choice, because it's in them. Most filmmakers I know would do this work for free, if they had to. I was actually into making movies before I got paid for it, and I make a living as a filmmaker now simply because I'm *lucky*. Filmmakers persevere because it's a form of expression, a way to communicate from their depths.
>
> It's not rational to be in this business. *It's beyond rationality*. I think most people who do this have a neurotic compulsion for approval from this great nebulous other, from society. "I wanna be loved by everybody. I wanna be known. I wanna be a star." It's simplistic what I'm saying: there are also other desires, like expressing creativity. But there are other ways to express your creativity, lots of other things to do. Somehow, there's something alluring about this movie business. Most people in this town, and I'm guessing here, feel that they're outsiders and are looking for validation from the great external *other*. For people who haven't felt being part of society, this is their ticket in. Because if you made it in this business, well, you're OK now.

So the people who addressed this topic say they stay on board for a multiplicity of reasons. There are practical reasons (the money), artistic reasons (visioning a compelling story), and professional reasons (practicing their craft on the set). Less tangible are social reasons (bonding with associates), psychological reasons (dominating a human collectivity), emotional quirks (craving acceptance), and others. From the responses beyond this question, my impression is that the excitement of shooting on the set was mentioned most often and is an over-the-top emotional high for many people. What we have here is an intriguing snapshot of a range of influences that drive directors in a work milieu that has turned increasingly bitter for many of them.

It's My Identity, Stupid

As I made my way through all my conversations, a notion that kept coming to my mind was *identity crisis*. Erik Erikson, the respected psychoanalyst who coined the term, was apprehensive about untoward consequences of what he saw as identity confusion and negative identity, glimmerings of which I detected around me.[1]

Let me explain. When in the 1970s and 1980s conglomerates, in a rapid-fire sequence, took over the filmmaking apparatus and, step by step, defined profits as their predominate and almost exclusive preoccupation, freedom began drying up for directors to have creative elements in their careers. Many inevitably have been left with a sense of "What am I doing here?"

From what I could tell, the people I interviewed had been motivated, to a greater or lesser extent, by artistic callings in choosing their career. The degree to which their careers have gone in a commercial direction was variable. But probably for all of them, their initial artistic ideals and intentions have remained in place as part of their concept of themselves.

Maybe *identity theft* is a better term for what the directors experience. The studios haven't pinched anyone's Social Security number or credit cards, but they seem to have purloined a measure of dignity and purposefulness from talented people, many in mid-career or after, leaving them without attractive options. Nobody can say this was done with ill intent. The studios are indifferent rather than malevolent in this matter, just as they are indifferent to the despoiling of American culture through their obsession with bottom-line dividends.

Parenthetically, most books on directing focus on techniques of the craft and bypass psychological mechanisms aimed at personal renewal and survival—as, for example, widely used texts like Steven D. Katz's *Film Directing Shot by Shot: Visualizing From Concept to Screen* and Michael Rabiger's *Directing: Film Techniques and Aesthetics*. Sidney Lumet does chronicle his conflicts and frustrations in his *Making Movies* and tells how the challenge of creating something "larger than life" spurs him to go on.[2]

Oh, To Be a Good Director

If surviving in the industry—successfully surviving, not just treading water—is a bit akin to doing the backstroke in shark-infested waters, what qualities must the director come up with to keep doing lunch *rather than becoming lunch?*

In the profession, there's no unified opinion on what chief character elements must be in a director's possession. Often directors are likened to martial chieftains leading their troops. Just as often, they are equated with the conductor of a symphony orchestra. "No!" says one publication put out by the American Film Institute; they are really more like the leader of a jazz band who lets each player have his own riff. In his film industry book *Reel Power*, Mark Litwak tagged them part artist, part politico.[3] And Elia Kazan, as recounted in chapter 1, generated an astonishingly expansive inventory of talents and skills that directors must master.

Storyville

Recall that in my survey I asked directors what *they* thought were the attributes of truly gifted directors, hoping they might shed some clarifying light on this slippery subject. I wasn't surprised to see that the largest number of responses by far centered on what can be thought of as *creative capabilities*: storytelling, imagination, and vision. According to many of my informants, a passion to tell a story is the fundamental ingredient in any top-notch director's makeup.

It's crucial to want to tell a story. Call it a sense of drama, and an ability to convey to the audience the pieces of information they have to have to understand this tale. That's why people go to the movies. The story must be a human drama that connects to the lives of the people in the audience and invokes them to respond with wonder and awe. You can recognize the storytelling passion in directors who like to talk about their experiences, to schmooz, tell a joke, have fun with life. The director has to put the audience into the subjectivity of the character who at that moment is the best character through whom to tell the story. A good director makes viewers follow the story with their eyes, yes—but also respond with their guts.

Some worried that bouts of narcissism can impede the narrative, leaving a few to wonder: "Is that a moth on the lens or is that object in the way just me?"

A first-rate director will make sure not to get in the way of the story. So much filmmaking that goes on nowadays takes you out of the story. It's so show-offy. It's "*Look how I can move the camera . . . Look at all the fancy shit I can do.*" I don't want the audience to be saying, "What a great director!" in the middle of a scene, when they should be saying, "*Oh my God,* I can't believe what just happened to this character!"

The aim should be to tell the story in a very different way—if possible, as it's never been told or imagined before.

A good director has a writer's sensibility. That means being able to tell a story in a fresh, exciting, nuanced way, drawing from literature, the arts, and theater. You have to have the ability to take the commonplace in life and make it seem altogether new. After all, there are only a limited number of stories, so the trick is to tell them in *unexpected ways,* like with poetry. I think the best directors were writers, or rewriters, and managed to put flesh on the bones of the script as the film was being shot. Think of people like Wyler, Capra, Kubrick, Hawks, and John Ford.

Beyond the story, there's the unique stamp that top directors put on the story. They project a distinct personality, sensitivity, and way of viewing the world. If you are not a storyteller, you can't be a director. But if you are only a storyteller, you are an insignificant director—you have no dimension beyond the story you are telling.

For me, the number one thing in a director is *vision and taste*. A good film has to have a style about it that no other director can duplicate, a sensibility that fuses the individual's personal imagination with the material. When I think of Coppola and *The Godfather,* it's so evident that behind that film was someone making decisions about production design, casting, editing, about music—someone with a consistent sense of taste. The same can be said for other auteur directors like Cassavetes, Altman, and Scorsese. And it's remarkable to me the way Spielberg got into the mind of a child in *E.T.*

You have to have a coherent point of view, let's say, a narrative force, that portrays the world on the screen in the way you see it, and you stick with that through all the pressures and distractions. I don't like to bandy about the word "vision" because that's so overused, but that's what it's about. Our frequently spoken professional argot captures the idea—"How do *you* see this?" I believe there is no such thing as *objective* filmmaking; the minute you decide where to put the camera, you've made an editorial statement that's totally personal.

Creativity and individuality get intermeshed with what studios will endorse. Different directors bump up against studios in different ways.

Hitchcock was someone with his own distinct style, and he also had control over his material. Nicholas Ray is an example of someone who had material *assigned* to him, because he didn't have much clout with the studios. Even so, he had such a strong personal style and affinity for certain themes that his viewpoint comes through in a diversity of genres, from westerns, to contemporary dramas, to musicals, to epics. In some ways, he deserves *more* credit than Hitchcock. You can also compare Orson Welles with Howard Hawks. Welles went out of his way to choose unique material and Hawks chose totally studio product, but he made it his own. Hawks had no money problems because he was part of the system. But he was an artist. It's a fact that for some artists, the system fits with their talents; for others, like Welles, the system definitely does not fit the talent.

Diplomat and Commander

The directors I interviewed clearly regarded creative capability as the highest-order attribute of gifted directors. What, you may wonder, would fall in line next? Actually, two traits emerged with about an equal number of mentions. One of them involves personal characteristics that make for good relationships with other people; the second concerns task-oriented skills for putting together a movie.

Not everybody can get along, we know that. Since filmmaking is a collaborative process, a collaborative art, it requires the ability to work in harmony with other people, unlike the more self-driven, introverted execution of a painter, say, or an inventor, who can go it alone to a much greater degree. In the interviews, three kinds of personal aptitudes, all people skills requiring diplomacy, came to the fore: sensitivity to others, being able to communicate, and having certain personality traits, such as patience.

On Sensitivity

I think a good director is part psychologist, part parent, and like them should have good listening skills and *empathy for other people*. The director has to build a congenial and cooperative atmosphere on the set and be a nurturing person who can bring out the best in actors and other creative people. That means recognizing talent and enabling it to flower. In my view a director needs to be personable, at least in the minimal sense of connecting with people on a one-to-one basis. You can only do that well if you are sensitive to human emotions and the predicaments of life. But some directors have succeeded by not getting along, by doing just the opposite. Otto Preminger was an arrogant, opinionated man, a Nazi, who thrived on tension. He prodded and tormented actors to tears, working everybody's energy up to an unbearably high pitch, ironically to the benefit of the film. So there are exceptions.

If you're a really good director, you have the ability to create an environment where others will *want* to do what you want them to do. Assuming there is a director's single vision at the outset, other people can take it beyond the director's capacity, beyond the director's imagination. I saw that Spike Lee really creates an ensemble with the people who work with him. When you've worked on a Spike Lee film, it's as though you've all been to camp together, and you've all shared something bigger than yourself. People develop a camaraderie, so they look out for each other and help each other do better. He has a great eye for seeing the potential in people and bringing that out, not *always* in a happy way, but who he is inspires people to be better than they've ever been.

On Communication

You need to be able to tell people clearly what you want and what you don't want of them. To do that I think you have to be clear inside yourself. That comes first. You have the job of communicating your vision to all kinds of people—executives, actors, crafts people, everyone on the set. With executives, that can be tough and take real sophistication and diplomacy. They speak a *different language* than creative people, so you have to translate. But they pretend to understand when they don't, which makes the translation task harder. Sometimes you just have to baby them.

On Personality Traits

If you don't have infinite patience, you can get in trouble. The director can't do everything and has to rely on a whole raft of other talented people to come up with something that's worthy. You have to keep yourself in check, sometimes, to leave time and opportunity for the contributions of other people to come out. Also, you need to have a certain level of humility, because that helps you look out for your actors and your crew. And a director ought to be able to go with the flow, fall into the adventure of making the movie, like Fellini seemed to do. At the same time you have to have an internal, driving desire to make movies, and the determination to stick with it through thick and thin. Richard Brooks said, "You have to learn to eat shit, *unsalted.*"

The notion of the director as a supreme human relations adjudicator came across to me in a tale one director told me about how he juggled the differing fervent views of the lead actors and the writer on the set. Julius Epstein, the esteemed coscribe of *Casablanca*, wrote the screenplay for the movie *Reuben, Reuben,* which this filmmaker was then directing. The last major scene was pivotal. Both key actors in it, Tom Conte and Kelly McGinnis, came to the director privately and said the scene was just not working for them.

There apparently wasn't enough space in the scripting for the emotional quality of their interchange to get played out. The couple had to work through the young woman's pregnancy, whether she should have an abortion, if the characters should see each other again. So the director went to Epstein and told him to take another look at the script to accommodate this input from the actors.

Epstein took the script home for several days and then came back with his judgment that the dialogue was as he wanted it: "The words are right; I'm not going to touch it. There is no more I want to add—that would be padding it. And there isn't anything I want to take out." So what should an earnest director do? The resolution was this: The first bit of the scene in question is played in the man's bedroom. Then the characters move out and continue to talk on his porch. He asks a question and then the sequence cuts to them walking along a railroad track in the countryside. Then they are seen conversing in a park in town. "The only thing I added was time, in a visual fashion, the feeling that they had spent part of the day together. It had lacked the element of time; now it felt as though they had given their problem a thorough airing." No words in the script were changed. But a few hours were shown to have gone by that allowed the emotional content in the situation to be realized.

It isn't hard to detect contradictions among the director attributes I enumerated—like hanging loose and holding fast. The sensitivity notion calls for being receptive to signals given by others, while communication involves transmitting signals outward to others. I'll talk about the disparities later; let's just acknowledge them for the time being and go on to the area of task-oriented skills.

Command Performance

Making a film demands that directors execute concrete actions that result in a finished product, part artistic, part practical and commercial, just as physicians are on the line to use both art and science to bring about better health in those who depend on them. To some degree, these are the kinds of actions that might be set down in a formal task analysis performed by a management efficiency expert who is breaking jobs down into their core components. The material here doesn't come together in that kind of systematic way, but it does provide an orientation to task skills.

Let's start with the skills of the craft:

You've got to know what music does, what scenic design can do, camera, sound, editing, all the components. So when they start the storytelling process directors can use all the tools. Take Jim Cameron with *Titanic*, for instance. Though he's a difficult personality in real life, his *mastery* of all facets of filmmaking, from the script through final editing, yielded a great picture.

I realize some people put a lot of stock in knowing it all, so to speak, especially working the camera, and I won't argue with them. But you have to consider that making films is so complex, you can never master it all—it's beyond mastery. So, no matter how good you are, you can learn on every film, and grow. You also have to be proficient in picking good people and on-board enough about the craft areas to be able to work through these people. Of course, there are some dumb directors who survive by luck and by *leaning on other people* for feeding them advice and fixing things up. Their films just become a composite of other people's abilities.

I think you have to have casting, acting, and pacing in your repertoire. To me it's essential to appreciate acting, even to have been an actor. You have to know what actors go through, and that means internalizing the tools of the acting profession. If I meet a young person who wants to become a director, the first thing I say is *take acting classes*.

We know that directors are often compared to a field general or the captain of a ship. I think this imagery symbolizes the director as a leader of a sizable work group charged with completing a pinpointed mission, and that's a complex undertaking that in reality goes beyond simple slogans. The needed leadership falls partly in the realm of command, which can have a charismatic dimension. But it falls also in the realm of management, which is more reflective and even bureaucratic. (We have already gone over the collaborative, interpersonal dimension.)

> You have to have command of the apparatus, to get the actors to do what you want, the director of photography, the crew. You want to get them to move toward making the movie you want to make. One part of the director's job is being a challenging leader—*tough* and inspiring, like a general driving the troops in battle. You may have to push sometimes. Being decisive is important in this. Otherwise, everyone will walk around in a state of confusion, and there are thousands of decisions that have to be made moment by moment. You have to make these decisions fast, because time is money—snap decisions, like "Wear the green outfit," or "We will shoot the river this time."
>
> In all of this, a good director makes people feel the project is significant and special, not like a factory job, so they will give their all to it. That means demonstrating discipline and an exemplary work ethic through your attitudes and performance. The director should be working the hardest—not taking drugs, not getting drunk on the set, not having affairs with actresses. If directors give the project proper respect, the people working on the project will give them proper respect.

Very few respondents actually used the word "managing." It probably comes across as mechanical to most directors, and "management" represents the antithesis of art, symbolized by the suits, whose mission it seems is to keep creativity in check. But the reality is that a significant part of the director's role is managing a complex workforce engaged in creative labor. And some directors recognize that.

> I think a big part of what I do is being a manager—managing people, money, and time. When I do that right, I have room to focus on the more aesthetic elements. It takes real organizational ability and political acumen to juggle the diversified talents on the set. I try to work these things through in a give-and-take way, but I keep the reins in my hands. For example, with my editor, we'll sit at dailies and I'll flag a take and say how I see the film being cut. But then I leave it to her to go ahead with the project. She can add something to what I start with. I'll convey that when I'm done shooting: "In three weeks, in five weeks, I want to see a movie . . . *your* best version of the movie. I don't care if you leave scenes out, if you rearrange things, because I can always retrieve scenes that are cut."
>
> Don't be mistaken, there are very smart people in the movie business, on all sides. You can't get away with being unpredictable. To be a good director you have to show up, do the work, complete the day. Your pictures won't make it, and *your career won't*, if you are irresponsible.

A half-dozen directors raised single points that did not combine with others into categories. A few are worth noting briefly.

One director thought that there were more gifted directors in the past, in the John Ford era. Nowadays, he said, many kids come out to Hollywood to "get laid and become rich." Another agreed that there are few 1970s-type powerful directors like Scorsese and Coppola coming along—and to make it worse, both those giants have told him that they would not have been able to build a body of work if they started in film today.

Another director lamented that the theater, with its serious focus on story and drama, used to be an important source of directing talent, but it is rarely drawn upon. Today, on the flip side, MTV is more often drawn upon by directors who can use razzle-dazzle camera techniques.

And yes, cycling back to Orson Welles, a respondent declared that filmmakers have to have great physical stamina, which ties in with the idea of *strong feet*. So Welles's assertion, in the end, is confirmed.

Who Made This Stew Anyway? A Question for R&D

Going beyond the listed attributes and to a culminating point, several directors made what I think is a familiar but crucial observation: that the director has to have a mingled collectivity of diverse skills that interconnect in complex ways. I'll go into that notion in detail momentarily, but first let's hear how it was brought out in the interviews:

> This process is so all-inclusive, so athletic, that it requires training and experience encompassing music, art, psychology, and previous movies. The filmmaker incorporates the priest, coach, guide, cheerleader, among others—and that has to include a diplomat, and a coordinator who can put many elements together into a whole. Sometimes I think it's like being the ringleader of a three-ring circus, keeping lots of things in the air at the same time, and seeing to it that all the performers are having fun too, while concentrating on making the audience have fun. All these things don't always hold together.

Indeed, at times, *ringleader* could take a back seat to warden of an insane asylum. A paradox for directors is that their role requires an extraordinarily wide array of talents, yet many of them are contradictory. Organizational theorists talk of "command" or "instrumental" features of leadership, which deal with surmounting the task, and simultaneously "nurturing," "group-building," "socio-emotional" features, which pertain to working together on the task. Among many directors and others, the command features are seen as masculine and the more people-nurturing features as feminine. But both are there side by side and intertwined. Or should we say that alpha and beta characteristics have to fuse within the single persona of the director?

We've glimpsed asylum wardens and circus ringmasters for clues to the managing of bedlam. What about R&D centers? Donald Pelz, a colleague of mine at the Institute for Social Research, University of Michigan, studied the leadership style that's necessary for research and development organizations, and I think his findings offer an intriguing clue to making sense out of what the directors were saying. R&D institutes are usually part of large bureaucratic operations, like conglomerate corporations and federal departments. They're charged with coming up with innovative, creative products—within targeted time periods and under strict budgetary restraints. Same as with directors. To do this, they work through a cross-discipline mix of imaginative scientists who collaborate with a polyglot support staff of engineers, technicians, lab assistants, marketing personnel, and many others.

Heading each product team is a project director—who, as I suggested, in some ways, maybe in many ways, is analogous to a film director.

It seems that two organizational cultures meet in R&D: a bureaucratic one and a professional (read artistic) one. The corporate need for order, predictability, and time and expenditure control clashes with the creative scientists' need for autonomy, elbowroom to experiment, and a "horizontal," collaborative style of work—not a top-to-bottom chain of command format. For a research scientist the idea of a strict boss is abhorrent—just as it is for an artist.

Dr. Pelz found that the best R&D project directors gave *blended* leadership. A domineering leadership style brought about apathy and resistance; hands-off, laissez-faire leadership often brought about what approaches chaos—together with dissatisfaction and low productivity. The best leadership style required mixed competencies that gave both "security" and "challenge."

Pelz's study showed that what works in practice is leadership combining security and challenge *at the same time*. It was that climate that the researchers found in organizations with the highest level of productivity and creativity.

Other research studies have come to the same conclusions: leaders having a mix of styles and approaches are fairly common and those bring about the best results.[4] Overall, I think the trick is to blend freedom and flexibility with structure and expectation, to stitch together a climate that promotes productivity and values and empowers people. That's a high-wire balance act, but I think it clearly defines the job description for film directors. That outlook is a way to make sense of the director's jumbled role repertoire.

Wedding "Creativity" and "Leadership"

The studies I mentioned in note 4 don't highlight the vision idea that the directors thought was paramount. But Warren Bennis does in his influential book *On Becoming a Leader*.[5] In his words, "the single defining quality of leaders is their ability to create and realize a vision." The capacity for vision in his scheme means imagining a story involving a desired future state for an organization. This involves dreaming up a mental image attached to reality rather than fiction, but it calls upon a kindred aptitude for creativity.

A recent trend in leadership studies is to focus on managing creative people. This has become a critical problem for businesses concurrent with the Information Age revolution and dog-eat-dog global competition. Cutting-edge organizations are looking for innovative people to help keep them strategically placed, and success in attracting and retaining such personnel requires a very different form of administrative oversight. A recent book, *The Talent Era*, outlines ways of managing such maverick employees, and gives ideas for directing creative people in the arts. Author Subir Chowdhury makes suggestions that echo what the directors were saying, and adds some new points. I'll touch on a few:

- Dispense trust automatically (don't make people earn it).
- Radiate respect (across the board, not for a select few).
- Foster mistakes (let miscalculations come out early rather than downstream).
- Be a guardian of creativity (by not getting in the way of people's ideas).

- Invite talents to say what they want of you (and deliver it quickly).
- Invite input openly (share the decision making).

This isn't the constellation of verities found in traditional management textbooks, but it mirrors and supplements the views of the directors,

If the "Good Old Days" Were So Good, Why Did They Change?

In reflecting on gifted directors, the filmmakers I interviewed mentioned people who came to mind as they spoke. This group was not formally nominated as the best of the gifted, nor were they mentioned to the exclusion of others. They are simply examples of gifted directors as seen by a sample of professional filmmakers.

Only a few contemporary directors were included: Robert Altman, James Cameron, Francis Ford Coppola, Spike Lee, Martin Scorsese, and Steven Spielberg. Foreign directors included Federico Fellini and Ingmar Bergman. Most of those mentioned were Americans from previous eras, specifically, Frank Capra, John Cassavetes, George Cukor, Cecil B. DeMille, John Ford, D. W. Griffith, Howard Hawks, Alfred Hitchcock, Sam Peckinpah, Nicholas Ray, George Stevens, Orson Welles, William Wellman, Billy Wilder, William Wyler, and King Vidor. Clearly, this is not a definitive listing, but it hints at the kind of filmmakers, and the composite of skills, directors hold in high esteem.

Since they were focusing on the American situation, it's not surprising that relatively few foreign directors were mentioned. What may be more interesting is that respondents mentioned much fewer contemporary directors. This could mean that the group as a whole believes directors were better in the past, or the responses may merely reflect that there has been an accumulation of good directors over the past century of film history. An alternative view doesn't seem to hold: namely, that our grasp of the art of cinema and the development of filming techniques has advanced to the point that there was a dramatic burgeoning of directors of distinction in the most recent period.

Whether in the past or contemporaneously, cinematic lore places facility in working with actors near the pinnacle of the director's trade. Hark, what's that rustling we hear? The troupers are getting restless; let's bring them to center stage.

~

CHAPTER THREE

The Actor Factor

Real acting can't be computer generated. Actors are real human beings with awesome talents. We have to be open enough to let them explore the part as they see it. Usually a particular way of playing a part is not wrong, just different.

—Nancy Meyers

"No! No! No! It's just not right!" The frustrated actor spins on his blocking mark defined by a chalk X roughly hewn on the cold slab of an outdoor stage.

His director: "But, Aris, you don't need to show more affection here. *It's only a platonic relationship.*"

"I'm telling you, Petris, it just doesn't *feel* right. I need to emote, even in the most ordinary, common, friendship-type of relationships. I love my friends, Petris! Why, on some level, I think I even love . . . *you!*"

The director rolls his eyes up to the heavens and begs for a deus ex machina to descend and airlift his impossible star out of his show and off to another universe.

Directors and Actors—A Dysfunctional Marriage?

The above scene took place at the time when the Hellenic gods still ruled. Twenty centuries or so later, not much has changed. Directors are addicted to trading war stories about their complicated relationships with actors, both the exhilarating highs and exasperating lows.[1] Some filmmakers who are can-do people, at home in all the technical elements of their craft, lose their cool when dealing with actors. They don't quite know what to make of them. Speaking of ancient Greece, I believe some nonplussed director must have run into this trouble when Thespis stepped out in front of the chorus in Athens around 500 B.C. and made himself into an actor. Why did that early stage director let him get away with that? And would the Greek player have given a hoot about what the director wanted any more than the "hotshot" thespians around Hollywood do today?

From what I can tell, the preparation of filmmakers in film schools includes heavy instruction in the craft and technology of directing. But many of these future Spielbergs and Scorseses get little acting training, so that whole area of the filmmaking process is quirky and mysterious to them. The visual dimension of camera work is one thing, and the rhythm of dialogue and the threadwork of human relationships is another. In her book *Directing Actors*, Judith Weston, who for years has taught a highly regarded course for filmmakers on this subject, concludes that most directors simply "do not have a reliable technique for working with actors."

In *Making Movies*, his sharply observed treatise on directing, Sidney Lumet states that actors have to rely on *themselves* alone as the instrument of performance, instantly communicating feelings and thoughts through a repertoire of human emotions—tears, laughter, sexuality, tenderness, anger.[2] With almost everyone else, filmmakers operate through materials and technology that they can manipulate: with the cinematographers there's the camera; with the make-up people, cosmetics; with set designers, the paints and props. The actor is naked before the audience, and the director has to maneuver through that nakedness. Veteran B-horror guru Roger Corman, I was told, wondered, "I still don't know how actors do what they do."

The status—real or self-perceived—and the whims of actors can spell trouble for directors. Stars receive exalted treatment from virtually everyone on the set, and at the same time they are often viewed as spoiled, egotistical, unpredictable children who have to be "handled." That alleged childishness includes an inclination by some actors to test the limits and behave outrageously when that path is left open. Also, A-List actors have enormous influence and can easily checkmate the director vis-à-vis the front-office powerbrokers.

The director-actor relationship becomes more complicated because actors' expectations of directors vary enormously. An actress I spoke with told me that Woody Allen, in his famously taciturn way, gave her almost no direction on the set. One of the few clues he threw her way, though, was "Talk fast"—a tidbit of advice that, in looking back, she now feels was tremendously valuable throughout her career. For some actors, Allen's offering would have been simply trivial and patronizing: no substance.

Actors typically want a lot of elbowroom to create their characters, and they reject directors who micromanage how they play the part. Gene Hackman has said that he never aspired to be a director because he didn't want some mid-level studio executive going over the dailies and telling him what to do next.[3] Obviously, he feels that as an actor he can defend his artistic autonomy against directors more successfully than he could against the suits if he were directing. But despite jealously protecting their turf, actors do want to be able to rely on the director not saying, "*Print it!*" before the performance is right, before it is the best the actor is capable of giving. At the end of the day, actors don't value a director who "lets them be" on the set and is willing to put a dog of a performance up on the screen.

Acknowledging the natural frictions in their relationship, all the filmmakers I spoke with agreed that actors have an outsized impact on films, financially and artistically, and that directors have a high responsibility to see that actors make that impact. So by what means can directors bring out the best in actors while operating somewhere between the extremes of hands-off aloofness and point-by-point imposition? To specifically probe that, I asked: "How are directors of most help to actors?" Their answers were intriguing and abundant. Let me try to bring order from the profusion of ideas that flowed.

It's Lonely Out There on the Set

Actors are rather isolated people, even on the set. They live in a bubble to wall them off from intrusions and distractions, not to mention dangers, from people who adore them or want something from them. In my research I found it much more difficult to gain access to established actors than high-ranking directors for interviews, and it was much more difficult to nail down an interview once the way was somehow cleared for a contact.

On the set, I saw tremendous reverence for the actors: people cleared the way to let them into or out of a room first, jumped to bring them whatever they might need, kept distance so actors weren't disturbed when they were reading their lines. *Awe was the typical attitude toward actors; fear was the attitude toward directors.* High-profile actors rarely had to carry anything or drive themselves anywhere. In all of this, directors are a main point of contact and the chief source of artistic validation for actors. The directors I interviewed recognized the special relationship they have with actors and considered it a critical element of their work.

> Actors are performers, and there on the movie set the director is the audience; they are performing for *you*. The bottom line is simply that this is a symbiotic relationship where actors need directors and directors need actors. As the director, you are an audience of one—you are *the* audience, symbolically and in spades. You have to supply the reactions to the actor in ways that are equivalent to applause in the theater. No one else will say anything; it's not their job and they know it. Actors look to you for approval and that's the only approval they are going to get in the moment.

An experience with a gargantuan-scale actor like George C. Scott (not just his size) accentuates the point.

> Once, I was directing George in *Inherit the Wind* and using the video assist, looking at the monitor in a side room. People were crowding around me, making the situation claustrophobic. So I picked up and walked to the set to view the scene directly. When the shot was finished, George leaned over to say how much it meant to him to have me there watching him. *And he began to weep.*
>
> Actors are looking to the director for an appreciative nod, for parental-type accolades. They are wanting for the director to yell, "*Print that.*" You know, actors are doing the scene out of sequence in the micro-moment and toward the discovery of the micro-beat. They have to rely entirely on the director's eyes and ears and sensibilities to know that this action is right and fits with the whole. There is an invisible thread between the director and the actor toward getting that perfect effect. They can just look at each other and know *they've gotten it*, without anything verbal crossing between them.

Is It Safe to Go into the Water Here?

The main theme coming through in the interviews focused on the issues of security and risk in helping actors. First, directors agree, they have to make actors feel secure, upbeat, relaxed—fully at ease in the situation. Second, with that as a platform, actors have to be encouraged to go to the edge, to reach deep within themselves and find hidden and even painful resonances there of the characters they are trying to portray. It's like tossing actors a life preserver, then cheering them on into shark-infested waters.

When you're an actor, insecurity comes with the territory. We know that actors are on fragile ground whenever they're asked to open themselves up publicly in fiercely honest ways, while at the same time, in all their bareness, facing potential rebuff by directors. Actors have an obligation to observe human behavior closely, the same way writers do, in order to reflect it accurately and compellingly. But they reflect it through actions and emotions that grow from their understanding of how people, including themselves, deal with the challenges of life. They are the messengers and the animators of the words of the writers, but their perpetual worry and conundrum is whether they have it right. The director, in a sense, is a stand-in for the writer in telling them if they have gotten it right, at least from where the director is going with the story. (Many writers, though, who have later screened their words on celluloid, only to see something they far from recognize, might disagree.)

Besides potential ego humiliation, for actors there's the material risk of losing out on future jobs if they mess up. Competition among actors is cutthroat. There are more than 45,000 actors in Los Angeles vying for a handful of choice parts.[4] Someone has said that actors are to L.A. what hungry people are to Calcutta. Sometimes it must feel to them like all the world's an actor. Then there is the relentless ritual of the audition. An actor is forever being tested for new parts by new people in different venues—and being rejected. Actors are like writers in that they have to be able to eat a constant stream of rejections.

Except for those who are at the top of the pile, actors are like perpetual wallflowers at the prom. Screen jobs generally are short-term, they are sequential, and they are uncertain. And all of that takes place in the unreliable make-believe environment that is Hollywood. Laurence Olivier was probably right when he called acting "a masochistic form of exhibitionism."[5] The directors I spoke with were attuned to this issue.

> Actors are extremely sensitive. They are out front as the most visible component of the film, exposing their inner person, and they can look foolish. I try to form a psychological bond as a friend. I try to be patient, and I'm playful and at ease with my actors. In many cases, with all their insecurities, you are Mommy or Daddy to them around the set. The bottom line: directors have to win the respect and trust of actors. If there is a wall between the actor and the audience, *there was a wall between the actor and the director.*
>
> You never should come at actors as a critic. If you reject their performance, they can take it that you are rejecting *them.* You must make them feel at home and free: pamper them, pat them on the back, even entertain them, give them a lot of support.

On the "Handling" of Actors

Now, it would be a mistake to read these comments and conclude that directors are simply endearing and cuddly teddy-bear types who love nothing so much as to envelop all their relationships in a warm glow. Anyone who has worked among directors knows that's a fantasy. There is purpose and there is discipline in all of this. The purpose is functional and evident: to steer or inveigle actors to perform in new, surprising, and honest ways that illuminate characters and irradiate films. That enhances the art of filmmaking and draws audiences who enlarge the profits of film studios. I don't want to shed darkness on this, but directors do ratchet up their reputations and paychecks by maneuvering around actors in ways that draw outstanding performances from them. Also, some directors think that giving actors a wide berth isn't setting them loose to go wherever they want. It's a way of bestowing responsibility.

> You've got to provide a *safe place* that will allow actors to expose themselves and tap into the richness of their own emotional life. They have to find the character within themselves and interpret that character *in their own way*. It's a truism that motivation comes from the real life and experiences of actors. And you want what they have to give you. A director somehow has to bring into play the fullness of the instrument that actors embody.
>
> You should sometimes go with something that you wouldn't ordinarily go with to make actors feel comfortable. Maybe it's agreeing to a costume that's not quite your taste. That gives them a sense that *they have some power* over their choices and that you have some confidence in the choices they make.
>
> Actors want a sense of freedom, so give them the space to do their own thing. They need to find their own moments and *sparkle in their own way*. If they're not comfortable in the situation, they're never going to get it right. I personally will never let them look bad, never damage them. Therefore they can *show me anything*, let themselves go, and try things they would otherwise fear getting into. I will *not* use it if it will embarrass or expose them.

There were nuanced views among the filmmakers on the amount of direction to give, assuming a context of openness or freedom. Filmmakers frequently noted that to get the job done, they need to give actors the least amount of direction necessary.

> Actors come to the movie set prepared to play the character. You ought to stand back and let them do that. You can do some shaping—a little more of this or that—but most of the time *stay out of their way*. Don't be *doctrinaire*.

But we are also told to keep in mind that the director has authority and an artistic conception to bring to life.

> An axiom of directors is, "Make them think the ideas are theirs." You are a puppeteer, in part. Rather than doing things that cause actors to resent and oppose you, they ought to be putty in your hands. What you have to do is get them facing the right direction, then let the actor find the exact road.

We'll come back to the issue of the director as the architect of the performance shortly, but first let's look at some intriguing analogies that directors brought forward.

Of Stage Directors, Symphony Conductors, and Athletes

One of my respondents, agreeing with the thrust of these comments, made an interesting distinction between directing actors in film and in theater. In theater, the audience is live and the actor projects to the balcony. The stage crew is out of sight during the performance, and lighting has a different logic and form. Also, there's a particular phenomenon of stage acting that many actors maintain makes the experience particularly electric and fraught with opportunity to prove the mastery of their craft: it's that mistakes made during the performance are fait accompli, uncorrectable. While the aim is the same, the live, in-the-moment environment of theater dictates a different approach from cinema. In short, stage actors have to be prepped to get it right without the cushion of retakes.

> I do not believe, and others will disagree with me, that the role of a film director is analogous to that of a theater director. A theater director has weeks and months to rehearse a play and can put lots of time into working with actors, helping them to do their homework for their characters. In film, you don't have the luxury of that; you may have two weeks for rehearsal and that's outstanding. Typically you have a week or less. *And sometimes no rehearsal time.* Time is always pushing, pushing at your back.
>
> In film you rely on the actors coming to the process with preparation—about the character, back story, intention, objective, all those details—so when they show up they are not floundering. They already have a point of view, and maybe you *shade* the point of view and you give them input. I think it's kind of like a conductor in a symphony who is telling the brass section to play the music not quite so loud or the strings to play with more of a percussive flair. You don't work with musicians on the techniques of playing the instrument. Film is rather a *conductor's* medium, where you shape the performance, not create it.

So film actors can't be broadly equated with stage actors, but one director I spoke with thought they were akin to *athletes*. Both have to perform, each faces an audience, and if they choke up they're going to blow it. Both sets of performers have to "practice, practice, practice" to reach peak form. And they have one other thing in common.

> Actors are like athletes in that they do their best when they don't think about what they're doing, when they just have confidence and *feel* the part. I've never seen a good performance by any actors who were insecure about what they were doing. It just can't happen. Because then they're thinking. And when you're thinking, if it's all going through the head, you're not acting. As many wise people have said before me, *acting* is *reacting*, and if you're looking over your own shoulder, second-guessing yourself, you can't do a good job.

Surrounded by Atmospherics

The director has to create an atmosphere on the set that is conducive to working with actors in a creative way. This was a heavy theme in my interviews. It isn't just a tête-à-tête between director and actor. There's a mélange of other professionals and crew members—set designers, costume people, electricians, sound people—who are involved. Innovations, and mishaps, can occur at any time while putting up the lighting, constructing set backgrounds, or arranging stunts and special effects. Chances are that if the director blows his stack every time someone makes a mistake, there's going to be an aura of tension in the air. And sets by their very nature are often hair-trigger tense even during the most halcyon of shoots. Additional tension is counterproductive. The director has to develop an atmosphere that promotes confidence and announces, "Chances are taken here."

> You can go on a set and tell right away if the environment promotes good work or not. You *feel it*. You feel a safe place for people to work. It has to have a congenial, comfortable, and interactive atmosphere, where you can see cooperative relationships in action around you. And there ought to be some smiles and laughter, even around serious things.
>
> The atmosphere I like is where actors feel they can try things out, where they can be joyful and open, and have license to express themselves in experimental ways, to improvise. Yes, the director *is* a father figure, but one who is there to *encourage* rather than criticize. I truly want to create a feeling of relaxation and fun on the set, but only until the scene is ready to shoot. *Then* I want absolute discipline. That kind of undisturbed opportunity to concentrate is another way to make the atmosphere comfortable for actors.

Of Tallies and Titties

One director observed that the atmosphere necessary for artistic productivity is dramatically different from the atmosphere for business productivity. One is experimental and allows things to evolve in unpredictable ways; the other is pre-programmed and tightly controlled. The climate the front office wants directors to promote can clash fundamentally with what directors feel is essential for creative work. In addition to being an artistic craftsman, a good director has to also be a sociologist of sorts or an OD (organizational development) specialist who can design an inspiring social environment.

> Directors have to establish a protected work situation. You see, this is not a business. The bureaucracy is a business, but directing a film is not a business. Art is *messy*. You can't dictate art like you can carry out a business plan, with bean counters using tally sheets and punch clocks. People have to make mistakes. They have to be able to fall on their noses and pick themselves up and start again. You have to bring about an environment to deal with that mess, without making it personal and problematic.
>
> Believe me, it's a mess. *It's a mess.* This one has a headache. That one's son kept her up all night. Someone else is at home ill. A lead actor thinks the script is shitty. Someone else doesn't like the color of the shirt or doesn't feel the costume is comfortable. And that one is protesting that he doesn't want to come in through the door, he wants to come in through the window. It turns out to be raining, and the scene was written to be sunny. The DP [director of photography] has daylight film in the camera instead of tungsten. It's just a fucking mess.

And if you came into it thinking it was going to be neat, this *isn't for you.* You've got to go into the mess and slowly work around it and solve all these problems. "All right, we'll work with the film we have, we'll rewrite the script so there's rain. And I'm sorry you have a headache; maybe you'll take some aspirins or slip into a nap."

You need an atmosphere that allows for all these problems to be solved. The mess is OK, just like a mess on an active person's desk is OK. If you're selling widgets, you don't want that mess. It's not cost-effective to the bureaucracy to have it. But being cost-effective is inimical to the arts. You've got to have a mess; *creativity goes hand in hand with it.*

A young female director came out with an interesting slant. She told me that to make the cast feel this is where you can take chances, you should demonstrate to them that you are willing to make yourself vulnerable. It isn't always a matter of "You go out on a limb and I'll cover your backside." Sometimes it's "Let's jump into this water together." She related a personal experience to illustrate.

One time I directed an erotica piece. Well, as a woman, for the first time I had to think of sexuality differently. When I went into the project, I knew there was going to be partial nudity, and I thought, "Well, it ain't my titties up there." As I began casting, and talking to the women, and doing the preparation work to make the project what I wanted it to be, I realized that it *had* to be my titties up there. You see, to make the actress feel safe, I had to be as vulnerable as she had to be. The scene was part of the movie, and the movie was part of me. I was responsible for it. It reflected me and would affect my reputation. It wasn't a case of me watching her expose herself; it had to be an environment where everyone working on the project was exposed. Just getting that into my head helped me to help the actress. No, I didn't take off my blouse, but I took away my protective wall, psychologically. *She wasn't alone.*

From the Directors' Toolbox

Directors had a lot to say about the specific approaches they used to get the best from actors, and their techniques varied a good bit. For example, a particular director at first suggested to me something as concrete and mechanical as blocking the scene correctly so that actors would move in certain ways that shape the flow of the story and establish relationships among the characters. He added that there's also a need to create special "magical moments" in acting, a skill that he feels is intuitive and almost poetic. As you will see, the suggestions and experiences I report traverse much of the ground between these poles.

Put on His Shoes or Hear His Tune

Under the broad canopy, one of the points the directors underscored was that they have to learn to value actors and understand the acting process. You don't have to put on the actor's costume; just get into his or her shoes. Marlon Brando once remarked that "An actor's a guy who, if you ain't talking about him, ain't listening."[6] Next to themselves, actors like to talk about acting: self and craft are interwoven. Actors I have spoken to stress that for directors to know and speak the same language as actors is important, both to sense what they are reaching for and to show that the director is on the same wavelength.

Actors are concerned about "choices" they have to make that tie in with the script and their own inner being. They want to clarify the "transitions" or beat changes, the emotional events that occur where their characters observe or discover or lose something critical. They need to know about the "facts" of the scene and how those channel the actions their characters might take. There's also "subtext"—unstated facts, things that aren't said but meant in the script. Those examples just begin to scratch the surface of the actors' vernacular and thought patterns. Directors held that, to connect with performers around these acting issues, they have to start with themselves.

> You should appreciate actors if you want to assist them. For *me*, I came to the realization in my first film that the acting process is difficult and special. It's just not easy for anyone to give a spontaneous, well-thought-out performance while going over the same material again in take after take, dealing with the director's notes, and dealing with the physical logistics of the scene. It's just *not easy* and I found I developed an early respect for the acting process. And I found I like actors, because I think for the most part they are concerned with the *honesty* of what they're doing. They want to know that what they are doing comes out of the inner recesses and motivations of the character they are playing.
>
> Basically, as a director, you've got to know acting. When young people come to me with an interest in going into directing, I right away say, "*Study acting.*" Roger Corman regularly used to send all his budding young directors to acting classes, although he claims to not understand the mystery of acting. That ensured that they knew what acting was about, even though Corman was making strictly commercial movies.
>
> I myself studied acting with Lee Strasberg and Stella Adler, so I know an enormous amount about the primary available acting techniques in this country. I know the vocabulary and how these techniques work, and because of that I know how to communicate with actors. And that makes a huge difference.

Directors insist that if you didn't study acting, you should at least pay heed to actors. Hear what they have to say, for thereby you'll gain a special kind of enlightenment. But only active listening can decode the message.

> You have to keep your ears open on the set so you can be attuned to what the issue or problem is if the actor can't access what you've been driving at. *Ask questions* to find out what they're thinking and how they would like to work. Not that I'll give them everything they're asking for, but I have to know where they're coming from. I try to accommodate them from what I hear.
>
> Beyond being a listener, I believe directors also have to be able to *hear* what people are really saying. That's because on the set you're daddy, and a lot of information that comes to you comes filtered through attitudes of deference or defiance that you have to cut through. So often with actors, to get at the need they're expressing, you have to filter what they are saying. Sometimes you have to disregard the way things are presented and just listen for the *music in the voice*.

Acting Is a Verb

Directors say that what they hear tells them that actors overwhelmingly want help in dealing with the characters they are portraying. In the modern era, most actors follow the Stanislavsky approach to understanding and playing characters. In this school, more familiarly known as Method acting, the performer has to read the spine of the character—meaning the overriding need or aim that drives the character in life and remains constant through the story. Then there are the character's objectives that are more immediate and specific, like wanting to go to bed with someone or to pay back a debt.

There are verbs or playable actions that have to be articulated to animate and display the objective of the character, such as deciding to beseech, bribe, or beat your wife's harasser. Also, the character confronts obstacles in moving toward objectives, such as a policeman appearing at the corner just when he wants to kick the crap out of the villain. By working their way through these concepts, actors discover or hone their characters. The directors spelled out assorted techniques they use in helping actors develop their characters.

> The director has to focus on understanding the parts, the characters, because actors want the most help in that area. That's why actors love to speak with *writers*, to understand how the writer conceived the characters. I try to expose actors to the widest range of possibilities about what that character may be thinking or feeling or going through to expand the range of options that actors can *draw on* in shaping their own performance. Then I tell them to keep flexible before they decide which way to go. One directorial responsibility is to ask the right questions. "Why do you want to play this so quietly?" "Are you cowardly?" "What is it in your character that makes you turn away from him?" If I ask pertinent questions about what they seem to be doing, that can be helpful.
>
> Directors should try to make the part *playable*, maybe suggesting particular behavior, a line of action, to bring out the part. The director has to find the right words to express how he sees the scene unfolding. For example, if the mother has just died in the story, the director doesn't say, "You're sad now." The words are more like, "In this scene you dread walking up to your mother in her casket, because you don't want to remember seeing her face for the last time that way." It's a matter of creating those kinds of evocative scenarios.

A few directors said it's necessary sometimes to take the actor in hand and actually produce the wanted emotion or state of mind. When they can't get across what they're after, no matter how many verbal attempts they make, they deliberately create the intended emotions in the actor through actions that provoke that response.

> On occasion you have to sneak up on a person and cause a spontaneous reaction, like slapping her on the wrist. I once *insulted* an actor and got him pissed off at me, and then said that's how I want you to feel in this scene. In another case, I asked one actor to make anti-Semitic remarks that another actor would overhear, because I wanted that second person to be furious with him in the hijacking scene that was coming up. But here's a precaution. It's OK to stir up an actor to get him or her into the part; but don't

do it as a regular procedure. A director friend of mine pushed an actor and flustered him to such a degree that he couldn't continue with the part at all. That holds up everything, costs money, and is totally counterproductive.

In a different project I surveyed actors and asked them the same question about how directors can be of most help. Actors made a similar point about *playability*—confirming from an actor's perspective what the directors said. One example decisively drives the point home.

> In each scene the actor has a part involving an objective in the story, something the actor *has to do*. The actor has to figure out how to carry out that action, and the director can help the actor work that through. You see, the actor participates in telling the story by doing something that is playable, just like people in real life accomplish things, reach their goals, by doing things. *That means verbs.* The director can assist not by saying something abstract, like play it "lighter" or "gentler," but by making the event an action, and a concrete one, with comments like, "Do it as though she might break if you touch her," or "Do it as a secret."

Casting Iron
Several directors insisted that good casting is at the root of good acting. Directors help actors not only by assisting them in their parts, but also by casting them astutely at the beginning. However, directors' authority over casting has decreased in recent years, especially for the starring roles in big-ticket movies.

In the old studio days, casting was easier in some ways because each studio had a stable of actors who could be assigned to parts by somebody's order (though that limited the range of who could be selected). Now, with actors and directors operating as free agents, matching up all the components of the film can be time consuming and arduous. And some of the complexities of casting, like physical appearance, ethnicity, and age, can determine who is chosen and what they bring to the part—which can have ramifications for the way directors have to work with actors during the shoot.

What does a director have to deal with in the casting process? Judith Weston has spelled out the essentials in *Directing Actors*.[7] First, the director has to focus on the actor's ability—not only acting skills but the actor's intuitive equipment (i.e., emotional range) and artistic sensibility (i.e., taste and sense of proportion). Next, is this actor right for the part—can he or she connect to the character's experience and the transforming events that will be depicted?

Weston believes the director has to consider whether the actor and director can hit it off professionally by asking questions like "Will this actor take direction from me? Can we communicate? Is there mutual respect?" Finally, how will this actor relate to the other actors and roles in the film? In casting, it's important that the ensemble synchronize with the individual roles. These rules of thumb are easier to write out than carry out, and directors have to work with the consequences in any case. It was obvious that directors in my survey were tuned in to the significance of casting.

Casting is probably *the key* to the acting component of directing. It's a good 70 percent of the job. Find the right person, right face, right timbre, right attitude. The acting flows from that. Once you've cast well for the roles, you can let the actors carry the ball themselves as much as possible.

But in a given moment in the same movie, a director, knowing what acting level is required, can have a very accomplished actor in one role and a person who knows nothing about acting in another. That inexperienced person may have the visual look that's right, that's why he was picked, and the director knows that he can get out of the person what he needs, with a lot of effort. If the person is inexperienced, I may be all over him.

Another technique, used extensively by directors like George Stevens and William Wyler, wasn't mentioned in my survey. Those men went on shooting take after take until they judged they had gotten what they were aiming for. Wyler seemed to know what he wanted, and knew when he had it, but he wasn't able to make that clear to anyone beforehand. So "Forty-Take Wyler," as he was known, just kept on rolling the camera until he decided he had the material to choose from. But don't knock him: he directed thirty-eight Academy Award–winning performances. There's a story they tell about Wyler working with Laurence Olivier, driving him frantic with endless retakes. Finally Olivier asked, "Willy, how *do* you want me to do it?" All Wyler could manage was, "Better."[8]

And Add a Firm Hand
Despite the thrust of most of these comments, a movie set isn't a utopian democracy where directors and actors exchange views over cappuccino into the wee hours. Work has to be completed, schedules have to be met, and someone has to be in charge of organizing a disorderly enterprise. Directors sometimes direct actors by telling them what to do concretely in the area of performing. The comments here and in the previous section may seem contradictory, but they are not. Directors have to be very definite, but they also have to be very open.

I think collaboration with actors is a good thing. *But toward one goal.* People will feel better about flexibility if they feel someone has the whole thing in hand. It's only when there are no answers given and no clear pathway that there is chaos and everyone tries to fill the void by performing in their own way.

A director has to know how to communicate and in a clear and concise fashion, has to know the script and articulate the vision for the picture and the scenes to the actors. All actors really *want* direction and guidance. We shouldn't be afraid of giving it to them and helping them work their way through roles that are challenging and also perplexing.

You have to keep actors abreast of the progression and of the whole. A movie is shot out of sequence. An actress I'm directing on Wednesday morning didn't work at all on Tuesday, so she didn't see what someone playing her husband did in the previous scene. If they were in a play together, they would know everything from A to Z, but in a film someone could be in makeup or not in the studio when a scene takes place. The director has to keep them in tune with the overall project, letting them know what other people have done, what comes before or after a particular action, and how this performance has to play out in the context of everything else that is going on.

It is important for a director to have a clear vision of the story and how things will unfold. That said, directors must also be prepared to talk it out and go for something else if that's the way the pieces fall into place.

Different Strokes

Directors didn't restrain themselves in spelling out concrete principles and tricks of the trade. But then they seemed to backpedal. They included a caveat: what holds for one actor doesn't hold for another—you have to fine tune your approach for each one. There was strong agreement that actors are creative, restless individuals, each with particular strengths, weaknesses, and peculiarities. That means a director navigates a different course with each one in ways that may appear inconsistent in the aggregate.

One actor may be a dedicated Method performer who wants to absorb the character, and another may be wedded to more classical technical acting, where gestures and voice tone are of the essence. She wants to "register" anger, rather than subject herself to it on the inside. Some actors want to always look good on the screen, and others want to embody the character, no matter how they look. One actor wants to follow the script pretty much to the letter, and another has to bend the words to his own personality.

In his book *The Film Director*, Richard L. Bare speaks of a few distinct types of ac-tors that directors encounter.[9] There's the temperamental, high-strung leading lady (think Bette Davis); the overzealous self-promoter who wants to make a small part memorable—even if that doesn't jibe with the other characters in the story; the novice who got the part because she knows somebody or has the right bust; and stars like Harrison Ford and Tom Cruise, who (at least in the past) wanted to be in the same bankable role in every picture. The directors I interviewed told me that they have to be able to shift gears as different actors come before their cameras.

> You've got to individualize in working with actors, depending on what they bring to the table. With a brilliant actor like Robert Duvall all I have to do is *hire him* and commu-nicate my vision of the piece to him and how I see his character. Besides that, I need to *listen to him*, because a great actor is going to have ideas about doing the character that go beyond what the director imagined, or the writer. With a beginner, I could be guid-ing him every step along the way—like doing line readings, telling him when to smile, if necessary. Often I start out by asking actors straightaway, "How are you most com-fortable in taking direction? What would you like from me?" That has worked pretty well in my films.

In one encounter a director gave a detailed example of how he worked differently with two actors in the same film. The illustration shows concretely how the internal architecture of actors calls for dissimilar approaches from directors:

> I was making a film once with Kurt Russell and Ray Liotta. Kurt was very much like Jodie Foster to work with, because both are creatures of the set. They were both trained

at Disney as child actors and very social and have been in the business forever. I think Kurt wants to join in with the director in making the movie. That's the opposite of Ray Liotta, who's a New York–trained Method actor and would sit quietly in character with his book most of the time. He had *thousands* of notes on his book, and he would ask me *hundreds* of questions. He went for thirty-five ride-alongs with the L.A.P.D. to get into the part. Basically, he's all about concentration and working from the inside out with his character.

Kurt does as much internal work as Ray, but he doesn't do it where I can *see it* happening. He would wait and put on his shirt almost at the last minute, because he was hanging out on the set and didn't want to get it dirty. And he would put on his character when he put on his shirt. Ray would be in character when he arrived to make up in the morning, and he was sort of in character through the whole shooting of the movie. So working with those two guys required completely different skills that tied in with their different ways of working. If I had made them both adapt to my own set style, I wouldn't have gotten as good performances from them.

To illustrate, I would answer *all* of Ray's questions. I would storyboard and have the visual script for the movie before me and show Ray how I was going to shoot it. Basically, it was responding to his every insecurity or uncertainty about what was going to happen. With Kurt, it was a matter of allowing him, or better, encouraging him, to collaborate. His style was to make the character his own, to suggest lines, to change speeches, to make staging suggestions, particularly in action scenes because he's done a lot of action movies.

Filmmakers take very different paths to the director's chair and bring different backgrounds and disciplines to bear on the job. The respected George Stevens started out as a cinematographer, and Robert Wise initially was editor for a round of films—including *Citizen Kane*. More and more directors begin and some continue as screenwriters, including people like Blake Edwards, Nancy Meyers, and Nora Ephron. And actors have broken into directing in increasing numbers, notably Tim Robbins, Warren Beatty, Jodie Foster, Clint Eastwood, Robert Redford, and more recently Denzel Washington (not to overlook Orson Welles).

Some directors bring an extensive theater background. Many come from film school—but not all. And of late, MTV and commercial TV are well-trod pathways for younger filmmakers. Add in the gigantic ego needed to dare to tackle the enormity of what making a mainstream movie has become—with the narcissism and idiosyncrasy that often go hand-in-hand with a large-scale ego—and you begin to get a picture of the diversity to which the directors in my survey alluded.

Directors made the point that they are cut from different cloth and work in unique ways. For example, one director told me that on his set nobody talks to the actors except for him, and he only talks to them using the name of their character, not their real name. Another likes to work the part out through the rehearsal process whenever he can. A third wants quiet, in-depth dialogue with the actor about the character, conducted out of range of everyone else on the set. The point is that in the individualizing that directors do, they bring their different directorial styles. In other words, they applied the same relativity to understanding actors that they applied to themselves.

There are many approaches, and each director has his *own way* with actors: just let them go; romance them; coerce them; don't say a word; guide them. There are "*good cop*" directors and "*bad cop*" directors. It's based on the filmmaker's background and point of view. Coppola draws on his theatrical experience. Altman says that it's about picking the right cast and then stepping back. Hitchcock wanted actors to fit into his screen imagery and was said to be dogmatic and to instruct, "Do it like this or like that." Also, I think by and large the writer-director has more respect for the script than directors who haven't written. The director's personality gets into this, too. For example, Woody Allen says very little; Steven Spielberg says a lot.

Basically, directors are interested in actors and the acting process to different degrees. Some directors, like Hitchcock, are more into the style of the movie and the *visual components*. Others are deeply tuned into drawing the performance out of actors and aren't concerned so much with the camera. George Cukor is a prime example of directors who are really sympathetic to the acting process. The same with some European directors, like Ingmar Bergman, Truffaut, Rossellini.

Creativity Theory out of the Limelight

In writing this chapter, my brain perceived a background noise telling me that creativity theory comes into play in this in some way. We have been talking about a helping process, but an exceptional kind of helping. In medicine, you help someone get well; in teaching, you help someone learn. Here, as a director, you help someone *be creative*. What in the world does that mean? It kept occurring to me that I should call up creativity theory to see how it might apply.

Risking the same side glances a writer sometimes endures when he or she shows up unannounced on location, this academician once again steps out onto the soundstage to draw some intuitive comparisons between his and the director's profession. So now, I beseech you—professional moviemaker, film buff, and film student alike—to consider the following: psychologists who study creativity make a distinction between *convergent* thinking, which is conventional, and *divergent* thinking, which is innovative. The first involves the standard problem-solving approach—narrowing down a set of potential solutions to a problem until they converge in an answer. The second and more imaginative way of thinking directs you to come up with a very wide range of possibilities that could feed into solving a problem. In that mode, you emphasize funneling out rather than funneling in.

Divergent thinking has different facets. *Fluency* involves arriving at several solutions in a relatively short time span. *Flexibility* means that you juggle many possible solutions at one time. *Originality* implies that you entertain ideas that depart from what other people deem acceptable.

Directors in the survey spoke of using these divergent approaches in their work. They try to encourage actors to consider as many ways as possible to interpret a character and to be flexible before making a choice. Recall:

> I think it's kind of like a conductor in a symphony who is telling the brass section to play the music not quite so loud or the strings to play with more of a percussive flair. You

don't work with musicians on the techniques of playing the instrument. Film is rather a *conductor's* medium, where you shape the performance, not create it.

Directors ask questions to help expand the actor's scope of thinking about a part. Further, they create a risk-tolerant zone that frees up actors to think "out of the box." And they call on actors to reach into their own personas to arrive at portrayals that are distinctive, different from what anyone else might conceive. Intuitively, directors seem to be following guidelines that creativity researchers suggest.

Broad study of creativity is relatively recent. The breakthrough can be pinned down to J. P. Guilford's presidential address to the American Psychological Association in 1949, when he documented the scantiness of studies on the subject.[10] He began his own work during World War II, looking not at film folk or artists but at fighter pilots. The U.S. Air Force asked him to try to find out why unusually intelligent and superbly trained aviators weren't equipped to deal with unanticipated problems arising when an airplane was hit and damaged. Guilford set out to develop tests that could predict which recruits would be able to factor originality into their flying competency. For a long time before that, work on creativity had been preoccupied with genius, with physician Cesare Lombroso relating genius to madness and eugenicist Sir Francis Galton to hereditary factors. Freud and his associates used the notion of the repressed libido to scrutinize cutting-edge artists like Leonardo da Vinci and Michelangelo.

One of the important twentieth-century advances was to conceive of creativity not as a trait but as a process. That has important implications for working with people proactively to produce creative outcomes. The phases of the process fall into a general sequence. *Preparation* involves gathering information about a domain or problem and becoming immersed in its history. Curiosity is a component of the preparation mode. (Let's relate this to a problem such as how to play a particular character—a policeman. Information-gathering might involve observing how cops work on the beat.)

Next comes *incubation*, when a person continues involvement with the problem but allows the unconscious mind to enter and play around with the subject being addressed. Sometimes taking a shower or driving a car can spark new ideas better than hacking away at it with pristine logic. (At this stage, a director can often be heard to say, "Sleep on it.")

A crucial following step is *illumination* or *insight*—the "Eureka!" moment that most people think of as the totality of creativity. Psychologists believe that this "Aha!" phenomenon breaks through when new ideas have congealed forcefully enough to ward off unconscious censorship. (OK, the cop in the story will be a crude brute, but use the investigative methods of a university scientist.)

Then comes *verification* or *evaluation*, where the idea is examined and tested consciously and shared with others to receive critical feedback. (Well, maybe this cop character is worth trying.) One pitfall here is accepting the idea without a really sober assessment; the other is to throw it overboard out of lack of confidence or too high an expectation.

These were the stages proposed originally by Graham Wallas in his respected book *The Art of Thought*.[11] A fifth stage has been added: namely, *elaboration*, which involves not only carrying the idea into reality, like playing the conceived character in a re-hearsal, but transmuting the character as he or she bumps into the "reality" of other characters and the unfolding story line. (The other parts can't react naturally to this guy. Maybe the cop shouldn't really use scientific methods; he should pretend to, but invariably botch them.)

Directors and actors do seem to go through these stages without having the rele-vant scholarly volumes around the set to crib from. Directors sometimes lead actors back to fundamental acting principles to bring the element of preparation—that is, training—to bear in working out a part. We all know the saying that creativity stems from prepared minds. Directors help actors through the elaboration stage of altering the conceived character when the chemistry with other parts isn't there. There are lots of examples of the other stages.

Creativity theory contains other elements, like attributes of the creative person, tests of creativity, and techniques for stimulating creative thinking. We can think about the theory of creativity, but there's also the "creativity of theory." If creativity theory got attached to the repertoire of directors, possibly through the curriculum of film schools, it could be put to work systematically by them and in an informed way. Executed imaginatively, I think it would be a bonus for filmmakers. Along with other instruments of the craft, it could become a powerful tool in their hands. I am aware that academics like me are not unknown to oversell the tools of their own trade, so let me label this proposal with the usual "use with care" advisory. Still, let's face it, given the notorious failure rate rampant in the movie industry, a few adventurous di-rectors experimenting with the idea probably wouldn't result in any real harm.

CHAPTER FOUR

~

Digital Rising—Independents' Day

Digital is all for the good. It brings in a whole new group of young people who can't get big financing. Many directors are scared of it, like some were of video-cassettes, scared it would cut into theatergoing. But people now collect videotapes like people collect books, and yet they still go out to the movies.

—Henry Jaglom

When Robert Redford stomps through the snow at Sundance, making his way to the latest buzz-laden Indie film, I'll bet he sometimes thinks back to a 1970 snowed-in night in Buffalo, New York.

Revved up by the box-office and critical success of *Butch Cassidy and the Sundance Kid*, the emerging screen star came up with the idea of doing a trilogy of films on the slippery character of success in America. The first was *Downhill Racer*, a character study of a cock-sure, determined Olympic skier whose driving ambition was to win the gold. Paramount released the movie, but in the guise of a macho action flick, and when the audience response was tepid, they put the marketing campaign into low gear. Redford had his heart wrapped up in this project, so he took to the road to fan interest in the movie.

That's where Buffalo comes in. His tour was interrupted when a heavy snowstorm there (is anyone surprised?) pinned him down in his hotel. That night he dined with the Paramount field representative who, compassionate soul that he was, set this young rising star straight. The rep gave Redford a piece of advice, roughly along these lines: "The studio isn't behind this picture anymore, pal. They've given up on pro-moting it. For your own good, you better stop heading down this blind alley."

That experience stayed with Redford—who is a determined uphill racer. Ten years later, he established the Sundance Institute, predicated on the notion that he and other filmmakers like him who want to deal with out-of-the-mainstream themes should not be trapped in a landscape of blind alleys. The age of contemporary inde-pendent film had arrived.

Two years later, in 1982, another milestone event took place that helps lay the groundwork for this chapter. The film *Tron* was released, starring Jeff Bridges as a computer genius who becomes zapped into an electronic world and finds himself a player inside a computer game environment where he has to win to stay alive. Director Steven Lisberger used computer graphic images in about 20 percent of the film to create and enhance the background and actors. This was the first significant application of digital effects in American cinema. *Tron*, a Disney production, was hugely expensive to make and did much worse than expected box-office. The bold special effects had the unintended consequences of putting digital moviemaking on temporary hold. But the technology Disney had developed to create *Tron* ushered in the age of Hollywood digital filmmaking.[1]

These two turning points, the start of Sundance and the making of *Tron*, and their convergence, changed the face of contemporary filmmaking, and the directors I interviewed spoke eloquently on both developments. When asked about their views on the advent of digital technology, their replies covered the digital revolution and its subsequent overflow impact on independent filmmaking. On the pages to follow I'm going to report their thoughts and, with your indulgence, try to chaperone you through the thicket of agreements and divergencies in their responses.

By way of a readers' road map, I'll begin by presenting some *core attitudes* of directors—pros and cons—toward digital technology in filmmaking. That will take us to the whole *independent filmmaking* phenomenon, its inception, and directors' views of how the digital revolution and the Indie movement intersect. The narrative road then swerves in a more practical direction, with directors recounting the advantages and disadvantages of *using digital technology* in their craft of making movies.

Digital–The Pros and the Cons

There's no doubt that the digital phenomenon is a red-hot topic in today's Hollywood, whether in the executive suites or at tête-à-têtes around swimming pools throughout town. But creatives are not all on the same page in their feelings about the new technology on the block. The directors who spoke with me fell into three clusters: a large group who were *enthusiasts*, excited and upbeat about prospects; a somewhat lesser group of *ambivalents* with mixed or wait-and-see feelings; and a small knot of *skeptics* who were less than hospitable or outright opposed. Their own words convey the pungency of these multiflavored opinions.

Two Thumbs Up for Digital
The *enthusiasts* had their clapboards ready for action.

> I love it. The cheaper and faster we can deal with the details of filmmaking, the more creative we can be. I think it's *terrific*, and I've gone up to the George Lucas operation to look into what they're doing there.

To me, digital technology is a great new tool and people fall in love with their tools. When I started out, people had to lug around two-hundred-pound cameras back then. Film editing in the 1930s and '40s required you to splice and cement on acetate, and every time you did that you lost another frame. You could lose a lot of frames and have a lot of black spots. The director and editor would sit there in the theater and have to look at all these black spots running across the screen. But they *did* manage to make good films—*The Maltese Falcon, Citizen Kane, Gunga Din*—that way. It's a matter of using the tools that are available.

Several of these directors saw expanded possibilities for the craft—increasing the variety of movie offerings and escalating the momentum of independent filmmaking.

Anything that puts a camera in the hands of more people is exciting and will be a revolution that makes for different kinds of features.

I don't want to be pinned down to making cookie-cutter films in Hollywood, and this makes that possible. I see myself as an *independent* filmmaker, not a *Hollywood* filmmaker. Each film is like a child and needs its own special individuality. Digital will give me an opportunity to do that kind of *individual* work. This change is bringing back the imaginative spirit, with honest filmmakers trying to tell little stories about people and the crises of life.

I can put my movie on my website, and anyone who is interested can see it. Think of Gutenberg. Digital isn't exactly on that scale, but before the printing press, only the wealthy had access to disseminating the written word. Before long, we'll be thinking the same way about film. Before digital only the wealthy had access to disseminating film.

Quite a few directors, the enthusiasts and others, not only think digital is potentially valuable—they are convinced that it is an engine on a fast track forward, the number one *New Thing* in filmdom.

Digital methods are here and they are not going to go away. They are the future. It's inevitable. You don't have to call it good or bad; it's just a thing happening out there. Digital has already changed the world . . . and it's changed the work of directors.

There's an endless argument about whether digital filmmaking can have the physical resolution to be as good as film. The answer is *not yet*. But it's getting closer to emulating film, and a time is arriving when lots of films will be coming out in digital format. Every theater eventually will have a digital projection system, and they will get their product via satellite. I know I have to get into it to *survive*. Otherwise I will be bypassed—it will be like joining a herd of dinosaurs sitting on the sidelines.

See, for younger people, digital is a natural look, with their CD-ROMs and their video games and their Sony PlayStation 2s. In maybe ten years, *regular film* will look absolutely weird to them.

An event caught my eye that adds credibility to the inevitability notion. With the release of *Lost in Translation* in 2003, director Sofia Coppola conjectured on why she chose to use celluloid rather than digital video for the production. According to a report in the *Nation*, she wanted the movie to have a nostalgic quality, to feel like a memory. Since she thinks celluloid won't be around that much longer, for future audiences the movie will have memory embedded right in its physicality.[2] For her, this may have seemed one of the remaining chances to shoot a movie in the classic style.

Sore Thumb?

Conversion to a new technology isn't easy or painless, even for those who appreciate its advantages. The directors acknowledged a cacophony of different opinions within their company of filmmaking colleagues and realized that there are costs in coping with change.

> I'm overwhelmed by the potentials, but I have some trepidation, we all do, and we're on a learning curve. There are lots of different schools of thought on this. At first, people were terrified, afraid of being outdated. But denial isn't the answer.
>
> That means that right now you have to sit there and learn a few new things—they're not that complicated, even though some folks love to make it sound as though they are. You know, it's wonderfully complicated the way the technology was conceived and brought to the point where it is now. But it's not actually hard to use from a director's point of view.
>
> It's funny, though, but no director has ever talked about this with me, or I with any of them. Directors don't talk technology with one another very much.

I sensed that even some of the directors who were advocates had a catch in their voice, a hesitation, which revealed an inner anxiety about going forward into the unknown. Relating it to my own experience as a writer, it's like getting an upgraded computer or a new word-processing program. You know that this will improve your work, but you hate what you're going to have to go through to master it.

One Thumb Up, One Thumb Down

Ambivalent directors, the second cluster in my interview group, gave voice to a division of thought about digital developments, both within themselves and among directors generally. They see merits to the change, but they have serious reservations about the direction it may take. They believe wisdom lies in pacing, not rushing in.

> Many of the directors I know seem to be interested and cautious, kind of fascinated by the potential but in a waiting pattern to see what works. We can't predict if the image will look as good as film, and this is a visual medium, where lighting and skillful photography have counted a lot. Myself, I don't think about it a lot. If it moves along and becomes a valuable way of making movies, I'll use it. But that depends on whether it won't compromise quality—just make it more financially doable to make good movies.
>
> As I see it, there are two camps. One camp that is excited about it, wants to explore it, and let it take off. They want to push the envelope of digital. The other camp is purist and worried and says, "How can they do this, it's changing the art, it's a different *look.*" They're apprehensive about the use of a smaller crew, the different approach to lighting, and unknown problems that may emerge. And, you know, few theaters are equipped to show digital films as yet.

One lesson gleaned from the last remark is that people who have a successful experience using digital methods come eventually to see the benefits to shifting over.

A Nose-Thumbing

A third and smaller group among the directors, a twosome of *skeptics*, disagree with the good reviews of their aforementioned colleagues. They take a dim view of the technology itself, or of the way it is likely to be used. First, they question the quality of the image that video-type equipment can produce.

> I myself love the look of 35 millimeter film, and that's where I want to be. I do see the benefit to being able to shoot as much footage as you want and to having people in the foreground in focus at the same time as people in the background, something that's hard to attain in standard film. Those are pluses.
>
> But I think in terms of telling a full, rich story that you want to see in a theater, I prefer 35 millimeter film. Those are the kinds of stories I want to tell and the kind of presentation I want to make. From what I've seen of the digital medium, it doesn't have that rich look that we are accustomed to experiencing when we go to a good movie. Digital is synonymous with being cheesy and cheap, without the texture that we associate with films.
>
> Right now when most directors see an anamorphic film—a widescreen picture and lots of depth—we have a feeling of success. When we see a digital film that isn't well lit and doesn't have a polished texture, we think low-budget, half-cocked. For myself, I want to be a successful commercially received director of quality films, and that's at contradiction with the digital aura of quick, cheap, dirty, and edgy. That's not who I want to feel I am right now. To me, a lower quality of screen vision connects with a lower-quality story, a lower-quality production.

The other critique from the skeptical wing challenges the assumption that an easier technology, ipso facto, is a plus. The very complexity and grandeur of making a movie has merit—it engenders care and dignity.

> I think there is something valuable about it being so difficult to make a movie. It's a craft, it's a profession; it's not just about any hotshot kid moving the camera around and shooting whatever's in range. There is something to the whole apparatus of the camera, and the crew, and the celluloid that requires you to really plan it out and convince a lot of people that this thing is really worth doing and investing in.
>
> I hope we don't entirely lose that special aura that making a movie has had. Yes, there may be instances where digital could be the best choice, like with the film *The Celebration*, where digital worked to great advantage. But I wouldn't use it in a period movie. It shouldn't take over. Mark me down as one of the agnostics.

One of the most powerful polemics by digital skeptics that I've run across was by critic Godfrey Cheshire of the *New York Press* in a two-part series ominously titled "The Death of Film" and "The Decay of Cinema."[3] Cheshire sees digital imagery as television imagery and argues that as digital spreads in filmmaking, it will naturally ape its television precursor. He points to research showing that film creates an alpha state of alertness in the brain, whereas TV invokes a passive beta state swathed in suggestibility. The "wasteland" content of TV in the future will be beamed to an audience of couch potatoes in movie theaters.

As television technology edges out film, the argument goes, theater owners will try to maximize profits through a cafeteria of big-screen showings of sports events, concerts, and special attractions like the Academy Awards, space travel news, and audience video participation games. Film, as we have known it, will shrink as a component of what movie theaters traditionally have been about.

What's surprising about the words of the two skeptics among my informants is not that they were spoken, but who spoke them. They were among the youngest of the directors I interviewed, and both were minorities—one a woman. People in the industry believe that there's wide support for digital methods, and new approaches to filmmaking generally, within those very groups.

My interviews uncovered a contradiction, or at least a balancing-out of that understanding. The data remind us again not to be glib in our assumptions about groups. Although young, minority, and female directors, in all likelihood, are heads-up about the digital movement, they do not speak with a single voice. The next minority or woman director you encounter is not *necessarily* going to be a digital aficionado.

It Depends on Who You're Dancing With

Sprinkled among the varying shades of opinion was an alternative perspective that served to iron out the wrinkles. This enfolded the old and the new technologies of moviemaking. Use both, these people were saying, depending on the purpose of the project and the effects directors are trying to create. This ecumenical view played down categorical superiority or inferiority between methods.

> There is a difference in the electronic image, but it's not better or worse—just different. From an artistic standpoint, I think of film as working with oil, and video as working with acrylic. You can do beautiful work with both; it depends on the artist. Directors working with digital should keep it organic to what it is and not try to mimic film with digital.
>
> Some people cling to the classic film look, just as there are people who keep to LPs and refuse to play CDs. It's an emotional attachment. Digital sound is not the same as analog sound; there is a distinct quality to each. You can't say one is better than the other.
>
> Digital filmmakers ought to see that it remains its own medium. It's so truthful and hyper-real—in your face. When an actor conveys pain, you can really see it; you almost squirm in your seat. In film you're slightly removed and protected, not made so uncomfortable. You have to decide which of these reactions you want from the audience.

Another mediating motif came through: storytelling is at the heart of filmmaking, and technology doesn't change or distort that basic mission. All new technologies have had to plug into that core element, whether sound, 3D, or color.

> These are really new tools to tell a story. It doesn't affect storytelling per se; it only affects the way the story is shot and distributed. Just like word processing is a new tool for telling a story with the written word. Maybe you can do it faster, but it doesn't set aside

the requirement to tell a story in an entertaining and meaningful way. The technology doesn't change the *work*; the work adapts to the technology.

The underlying process of creativity that has been around from the days of Sophocles and the Greeks—portraying human emotions like fear and pity—are still with us, but we have more choices in the means of expressing our creativity and exhibiting the results. That's a bonus for independent filmmaking. The director at core is a storyteller, not a technician. And the craft of telling a story is behind what makes you unique and gets you work.

I was struck by a statement by George Spiro Dibie, then president of the International Cinematographers Guild, on what to him is important in shooting a film. I read him to advocate a professional stand, to invoke excellence as the chief criterion to apply concerning use of a camera. "A minuscule shift in focus, camera angle, or movement can irretrievably alter the flow of a story, as can a blush in someone's cheek, a glint in an actor's eyes, and someone barely concealed and then revealed in the shadows."[4] This says to me that whether you choose to do film-based or digital-based shooting, what counts is doing it well. That's another mediating position.

The Independent Filmmaking Movement—Origins and Permutations

So much for basic "for" and "against" attitudes toward digital. Through these discussions, a slew of notions about independent filmmaking kept surfacing. Before going ahead, I think it's important to fill in some background, historical and contextual, about the Indie movement. You'll have a better handle on what the directors are saying on this when I reintroduce their comments.

The synergy between digital and the Indie field is obvious to everyone; not so the concept of just what independent filmmaking is and is not. Discussing the Indies is tricky because nobody can really define what that means anymore. It's like trying to define a shapeless mass that's in motion and changing rapidly as it goes.

At the beginning of the chapter, I called up significant dates, and I'll do the same again here. In 1989, the release of Steven Soderbergh's *Sex, Lies, and Videotape* transformed the independent movie field. Independent films had been defined as small pictures on off-center themes made with tiny budgets for fringe audiences. Then Bam!—suddenly we had an Indie blockbuster that grossed over $24 million in North American box-office receipts. The distributor, Miramax, apparently had an alternative vision for independent films. They could be lucrative, made with larger budgets, and attract high-profile stars in leading parts. Indie didn't have to mean small and marginal anymore.

Cassavetes and the Birth of Indie (A Man under the Influence)

That same year marked the death of a pioneering giant of independent film, John Cassavetes. Just as Soderbergh had ushered in the era of the new independent film, Cassavetes, I believe, was the founding father of the earlier and original modern independent film movement.[5] When I was going to graduate school in New York City in the 1950s, you pretty much had to turn to foreign films to see noncommercial movies with substance, trekking to a few art-house theaters on the Upper West Side and in Greenwich Village.

It was stunning, then, to encounter American filmmaker Cassavetes's remarkably innovative and personal films, like *Shadows* in 1960 and *Faces* in 1968. His films were bleak and improvised and intensely emotional, depicting human relationships with raw and searing truthfulness. Going to these films was like seeing *Who's Afraid of Virginia Woolf?* over and over again with different characters in different social situations. His films experimented with all the earmarks of what became independent film: jerky handheld cameras, a grainy 16mm look, gritty city streets, random noise, lesser-known actors. He operated with shoestring budgets, pretty much self-financing the work through his respectable earnings as a sought-after actor.

Cassavetes forged ahead, a solitary figure on the Hollywood landscape, with maverick films like *Husbands* (1970), *The Killing of a Chinese Bookie* (1976), *A Woman Under the Influence* (1974), and *Opening Night* (1978), among others. The fact that Cassavetes began work on *Shadows* two years before the release of *Breathless* by New Wave poster-boy Jean-Luc Godard only underscores his place as a cinematic trailblazer.

Of course, other Indie-minded directors surfaced at this time, but none had the impact of Cassavetes. Greg Merritt, in *Celluloid Mavericks*, names some of those he considers "ahead of the curve" groundbreakers: Shirley Clarke, Sam Fuller, Roger Corman, and Monte Hellman. Later, important contributors to independent film who often get tagged with founding-father credit did not release their breakthrough films until the Indie ferment of the 1980s; the roster includes John Sayles (*Return of the Secaucus 7*, 1980), Jim Jarmusch (*Stranger Than Paradise*, 1984), Joel Coen (*Blood Simple*, 1984), Spike Lee (*She's Gotta Have It*, 1986), and Gus Van Sant (*Drugstore Cowboy*, 1989).[6]

Before Cassavetes, independent film in America did have a pre-existence, but in an esoteric and obscure form, going under a mixture of names like *experimental, avant-garde, underground film, counter,* and *pure cinema.* The venue for exhibition was largely museums, art galleries, and university lecture rooms.[7] These films wanted to be more than different. They aimed to radically subvert the conventional style or politics of film. The filmmakers often used abstraction, distortion, and nonnarrative approaches, as in Maya Deren's *Meshes in the Afternoon* (1943), a short that played with time and space to fabricate a lyrical twilight space between dream and reality. Andy Warhol's creations at The Factory represent the genre, as do those by filmmakers like Stan Brakhage (*Sirius Remembered*, 1959), Jack Smith (*Flaming Creatures*, 1962), and Kenneth Anger (*Scorpio Rising*, 1963).

What Cassavetes managed to do was bring independent film out of the museums and university halls and into art-house theaters, where larger audiences of serious filmgoers could see them in the form of entertainment (rather than as pure cultural experience) on a Friday night date. Soderbergh took that a big step further; he propelled independent film into the malls and mainstream theaters, where the films attracted still larger audiences.

Soon after, Quentin Tarantino slammed this progression into overdrive with *Pulp Fiction* (1994) and its worldwide gross of well over $200 million in ticket sales. The studios and their conglomerate owners were beginning to say, "Hey, there's money to be made here," and took steps to own and finance the more aggressive, profit-generating Indie distributors—ingesting them as subsidiaries. There were marriages and a blurring of movie styles, until now, when almost every big-time Indie company is a studio subdivision, with Miramax and Disney the prime examples. The line between studio and independent has become increasingly indistinct.

A sizable flow of solid Indie films came out through the 1990s and into the present, many drawing respectable audiences. My own selective list includes: *Ulee's Gold*; *Gas Food Lodging*; *Stand by Me*; *In the Bedroom*; *Boys Don't Cry*; *Dead Man Walking*; *To Sleep with Anger*; *Rambling Rose*; *Leaving Las Vegas*; *Sling Blade*; *Magnolia*; *Welcome to the Dollhouse*; *Traffic*; *Crouching Tiger, Hidden Dragon*; and (symbolically?) *High Art*. Add your own choices. We should also give notice to the longtime uninterrupted flow from stalwarts like Woody Allen, Robert Altman, Henry Jaglom, and Wim Wenders.

Where, Oh Where, Has Indie Gone?

Some of the directors I spoke with had a bittersweet take on the revolution in independent film that was sparked by Steven Soderbergh and the Harvey Weinstein/Miramax machine. They are buoyed by the increased prominence and wider audiences for Indie-style films but distraught that the studios have taken over all the important independent distributors as subunits, subsequently watering down the Indie character of films that make the cut for distribution. This excludes many small relationship-oriented pictures that have been a staple of the Indie community.[8]

The comfort level of the parent conglomerates doesn't jibe with the riskier, edgier, more original, less niche-conscious, and more modestly budgeted films that are traditionally Indie products. A few directors who came from independent filmmaking backgrounds had bitter views on these developments and elaborated on them. They believe it is becoming more and more difficult for committed Indie directors to survive in this new environment.

> Real independent film was around until six or seven years ago. Then the conglomerates took over independent distribution companies: Time-Warner/New Line Cinema; Viacom/October Films; Disney/Miramax. True independent films are now made by recent college graduates, who go to their parents and aunts and uncles for cash, get hold of an American Express Card, and shoot a film on video for $5,000. Those films are not available to be seen nowadays. Lots of Indies are being made, but they are not being distributed.
>
> The distribution of films with artistic merit took a slide once the conglomerates took charge. The bar as to the requirements for an Indie picture making enough money to qualify became higher. Innovative films do not fit the formula for what acquisitions people think will be good box-office material. Now many independent movies have to be like *Happy Texas* or *Chocolat*. Those are like what the studios were making fifteen or twenty years ago—commercial-type movies with a slight edginess to them. They are

hardly innovative or high in aesthetic merit. True independent films, ironically, seem to be independent of audiences who are allowed an opportunity to see them. They don't get shown.

That's what Jonathan Rosenbaum says, and he's one of the best film critics around. He tells us that commercial-flavored Indie films are being distributed; artistic films hardly at all. Excellent offbeat movies like *Panic*, *One*, and *Croupier* are stiffed altogether or get distributed poorly.

Great movies made in the early 1970s during the second "Hollywood Golden Age" wouldn't make it into the theaters today. Bogdanovich has said that the *Last Picture Show* with its pushing-the-envelope themes and absence of stars would have gone directly to cable, if even that. *Midnight Cowboy* might not be seen *at all* now.

Some of the edgy independent movies that get picked up tie in to some niche market that is awash in adolescent rebellion. A lot of them exude postmodernism and belong to a sewer culture. But studios see the themes as commercially viable. Some others perceived the same way are gay-themed films and political protest.

Many young independent filmmakers seem to be going through a prolonged adolescent rebellion against their parents and society, with little talent or life experience to guide them in what they are doing. They are not culling from deep-down rich experiences and the good classic filmmakers. The romantic idea of Indie film as the haven for cineaste aspirations is a bogus idea. It doesn't exist anymore.

This critique hits hard and strikes valid targets, but I wonder if it overreaches in positing a virtual total blackout on distribution of good independent films. Despite the commercial filter of distributors, some deserving cinema slips through. Consider the collection of recent solid Indie pictures I listed a few paragraphs back.

I've heard the Indie situation analogized to the theater. In the past, studio movies were shown at the mainstream movie houses ("Broadway"), and the Indies in small art cinemas ("Off-Broadway") together with foreign films and successful documentaries. Now the big studio films still go to the "Broadway" mainstream theaters, but it's the studio-sponsored Miramax-type Indies that get shown in the smaller "Off-Broadway" theaters (plus in some larger venues for the *Shakespeare in Love*–type offerings). "Real" Indie films are put into quarantine at "Off-Off-Broadway" venues—playing here and there at assorted film festivals to esoteric audiences. The analogy breaks down at the point where a smattering of these do indeed make it into the other two venues (like *Stand by Me* and *Boys Don't Cry*).

Nonetheless, distribution is truly a bottleneck that is strangling the exhibition of a wealth of Indie works that deserve to connect with audiences. And some committed independent filmmakers, say a Jim Jarmusch or Jon Jost, are pretty much closed out in this climate. There'll be more on these issues in the next section.

The Indie/Digital Connection: Democratization or Devastation

Independent filmmaking and digital technology converge at the point where the low cost and ease of digital methods put cameras in the hands of a wide cross-section of the population. This checkmates the long-standing monopoly by studios over the production of movies. I encountered a bittersweet attitude mix among directors on this new state of affairs. Directors who commented on the topic gave high marks to the idea of democratizing filmmaking, but they worried about the glut of independent movies the mass of budding filmmakers is generating. I'll report their good feelings first and then the downside.

Film has long kind-of been the art of the rich, of the upper middle class, because the people who could afford to make films were people who could afford to go to film school. You had to be able to go to private universities like USC or NYU, or had to have rich friends who could give you the money to make films. All of a sudden, you can dig up two or three thousand dollars, borrow or buy a pretty cheap DV Canon or Sony camera, get a computer setup, and for ten grand you can *make a feature*. Realize, only ten or twelve years ago, shooting *minimally* in 8 or 16 millimeter would have cost you forty, fifty thousand.

Look, anything that puts a camera in the hands of people—including the kid next door—and makes it easier for them to make movies is exciting. That aspiring regional filmmaker in Toledo, Ohio, or Kennebunkport, Maine, who wants to make a film now can make a film.

I'm ecstatic that high schools can have a media lab and offer video production courses. For fifteen or twenty thousand dollars you can outfit a school to do that, at least at a basic level. Film and video are part of pop culture, and kids should have an opportunity to get into it regardless of where their school is located, a poor neighborhood or an affluent one. Not having those facilities at some schools is unfair, just like having computers only at some schools is unfair.

Now for the misgivings. Democracy can be messy, and democracy with cameras doesn't escape that risk. Will the quality of film likely rise and will the chances of audiences getting to *see* high quality film increase?

With the deluge, I don't know how a place like Sundance is going to cope. Even now, it's getting to the point where it's beyond comprehension, the number of films that are submitted there. It's a veritable orgy. Imagine what it takes to look through all that and judge *talent*. As this doubles, triples, quadruples, the more competitive it is, the harder it will be for good people to poke through. Distribution of all of this is seriously bottlenecked.

I can see that brand names are going to become even more important—stars will become more important—because that may be a way to distinguish between the offerings. When people want to go to see a film, they don't relish sitting through a thousand to find one that seems right. They need some kind of sifting *process*, and past history has shown that stars make a difference. Ironically, we may find stars getting more important to the Indie field and studios getting more important as filters.

I think it's really a *problem* that anyone can make a movie. You have to have some tangible talent. To me, it's a bit like the Internet. The Web can be the best thing in the world if you know how to manage it, but it's amazing how it's filled with *garbage*. You can waste your life on the Internet. I keep stumbling upon trashy websites that are written by idiots. The same applies to movies. There can be thousands and thousands of independent movies now, and I have been looking at a bunch of them. What I see is a lot of garbage.

Figures from Sundance substantiate qualms about the numbers. Attendance at the 1993 festival was 5,000. By 2003, attendance had jumped to more than 20,000—a four-fold increase in ten years. The madhouse atmosphere of late is hardly a secret. Sundance's kid brother festival, Slamdance, had 2,800 feature submissions that year. Geoffrey Gilmore, who works at running the Sundance Festival, estimates that of all the independent films produced in a year, only seventy-five to one hundred of them win a theatrical release.[9] And those are not necessarily the most distinctive.

Dissecting the Distribution Conundrum

Why don't more of these films get shown through normal theatrical distribution? Therein lies a long tale, which I'll spell out because it was something I wanted to understand better myself. The Indie field surely has been on a roller coaster. It came out of nowhere—with Cassavetes leading the way—and rode high in the 1980s. Suddenly a market of opportunity opened, and Indie distributors jumped at it—New World, Vestron, De Laurentis, Cannon, Orion, and others.

The 1980s found the majors temporarily easing up on production. Reagan's economic policies were causing uneasiness in business circles, especially the swelling of interest rates—which put a damper on borrowing. The disastrous fiasco of *Heaven's Gate* had already intensified the "proceed cautiously" mentality of this insecure industry. Simultaneously, theater owners had gotten into an *expansionist* mood, using financing from conglomerates that had begun to colonize Hollywood to multiply the number of theater screens. The emerging home video and pay cable venues were starved for product for their growing audiences. In this environment, the Indie distributors were delighted to fill the vacuum. But they expanded too rapidly, oversaturated the market, produced too few hits, and took too many business risks.

Now there was a surplus of product from the combined output of the majors and the Indies, and the majors were also skillfully moving in to take control of the home video situation. The Indies couldn't compete, and over the years there wasn't enough cemetery space to accommodate their casualties. The companies I previously mentioned hit the dust, joined—right up to the present time—by Skouras, Savoy, Triton, Hemdale, Island, Shooting Gallery, Propaganda, and others.

What makes the distribution situation so terribly problematic? Why can't truly independent distributors get leverage for their products? There are, in reality, a finite number of theatrical venues, putting a lid on the number of features that can be shown at any one time. Why do the studios have a stranglehold on those theaters? They don't own them! What they do own is the means to satisfy the exhibitors' passion for a flow of films that fill the seats and sell popcorn. The majors can supply a fairly steady stream of product over the whole calendar year, including lollapalooza blockbusters that keep the box-office registers clanging. Independents can't compete with that. They can mainly fill the down time and occasionally deliver a hit.

So they are second-class operatives who have to bargain and cajole for a place at the marquee. Being marginal and vulnerable, they don't get as good a financial deal with exhibitors on divvying up the profits, and they can have grief prying loose their share—which freezes them in a fragile financial state. If an Indie company decides to contract with a major to distribute the movie for them through its existing channels, there's going to be a roughly one-third distribution fee that comes off the profits. It's a wonder the graveyard isn't more crowded.

This story ties back to where I left off earlier, with Steven Soderbergh's *Sex, Lies, and Videotape* unexpectedly drawing crowds of paying customers to the box office. The majors sized up that a new breed of Indie movie had come into being, and they calculated that it ought to become a component of their distribution wares. These films could bring in audiences (and revenues), satisfy the exhibitors, and diversify their product line. And they realized that sharp and enterprising Indie distributors, with Miramax out in front, had a handle on the product line and would be excellent allies. So, as mentioned previously, they bought them up and made them appendages.

Now for Indie films to qualify for the distribution queue, they had to be able, as never before, to fill seats and satisfy exhibitors at a combination of art theaters and mainstream movie houses. The remaining "pure" Indie distributors, like Zeitgeist, Artisan, and Lion's Gate, wanted in on increased revenues (their take was based on the percentage of tickets sold) and jacked up the commercial-side requirements of films they would agree to market.

You need to join together the explosion of independent film production as a result of the digital revolution with the shriveling of outlets for noncommercial films in the theaters to sense the mammoth backlog of undistributed Indie films we have now. It's as though the mouth of the distribution funnel became a vast savanna, while the neck thinned to a single reed.

Since the Indie distributors are no longer a strong channel into exhibition, other channels like the Sundance Festival and its clones have become a substitute, but not a very fertile one in relation to the pileup of contenders. If a lucky Indie production does make it to a theater, the stay is likely to be very short, maybe days. It's got to find an audience right away (there's no time to cultivate one), or it will be moved out to make room for another one waiting in the wings.

The new-style distributors, who are affiliated with the studios, dominate Indie distribution (picking up many of their products at the festivals). Industry folks have come up with diverse language to name these hybrids—mini-majors, neo-Indies, Indie-studio companies, or Indiewood operations. Some people talk of the Hollywoodization of the Indies and others remark on the Mirimaxation of the studios. In any case, there's a good bit of imitation and acculturation going on.

From all of this, a new kind of hybrid movie is being promoted that combines noncommercial and commercial characteristics. At this time, the menu of filmdom has big splashy studio movies on one end and, on the other, highly offbeat movies (preponderantly digital) that rarely get distributed. In the twilight zone between are the intermingled hybrids: say *The Brothers McMullen* or *In the Bedroom* or *Leaving Las Vegas*. Some industry types embrace these films as Indies, others decry them as commercial movies, another group sees the grouping as true hybrids, and other observers pronounce them indefinable. In a word, there's confusion.

Sundance's Geoffrey Gilmore has pinned down some of the sources of confusion.[10] To paraphrase him: we used to define an independent film as one made by an independent filmmaker; now the Ang Lees, David Russells, and Steven Soderberghs do studio films as well as Indies. Independent films had to be free from studio financing; now the hybrid companies all have studio funding. Indies formerly had to be made low budget; now the dollar ceiling has been blown by the Fox Searchlights, Paramount Classics, and Sony Pictures Classics. Indie filmmakers were supposed to have final cut; now many don't, but A-List studio directors like Steven Spielberg and James Cameron do. From Gilmore's description, we can only conclude that the whole thing is a can of twisted celluloid. Phone Independent Feature Project/West in ten years to see how this all works out.

Meanwhile, look for the small Indie filmmakers to break free of the distribution blockade by exploiting other forms of outreach—cable TV, the Internet, DVDs, special-interest DVD clubs, specialized distributors like the political dissent–focused Independent Media Center, satellite distribution in baseball stadiums and public parks, empty lots, and other channels of outreach—who can imagine them?—still to be invented. Running parallel is a discernible rise in art-house theaters in cities like Denver, Albuquerque, Cleveland, San Diego, and Boulder—with amenities like coffeehouses and links to schools around film tie-ins to the curriculum.[11]

Using Digital: Advantages/Disadvantages

Following the road map I set out at the start, let's steer in a practical direction. I described the pro and con attitudes of directors toward the digital revolution earlier. Here I am documenting the advantages and disadvantages they perceived in using digital technology in actually making movies. The advantages that my informants ticked off cover the spectrum of filmmaking from shooting to editing to distributing. I'll lay out all their comments and then add my own when the directors have had their say. I'll do this later, as well, with disadvantages.

See the Advantages—All in a Row
A Penny Saved Is a Penny Saved

> Digital films are definitely cheaper to make: the equipment, tape, lighting—the works. With digital equipment I can make a $1.5 million film for $300,000 and even keep the same level of cast. If distribution channels continue to open up, I'll be able to collect a lot of that back.

Shooting Was Never Like This

> I loved *The Celebration*. Thomas Vinterberg put the little camera in places where you just couldn't put a standard film camera—on the floor, in a corner, you know, up on the ceiling. Off somewhere with his hand cupped at a weird angle. The portability lets you get shots that you just couldn't get with a more cumbersome piece of equipment. There's freedom of movement and freedom of lighting. Because the camera is totally unobtrusive, you get access to many more people for all kinds of stories. Also, video assist allows you to frame the shot in the way it actually will be seen.

What's Special about Special Effects?

Digital tools can actually save your ass in certain situations. I've seen them insert an actor's head on a double's body in a scene that was dangerous for the star. An actor can walk into a lion's cage and be safe because it's not a real actor. Or two actors who do their parts separately can be put together in the same scene. You can make radical changes in your film without having to reshoot scenes.

Digital allows you to do backgrounds that are spectacular or tricky and that would be cost-prohibitive otherwise. The Ancient Rome backdrop in *Gladiator* wowed the audience and drew them right into the picture. With *The Perfect Storm*, a lot of it was shot in a tank, where you could generate eye-popping impressions, like huge waves, and it was safe.

There can be a new ending for *Casablanca* with Bogart and Bergman walking off into the sunset together. Or you can play *Gone With the Wind* with Sylvester Stallone doing the Clark Gable role. Also, weather doesn't have to be the bugaboo it has been—just insert the *weather you want* into the scene.

All That Footage!

It's great to be able to shoot as much footage as you want and not worry about cost. That gives you more to work with at the end. You can shoot for eighty minutes without stopping, where with normal 35 millimeter you can film for only 10 minutes. That's good for actors, because when they're cooking in the part, they can keep right on going without breaking their pace or mood. There's a rehearsal-mode feeling to this—if the scene doesn't work, just go ahead and do it over again. That makes the actors more relaxed.

To the Editor

I think it's revolutionary the way editing on a computer has changed filmmaking for the better. In the last ten years we've gone from a film-based system of cutting film, which was the method in almost ninety-five years of film history, to a computer system. It's made an enormous difference in quality.

Film editors used to make decisions to not revise their work, because it was too hard. It was just too hard to put new film pieces into the film. Now, with the computer, it's instantaneous. You can try all kinds of different things. I compare this to when you were writing and had to type a whole new draft every time you revised something.

My wish has always been not to spend years in the editing room. Now you can try more things because you don't have to cut film and put it together again, which is time consuming. You get to view what looks basically like a TV movie until it is locked. But it's faster to work through. And it's great to be able to cut and store pieces and put them back in later if you want to. Arduous editing does not equate to "good movie."

A Contribution to Distribution

In the next five or ten years people, more and more, will have home theaters because of satellite and because of DVD. You will be able to bring a first-class small theater experience into the home.

The day will come, mark my words, when theatrical films will be distributed by satellite. You'll move from videotape to movie-house screens—without ever going into film. And it'll be a perfect picture every time.

One promoter I know of is distributing film in baseball stadiums after dusk. He has had 50,000 people at a showing. We have to open our eyes to different ways of distribution. That way, all directors will be able to tackle new film content and not have to keep to the same tired formulas and be tied to conventional marketing and distribution.

And More Pluses

This is a strong list, but there's another benefit being talked around in the industry—previsualization. It's a digital procedure that allows a director to depict the film with real specificity before any shooting begins. The director can call up a detailed high-tech outline of the movie similar to but different from the way storyboards typically have laid out the plot line in a series of comic-book-like panels.[12]

Now directors can have a synthetic but precise and comprehensive piloting of scenes, including the props, camera angles, lighting arrangements—maybe the trajectory of a car chase. The director can plan a shoot with enormous efficiency and in a way that optimizes the chances of achieving the best results. Or to discover beforehand that it isn't technically feasible to do it the way it was conceived. Previsualization isn't cheap, but it can save a lot more money than it costs (especially when you calculate that a fairly typical Hollywood shoot runs about $100,000 a day, maybe $6,500 an hour).

In support of what the directors said, I've sensed a good bit of enthusiasm among industry people for the cornucopia of footage from which they can now choose. And for the gift of time they have for continuous camera work before having to reload. With celluloid, a hard-up Indie director might shoot on a 5 to 1 ratio—five minutes of shooting for every minute that eventually ends up on the screen. A studio operates closer to maybe 12 to 1. Now, with cheap videotape, limits are melting away. A 75 to 1 ratio isn't rare.

So the contemporary director isn't automatically restricted in footage; the problem has shifted to potentially becoming sloppy in judging what and how to shoot, and then being buried in tape during editing. There's a natural temptation to skip the important headwork that once had to go into preplanning scenes and instead basically construct the picture post-hoc in the editing room—correcting mistakes by wiping them out digitally. (Is this a matter of shifting creativity to post-production or shirking creativity in the shooting of the movie?)

The blessings of a longer shoot time leaped out at me when watching the astonishing ninety-six-minute continuous take by director Alexander Sokurov in *Russian Arc*. The director shot his entire beautiful movie tackling Russian history, art, and culture in one seamless pass through the Hermitage Museum in St. Petersburg, with the absence of any editing.

The Other Side of the Coin: Digital Disadvantages

Despite the accolades, nobody I interviewed thought the digital age would usher in a state of picture-making Nirvana. Indeed, several directors pointed to significant defects and booby traps. On the whole, though, the group enumerated more advantages than disadvantages, and with more enthusiasm and verve. But a downside there was.

Reveille for Collaboration

I worry that ultimately, fifty years from now, one hundred years from now, one person might be able to sit in a chair in front of a computer and do the whole movie almost *single-handed*—the characters, sets, actions, dialogue. That's the George Lucas stated dream. Like so many things he has done for and to the industry, that, finally, is a very negative idea.

True, this is an alternative way to make movies, but I don't want to lose the heart and soul of filmmaking, which is the collaborative process—where all those creative juices come together and are stirred in the same pot. This involves teamwork, sharing, caring about each other and the common goal. I do only one piece of it. You need these diverse and special contributions for really creative work. You can mechanically create anything you can think of now if you have enough money, but that may not be much fun to shoot.

Boosting the Artificiality Quotient in Tinseltown

Digital and fakery come together when you exaggerate special effects, and I think that audiences recognize that. We've already reached a kind of saturation point. They can create huge armies that attack each other, but there's a real phoniness about it.

For an actor, that can be deadly. It requires acting against *nothing*, and that's very difficult and unreal. That's one of the reasons *Pearl Harbor* had such a mixed reaction. Everyone said the effects were great, but the love story was *pitiful*. I'll admit that the effects were incredibly impressive, but when you lay them out one after the other, you can see how phony they are.

Directors can come to depend on explosions and razzmatazz, at the expense of basic human drama that is expressed by actors. Film has to help us understand fundamental human experience, who we are, and where we came from. Dramatic power in *Pearl Harbor* would mean creating a sense of real people caught up in an awesome moment, in this case a historic moment. The film struck out on that.

Digital smoke and mirrors isn't liberating to the artist. It's just a reductionist idea that in the end gets you into making *Star Wars* over and over; but you can't make *Citizen Kane* that way. And, frankly, I don't give a fuck about two thousand versions of *Star Wars*. I'd rather have one *Citizen Kane*.

Gaining Time/Losing Time

Because digital's so fast, the studios will assume that filming can be completed in a much shorter time, and they'll demand that. Even more than now, they won't give directors time to think about what they're doing, to finesse the structure of the movie and try it in different ways. Cutting back on time is something we will fight, but they'll fight back.

I wouldn't be surprised to see the ten-week time allowed for editing scaled back a lot. In truth, you literally don't need that much time with AVID editing, but it's *nice* to have. And studios nowadays want to test the movie almost instantly. With digital you can work something up that looks like a movie quickly, but that's very dangerous.

The coverage is nice and smooth, and there's a dissolve, and there's a this and a that, and so you can actually get a movie on to high-definition tape and get it in before an audience with canned music within a few weeks of finishing shooting. But that's mechanical; it lacks a point of view.

The disadvantages were relatively few. It's not hard to add others. For example, Michael Allen, in his book *Contemporary US Cinema*, makes the point that digital technology can fragment and unbalance the filmmaking process.[13] It shifts the line between production and post-production, especially when digital effects are involved. Technical specialists create a high or even major proportion of a big action movie in post-production. The work is frequently done at small, specialized companies separated from where the project is centered. This reduces the control directors have over the film, except if they can boast the competencies of a George Lucas or Ridley Scott.

Another problem involves companies that make "sanitized" versions of films. These companies, originally based in Utah and Colorado, will camouflage nude scenes in a *Titanic* or blot out violent battles in *Saving Private Ryan*. These companies and their software—MovieMask, CleanFlicks, ClearPlay, Family Shield Technologies—are becoming a tech-age dagger aimed at the artistic and intellectual rights of filmmakers.

It's easy to point to other problems: the pirating of videotapes; loss of work among blue-collar set builders and lighting technicians; glitches arising from incompatible digital operations—such as a camera shutting down because of a hostile signal from a burglar alarm or cell phone. Some of these shortcomings surely will be worked out or reduced through sheer familiarity with the technology. For example, October Films kept it hushed up that *The Celebration* was shot in digital, worrying that the public wouldn't give it the same reception as a movie on film. That kind of apprehension is becoming a thing of the past, in part because of how well that film was actually received.

A Forecast and a Conclusion

Every new technology exists in a state of high risk. Some, like the cordless telephone, catch on right away; others, like the picture telephone, get stopped in their tracks for a time, or die altogether. So where does digital filmmaking stand? What are its prospects?

Everett Rogers, a professor at the University of New Mexico, is a widely recognized theorist on changes in technology and social practice. His book *Diffusion of Innovations* is a bellwether in the sociology of technological and social innovation.[14] I looked to it for clues on the outlook for digital filmmaking.

Based on his research, Rogers proposes that five attributes of an innovation are key in whether potential users accept it and put it into practice widescale:

1. The relative advantage of the innovation.
2. Its compatibility with the values and beliefs of users.
3. Its level of complexity.
4. The degree to which it can be divided and tried.
5. The degree to which it can be observed.

Looking at these criteria one by one, I predict there's a high likelihood that people in the filmmaking community will make a full run with digital methods.

Relative advantage means that users perceive the innovation as being better than an idea or method it replaces. The directors in my survey clearly perceived more advantages than disadvantages—the weighting and tone of their comments, as I heard them, was decidedly in the pro direction.

The relative advantage theory holds that economic factors are crucial; that potential users respond with open arms to a reduced cost in production. The directors I talked with were excited about cheaper equipment and quicker, simplified procedures that go toward budget slashing. Those with specific Indie interests waxed most eloquently, but digital potentially can lower costs across the industry.

As for *compatibility*, Rogers posits that when an innovation is out of sync with the outlook and norms of the adopter community, it will have a harder time of it. On this, my informants made a significant point, I think, in stating that digital methods reinforce the core objective of filmmaking—telling a story. Since, as they said, digital technology really gives them increased means to accomplish their storytelling mission, I don't envision a pile of impassable boulders on the road to adoption.

Complexity, as Rogers defines it, deals with the degree to which it's difficult mentally to grab hold of something new. When people can't understand the how and why of a new product, they turn away from it. The greater the complexity, according to Rogers, the lower the adoption rate. One of the directors made the point that digital technology was terrifically difficult for engineers and scientists to conceive and make operational but now is extremely easy to use in practice. Commenting in the *DGA Magazine*, director Allison Anders had this to say about digital: "It's so easy for me to speak the language. It's just an easier kind of technology—something I understand. Film . . . was so entrenched and rigid. I had to leave it in the hands of my DP."[15]

What about what Rogers calls *trialability/divisibility*? Can users break the innovation down and try it out at first in parts? That helps an uncertain consumer of the product decide whether to go with it. With a new refrigerator, you have to take the whole contraption home—not just the icemaker, or main cooling section, or freezer, or ice-water dispenser. Digital has a remarkable capacity to break apart for differential use. Some people have taken advantage of the editing feature for years. Others have selected the camera, or digital effects, or the video viewer. The technology can march forward in stages. There was a suggestion in the interviews that people who use digital become more favorable toward it.

And so to *observabilty*. If the positive results of an innovation are immediately visible, people are more likely to adopt. You can flash a digital image on a screen and see whether you like it. Done. Take an educational innovation like New Math or Whole Language. It can take years and years of accumulated test results before the outcome is known, and then people will go on haggling about the meaning of the statistics for more years. Digital is in a good place on this score.

Digital is in a good place, in general, with the Rogers paradigm. He would probably predict an expanding future for digital in filmmaking. I go along with that. And the directors who made a point about the inevitability of this new technology also agree. The outlook is sunny, although in a grainy kind of a way.

That's my forecast. Now for a brief conclusion. As I found myself thinking about the contemporary digital invasion of the land, it seemed to me this aggressive technological upstart was opening up all kinds of new ways of conceiving of filmmaking and of the industry—ways that go beyond the technology itself and that don't depend on it directly. The experience with digital innovations has begun to generate out-of-the-box thinking on new ways of distributing films, of editing them, of presenting imagery and combinations of images on the screen—real and contrived ones. I wonder if the only way to imagine creating virtual reality will remain in the digital domain.

I found a compatible intellectual soulmate in film scholar Thomas Elsaesser, who co-edited a book of cutting-edge essays on screen arts in the digital age, *Cinema Futures: Cain, Abel or Cable?* His writing concentrated on interconnections between film, TV, and the Internet, their "convergence" and "divergence." But what I appreciated most was Elsaessar's language, to wit, that digital serves "as a 'tool' not for making movies in a new way, but for thinking about them in new ways."[16]

The conversation we have had in this book so far has touched on some of these derivative ways of thinking, especially on alternatives for distributing films—options that break the grip of the majors on the mechanisms of distribution and allow new voices independent of the studio system to reach audiences. Some of these alternative channels (the Internet, cable TV, DVD clubs, outdoor venues) are exciting and, over time, no doubt will lead us to discover still others.

As a result of digital influences, we've come to think in fresh ways about the people who create movies and to realize the value of expanding the pool of eligible "auteurs." At the same time, we confronted the question of how wide (or narrow) the qualification should be for the title "filmmaker."

Digital technology asks us to reexamine the time balance that ought to go into production vs. post-production. More than ever before, filmmakers recognize the extent of creativity that can go into post-production fabrication of the movie. Post-production, it turns out, does not necessarily have to be a brief appendage to the all-important shoot. (Or should it continue to be that?)

It's clear that the time ahead will generate a raft of new questions, possibilities, and further experimentation. What will come into being—remarkable and mundane, fruitful and abortive—remains a mystery. We can predict fairly confidently a smooth course for the fast-moving digital ascent, but we can't identify the offshoots I've been talking about. I'll close on that note. I'm content for my conclusion to not so much map what we have already come to know but ponder intriguingly what we yet may learn.

~

CHAPTER FIVE

Stalking Creative Freedom

At the core, you are making the movie for yourself and the audience. And if you haven't made a movie for yourself, you are making a big mistake. Because if you haven't made a movie that you wouldn't personally go to see, you should be ashamed of yourself and you shouldn't be making a movie.

—Joe Dante

Spring, 1964! Less than thirty-six months earlier, a nation was transfixed by the challenge when John F. Kennedy assured America that "this nation should commit itself to achieving the goal, before this decade is out, of landing a man on the Moon and returning him safely to the Earth." But more than 2,500 miles away from the future launch pad, another stratospheric challenge was registering on the collective radars of the Hollywood majors. Frank Capra in essence told the studios: *Choose any director in the world to come in and finish up the picture, and the Directors Guild of America will cover the full expenses.* That's how filmmakers won the right to make a "director's cut." It's incredible to realize that this happened more than half a century after the dawn of the motion picture industry. Of course, for directors, advances in creative freedom didn't automatically come with the territory; they had to win whatever they could in battle with the tightfisted moguls.

From the Cruelest Cut to the Director's Cut

In the early 1960s, directors made only a rough-cut version of their film and passed it on to the studios to complete. They were then limited to making suggestions, whether beseechingly or insistently, to the associate producer for further improvements. Directors experienced this as a painful infringement on their creative prerogatives. They wanted more and, through the Directors Guild, set up a Creative Rights Committee, chaired by Capra.[1] The studios weren't interested at all in this "director's cut" notion that Capra's maverick committee proposed, responding with knee-jerk apprehension about driving up post-production costs (and likely with ulterior motives, not excluding a deep-down fear of someone subverting some of their clout).

Capra, true to form, devised a dramatic and compelling scenario: the studios and the DGA together would compile a list of the top twelve directors worldwide, and if any studio director delayed post-production—as feared by the companies—the DGA would immediately fly one of these eminent directors from anywhere on the globe to Hollywood to promptly complete the picture. The studios apparently were impressed with this audacious proposition and came around to agreeing to the principle that directors are entitled to compose their own personal version of the film as a step in the process of preparing a film for distribution.

A Slippery Slope

Many of my director interviewees felt that the right to a director's cut is far from film-making nirvana.

> It's a *constant* struggle to get the picture you want, a tug-of-war with producers and executives. Directors are really employees, and the companies are the legal determiners of what the film becomes. Throughout the process you're forced to try in every way you can to put your stamp on the ultimate film and make it come out the way you intended. The producer wants to make one movie, you want to make another. But there are other intrusions. The star thought we were doing something else. The writer doesn't like what's going on and goes behind the back of the director to complain to the producer. The actor's best friend slash sycophant slash manager is looking at dailies and saying, "Oh, they're not making you look good." Ten thousand things can happen because directors don't have the authority they should, and this is precisely why movies are so stinky. Any director with creative commitments has to use a lot of *self-survival skills*—you know, diplomacy, compromise, bullying, deceit—to come out anywhere near where he was headed.

Actually, you may be surprised to learn that, in the earliest years, directors had a great deal of control over film. But since that time, their authority has taken a downward trajectory. At the beginning of the silent era, the director played multiple roles: devising the story, working the camera, directing the actors, cutting the film, even designing the costumes and the sets. For a time, D. W. Griffith personally directed every film produced by Biograph. Studios were small operations with a businessman at the top and the multitasked director working directly under his supervision. Directors like Griffith made advances in narrative camera work and film cutting, virtually inventing a new technology that they pretty much monopolized. They improvised shifts in camera angles, parallel action, intercutting, crosscutting, rhythmic editing, close-ups and full shots, and other cinematic breakthroughs. The default result: studio heads weren't in a position to tamper very much with the finished picture that the director gave them.[2]

All of this began to change toward the end of the silent period and the introduction of talkies. Larger numbers of people were going to the movie theaters, which in turn propelled an expansion in production. The studio heads couldn't oversee the entire operation anymore, so they hired middle managers to assist them, people they called *supervisors* then and who we now call *producers*. These supervisors didn't have a lot of technical or artistic ability, not to mention influence, but as their departments became larger and more factory-like in mass producing pictures, they subsequently became more powerful. In their middleman position, they took to representing the interests of the front office in the everlasting skirmishes between business-minded studio bosses and creative-minded film directors.

The coming of the talkies further undermined directors: suddenly screenwriters were needed to prepare polished scripts. With silents, directors created the story, often shooting off the cuff or working from a slim outline. Now the story had to be well structured, with winning dialogue among the players. Playwrights and novelists were imported from New York to develop the stories—but assigned to work under the producers, not the directors, contrary to the logic of melding the key creative elements that go into shaping a film. The norms that developed then continue in the industry today, keeping the writer and the director at arm's length until the script is ready, in that way putting control of the story in the hands of the producers and, through them, the executives.

We need to remember that in the start-up years of the film business, producers and writers were basically nonexistent, and directors had enormous latitude and authority. This authority receded over time until the creative rights of directors, as we saw earlier, became crystallized contractually in the prerogative to produce a director's cut of the film. The producer, of course, is free to revamp that cut, and the executive suite has the ultimate say. Our directors saw the current landscape as less than egalitarian, with only a handful of directors today getting final cut. Where there were once eight to ten, there are now fewer than five or six, names like Spielberg, Cameron, Lucas, and Scorsese.

Precarious Help: The Directors Guild and the Berne Convention
The current DGA Basic Agreement with the producers allows directors a ten-week period following the close of principal photography to edit the film. The agreement calls for an editor to assemble rough sequences requested by the director and states that "The director shall then make whatever changes he or she deems necessary." As I read it, the key stipulation is that "No one shall be allowed to interfere with the director of the film during the period of the director's cut."[3]

There are additional details, but that's what directors have as a baseline guarantee. Still, there's room to maneuver in this. The terrain in this slippery slope between the rock-bottom right to a director's cut and the heights of a decisive say on final cut is murky and open to negotiation by individual directors. I couldn't resist probing into that territory with directors, and in a moment, we'll take a look at the candid and surprising responses. First, to put this in context, I'd like to briefly explore the background of the creative freedom issue as brought out in the observations of some of the directors.

One director commented on the legal and economic context for understanding creative freedom issues, going back to the 1886 Berne Convention for Protection of Literary and Artistic Works. Most countries—ninety-six currently, including the United States—subscribe to the Convention, which requires member nations to recognize the integrity of authors, broadly defined (including filmmakers). The aim of this treaty is to guard creative professionals against exploitation, giving them exclusive rights to "translate, reproduce, perform, or adapt" their works. With no deficit of passion, this director went into considerable detail in discussing the document, and therefore, I'm compelled to give him his due.

It was Victor Hugo who originally organized writers and artists for protection of their rights across national borders. Various clauses have been added to the Berne treaty over time, but the basic concept has been constant—authors can object to alterations to their work that is damaging to their *reputations or honor*. Most of the world respects that treaty, but the United States didn't sign until 1989. This country would not admit that the author is the actual author. We are wedded to the work-for-hire idea, a doctrine that gives the employer ownership of the copyright and all the rights of authorship. Laws in this country supersede the treaty and make the corporation the sole copyright owner, not the individual who conceived the work. That's an attitude of studios that carries across the *whole* filmmaking process. And that's what ties the hands of the director creatively.

The controversy about violence in movies illustrates how the creative rights issue gets played out. Film companies know people are attracted to blood; it's an *instinct* in us, something genetic in our nature, something that draws us to violence and catastrophe. We slow down to view a traffic accident on the highway—and bring on more accidents. The film studios deliberately promote violent films, even if they often deny that in a smokescreen of self-serving language. When there is an action scene, like armies clashing, cars crashing, cops firing their pistols, the studios view that as a desirable element for marketing films and *see to it* that films get to look like that.

When Congress dialogues with CEOs about this, with a concern about children, let us say, movie executives are not able to come to the heart of the moral dimension. Their loyalty is to the stockholders, and it is to them that they are responsible. The executives serve indirectly, by law, *as the authors* of the products they disseminate.

If the U.S. adhered to the Berne treaty, which marked the individual creator as the author, Congress could hold that person responsible for ill effects, though not necessarily going to the point of censorship. But the CEO is an elusive, faceless functionary who can duck behind the corporate veil. Portrayals of violence certainly wouldn't vanish from films if the individual artist could be singled out as the person responsible. As it is now, producers and executives can rewrite and reshape films to the level of total aesthetic and moral bankruptcy and keep the director's or writer's name there on the credits. They never announce that the film was *dumbed-down by Executive X*. And they don't want the director to attach a pseudonym to the trash they fabricate.

Congress is looking for a villain, but Congress itself is the guilty party, because it has promulgated the philosophy that set the corporations loose on the world to make money, to raise stockholders up as the one and only point of reference—or they are *breaking the law*. Executives are comfortable with this, because most of them are fixated on the dollar, with the larger human and moral concerns in the background.

I know that life involves individuals facing dilemmas and having conflicts, and this sometimes results in human explosions. We have seen that in classic drama over the ages—a fascination with violence has always been with us. But by removing the greedy propensity of the corporations to magnify and exploit this and giving directors more rights in their creative output, we would have a better chance of having a better balance.

That's one artist's view of the legal/philosophical edifice surrounding creative freedom. Another director painted a more personal picture, showing the on-the-job dynamics that conspire to tangle and restrict filmmakers in getting to a director's cut.

You're hired as a director and you're supposed to have the vision of the film you want to make, without being too artsy-fartsy. How to achieve that is really a problem for a director, because there are compromises to make *on almost every level*. It's not your money, so studios want creative input along the way—very few of us are a Steven Spielberg with full control.

It starts with the script; either they hand theirs over to you, or they want to sign off on the details of one you bring. Then you go on to casting. The director wants the best actor for the role, and that's a rare happening in Hollywood. Because it's not about getting the best actor; it's about getting the best *star*. It's a commercial issue, because there's no question that stars make a difference in the potential earnings of a film. So it's a serious consideration, and it's always a compromise situation, a matter of whether you'll get a compromise that works, whether you're lucky enough to get a star who will be good for the role.

Then you start shooting, and that's the best time, because you've got them a little by the balls from a money angle, because it's really hard to replace a director on the spot. So you really have the most power during the production phase. Even the cheapest film will cost ten thousand dollars a day, and big films can be a half a million dollars a day. To replace a director in mid-shooting means millions of dollars, generally, 10, 15, 20 percent of the budget. Even though you're in more control, that doesn't prevent studio people from commenting on everything and going over the dailies and drowning you with suggestions.

A lot of directing is knowing what your powers are and where and how you have to compromise to make it work. Getting the most you can, knowing what your limitations are, that's the real art of directing. You're not going to win everything. Some young directors think they have to fight every battle. If you fight each one, you're going to *lose*. It's about winning the war as best you can, and also figuring you're going to lose some battles.

But you've also got to always remember there's payback. So if you piss off an executive during production, once you're in post, they can kick your ass out of the editing room and do whatever they want. They can also get back at you when you're looking for your next picture. But you don't worry about that when you're making a film. Everyone understands that there's always fights, but bottom line is money. If your film is successful, you can be the biggest prick in Hollywood—and some directors are the biggest pricks in Hollywood—fact is, you will work forever if you make money. What goes on and is said in these battles doesn't really matter. You can be the nicest guy, the most creative visionary . . . but if your film doesn't make money, it doesn't matter. So while filming, your whole concentration is on making this film as good as it can be. There's no time then to worry about the next one.

The Studios: Good Cop or Bad Cop?

In the insights to follow, we'll return to many of these points. But notice, if you will, that this vivid depiction of the hard realities of directing gives a different slant on the guarantee of a director's cut. Directors, it turns out, aren't free and clear to do *anything* they want leading up to their cut. In fact, it's an ambiguous situation. The right is there, but it still has to be earned and fought for all along the way. There was consensus among all the directors I talked with that there is an uneven power balance between directors and studios: the studios obviously have control and ultimately call the shots. Directors have to struggle ceaselessly to achieve the film they envision.

Interestingly, there was a division among the directors about how to view the context of that struggle. I was surprised to find that they broke into two distinct and divergent camps, which I'll call *View A* and *View B*. View A people carry the brass knuckles. They behold a tough, contentious battle between folks with basically different interests. You slug it out with tough studio overlords obsessed with profits to maximize what you can get from the other side in order to advance your creative vision. There's an adversarial tone to this. View B people carry the olive branch. They conceive of a collaborative relationship where you try to find a compromise between studio execs and filmmakers who have a lot in common around the making of movies but slant in somewhat different directions. Here you aim to find a mutually agreeable midpoint that preserves the core of your vision. The tone is congenial, with lots of give and take. There was a roughly 50/50 split on how the A and B camps lined up.

First, let's share some blows with View A.

> You're butting up against a bureaucracy, and the situation is really intense. There are a lot of *frightened people* running the show. Where they are coming from has nothing to do with art and quality; it has everything to do with fear and anxiety. You use all your powers to bring these terrified people around to your way of thinking. Basically, you use whatever means will be successful. *All's fair*. This is a matter of self-survival. It's a horse-trading game. There are so many people in management who want to urinate on your film and put their mark on it. You've got to be shrewd and heads up all the time or else you can end up giving away so many chips that you're really not in the game anymore.

> Of course, executives vary a lot; there are maniacs and dedicated film people. But executives usually have a *hundred different agendas* beyond the story itself, like the marketing potential, how the film will affect their future in the business, whether their wife or their friends will like it. You have to figure out whether they have the best interests of the film at heart.

> You know, the system has everyone trying to get the upper hand. Executives push you to underbudget your movie, and then you go over schedule. A movie that's on schedule, they never say, "Gee, dailies are terrible." They can't. As soon as you're over schedule, everybody has an opinion about dailies. You get phone call after phone call. I try not to answer them.

View B people have a clearly different slant:

Most companies want to make the director happy and have a relationship they can continue. Barring a director whose ideas are way-out radical, they want to *accommodate* directors and help them survive. Once the project is under way, you can usually make the
picture you intended. It's give and take. I never was forced to accept something that I
really rejected and objected to. If the film is edited well and keeps to the story and concept you agreed to, producers will be reluctant to tamper with a director's work. If they
do, they are taking a chance. Often, it's the *star* who will be adamant about changes.

Good directors balance the relationship between the company and their own vision.
I think that's the director's job. Some directors feel it's them vs. us—the money people
vs. the art—but smart directors find a way to put everyone on the same page, or make
people feel they are, so that money people are protecting the director's vision. Being
committed to the integrity of the project means giving in when you are wrong, knowing
when you have to compromise. If you won't budge in the direction of making the movie
more watchable, or you are totally wishy-washy about what you think, the studio will
tell you what to do.

You've got to be smart to keep your creative force as a director. You've got to *grow up*,
get to know the game, and get to play it astutely. That means doing a lot of convincing
of people, winning them over. You shouldn't be an asshole and piss off people who can
hurt you. You've got to get decision makers on your side. It stands to reason that if you
get into an adversarial relationship with them, they will fuck you. People who have
power *use it*. Experience will tell you how to navigate these waters.

I work within the system and understand the system. Directors who fight the studios
aren't going to work a lot. When the audience doesn't show up, the director will learn that
previews serve a purpose. I go to previews and watch audience reactions. If it doesn't
work, I take it out. Nobody told me I have to do that. I'm not making a movie for me,
my father, my mother, and my sister. I want as many people as possible to come to the
film and enjoy it.

To Get Your Version of the Movie

So, with some crossover, directors hold two alternative views about the environment
that surrounds their ability to fulfill their cinematic visions. But beyond that divergence,
they are in total agreement that a *passive stance in all of this leads nowhere*, that they have
to use a grab bag of tactical moves to head the film they want to make in the direction
they want it to go. I put this question to them: "Given that few directors have final cut,
how do they attempt to optimize their creative freedom?" Their responses ranged widely,
from persuasion to psychological seduction to political manipulation, thereby constructing an image of the director as a multi-personality character—part Elmer Gantry, part
Sigmund Freud, part Machiavelli. An overarching point is that directors think the situation has to be approached from the standpoint of strategic thinking.

How to optimize your creative control? That's an art. There is no answer; every situation is different. It's about people management. Winning battles is a political matter, the

politics of organizations and individual people, and you work with different producers and executives and stars each time. You have to be savvy about how they will react to certain material and approaches. You know, you develop a sixth sense about what producers may accept. The chemistry is different from film to film—there's no formula. And your own particular power changes coming into every situation. You've got to assess the situation in terms of the power of everyone in it, especially the studios and the *stars*; those are the two big powers you have to deal with. They can mess you over.

You should pick your battles and strategize depending on your status at the time, when you think you can win. Your status depends on innumerable factors: for example, how much the star likes you and will stand behind you, whether she'll say, "If you mess with him, I'm walking." *That's golden.* Your stock is varying day by day, all the time. And you try to maximize the amount of control you have, keeping in touch with where you are. It's like a big pizza pie, and you have to figure out how many pieces *you* can get, depending on *them*.

What specific control-optimizing actions do directors instinctively take or recommend? The directors set a whole range of possibilities on the table. I believe these suggestions, with the wealth of experience behind them, have the making of a veritable field manual for film-school students on maneuvering film projects through the maze of the system. I'd bet students probably need more of that, given that their schooling is strong on technical competencies but short on the human and organizational skills that will permit them, as a matter of *realpolitik*, to actualize their vision.

I'll start with the obvious notion that filmmakers have to exert *personal influence* in the situation. According to my informants, that means using fully their powers of persuasion, capitalizing on their persona—their personal assets—and attuning their personal deportment to greatest advantage.

It's a matter of being passionate with producers and executives about your vision and enrolling them in that vision. You should be working to get them excited about what you are attempting (but first be clear about it yourself). Show them it's in *their* best interest to do it the way you want to do it. Listening carefully to what they say is valuable as such, but it's also a way of knowing how to push the right buttons to win them over.

Build on what you personally bring to the situation. The director is the one who sees the whole picture—and *someone has to do that*. Committees can do a certain amount, but there has to be artistic continuity for the picture to hold up and be successful. Only the director can accomplish that. Also, directors have a kind of power based on their charisma and stature. There are some celebrity directors, like a James Cameron, who has his own star power. You also bring power depending on whether it's your own script, your past history in filmmaking, whether you've done a film with a big star before. Those kinds of things.

You've got to play the studio games. It can be *stupid* things like where you sit at the table, the clothes you wear, and how you express yourself. For women, those kinds of things can matter a lot in getting their way. One angle is coming across as an important and capable operator. Another is not rubbing big shots the wrong way. There was a producer I knew who made sexually embarrassing remarks, but I judged it would be better in that situation to ignore him rather than take him on. He was an older guy who had been around a long time, very set in his ways, and I was pretty much getting what I wanted from him. You've got to know *when* to make *what* moves.

Some directors focus on steering the filmmaking process itself along lines that work for them. There are actions they can take that impact the process in both the production and post-production stages. With an ostensible collaborative cover, which may be one more tool in the political arsenal, they work decision makers into the shooting stage to make them stakeholders in the director's cut, and they work themselves into post-production decisions. Here's how they do it:

I try to bring producers and executives into the process while I'm shooting, using their notes when they make sense to me and having them feel they are true partners in what I am doing. You can also accommodate some of their ideas, but draw them into the larger picture, give them the illusion that what is on the screen is theirs. My standard practice is to work step-by-step with the producer all along the way to the director's cut. You certainly should at least show the producer your film and have some back-and-forth about it before turning in your cut. In that way, when that cut is complete, the producer has already had a hand in it and has some investment in its fate. Since he or she has had a say, it won't be in the cards to simply dismiss the director with, "You're finished now; see you around. I'll take it from here."

Another reason to get the producer as your ally is that if the two of you are in disagreement on the material, and the studio people sense that, then they move in like a pack of sharks. They'll fill in the gaps and make the decision about what the film should be. I've seen it happen many times. Neither the director or producer gets what they want, and it gets turned over to someone else to decide. I've come a long way on this from when I started out. I'm not shy about showing my film and getting allies instead of keeping it fenced off and protected in the darkroom.

You can also ally yourself with a high-profile actor. If you have a good connection with an Arnold Schwarzenegger, it can carry a lot of weight for you to get him on your side in a disagreement. Your connections with other people, like a well-placed attorney, a strong agent, or some other third party, can also be a real bonus.

Through Directors Guild stipulations, the director legally has ten weeks to edit the film and turn it in to the studio. I never *deliver* the director's cut, because that signifies that I'm finished. I keep things fluid. I position myself so that I have influence over what becomes the final version of the movie. Often I bring the producer in during my editing. If there is a big scene I want to cut out, I ask the producer to take a look at it and give his opinion. That keeps everything open ended and in constant flux and development.

When I turn in the cut, I convey the idea that it's a somewhat *temporary* version—we have some additional things in mind musically, there are certain visual effects that could be added, a short scene could still be flashed on the screen. In that way, I insert myself into the whole post-production operation and keep my hand in on what will become the final cut of the movie. I'm there going through every cut and every nuance. Some directors back off after turning in the director's cut, but if you want to shape the movie to be what you want it to be, you need to find a way to stick with it through post-production. And you generally can do that if you keep yourself involved.

You Say "Producer"—I Say "Protector"

Directors singled out producers as crucial to advancing their vision. Several directors spoke of the producer as ideally being a natural protector and advocate of the director vis-à-vis the studio, someone who wards off unnecessary intrusions or pressures. They said that you *should choose a producer carefully*, someone you can trust, that you should be very wary when getting involved with a new producer, and that whenever possible, you should follow the practice of working with someone you worked with successfully in the past.

But the right money configuration is as important as the right producer in giving a boost to creative freedom. Money matters figured in several different ways. Box-office success confers its privileges, and there are benefits to low-cost productions, as well as to making sure you are operating under a realistic budget.

Artistic freedom stems from power, mainly the power to make money through the films you create. If you bring in a ton of money, the studios will *listen to you* and give you leeway. You'll carry weight in getting what you want because they fear losing you and the cash you generate. Simply put, to optimize having your way, be successful at the box office. *Money talks*. There's also artistic power in this stew, and that comes from being able to cause people to laugh, to cry, to turn their thinking and emotions inside out. When that kind of power draws crowds into the theaters, it drives up receipts, and that buys a director freedom to do what he wants. But it's conditional and transitory. If your audience declines with the next film, that freedom declines also. I know that what directors hope is that they'll gain the trust to do it their way, but the only way they can gain that trust is through consistently producing hits that make big money.

As a rule, the higher the budget, the less freedom for the director. A big studio with millions of dollars on the line will try to influence you more than in those situations where there is less money involved. With a four million dollar film, the director has more room to maneuver creatively. Even with as much as sixteen million on the line, the makers of *American Beauty* (1999) could risk doing something out of the ordinary. As you go up from there, the director gets more and more boxed in. You always have to put the director's artistic freedom in the context of investors and their worries about making a return on the investment. If you want to leave more options for yourself, keep the budget low.

I have final cut because I choose to make low-budget independent films. For an artist, say a painter, the notion that *someone else* finishes your painting is absurd. Inexpensive independent filmmaking gives a director a measure of control as an artist. I myself aim at a smaller portion of the audience. If my films cost 10 percent of what mainstream films cost, I only have to reach 10 percent of that audience. The more intelligent and involved audience wants films about human relationships rather than car chases, and they are the ones I want to reach. So I *embrace* the limitations of my budget and go ahead with it rather than see it as a crippling restriction. The reality is that directors can gain more control if they are willing *to give up some of their perks*. If you shoot for four million, you can push for final cut, and any film worthy of being made can be made for four rather than forty. Orson Welles made a film, *F for Fake*, which cost almost nothing because he relied on found film, and he considered it one of the best films he ever made.

In any case, you have to try to set up a budget that matches the requirements of the film. Directors are always under heavy pressures to complete the film in the amount of time that was allotted to the project. If the budget is out of whack, too small for what you have to do, you're automatically operating in an atmosphere of compression and tension, and you've got to make compromises you don't feel right about.

Make the Picture You

Another strategy suggested for controlling the film is *to impose the director's imprint on it in as many ways as possible*. The more ways directors brand the movie, the more likely it is to stand up against anyone's attempt to alter it.

You can hire people who will impart as much of your vision as possible on the film. I mean casting, choosing the editor, the cinematographer, makeup people, props. Another way is to master a bunch of filmmaking skills yourself. For example, Michael Mann really knows photography. If you can deal with the camera, you don't have to go through anyone else to get your look on the screen. Being an expert editor is another way to gain leverage.

Or you can write the script, and many directors do that now. By producing the script, I found that I not only could control my own material but also even force the hand of studios to hire me to direct. Being a storyteller *on several fronts* protects your vision. Of course, that can be great, or it can be your downfall. Sometimes you need other people to spell you and offset the places where you can undermine yourself. From my experience with him, I really think Spike Lee does best in projects where he *doesn't* write the script.

Add a Dose of Deception

As many admitted, directors often use tougher measures. They can contrive the situation so things are forced to come out in a predetermined way. This involves aiming high by taking the low road. In doing this, the director artfully constricts the options that are left for anyone else after principal photography is finished. Not everyone does it, but those who do think it's legitimate.

I try to protect my vision by shooting each scene with only one or two setups, and I explain that that's the way the scene works best, that I don't want to be too "cutty." When I'm finished, there is only so much that can be done with it. There is no way anyone else can cut it without still leaving it *what it is*. I've always tried to make sure that my cut of the film is as tight as it can be within the running time I'm aiming for. I don't like to give producers a lot of extra material to deal with. Here's an example I once witnessed with someone else. A director I knew decided he was going to do a scene in one take, a complicated scene involving four or five different people, so it was quite ambitious. I was his AD [assistant director] at the time and asked whether he wanted to get any coverage, just in case, and he answered no. When I asked why not, he said, "It's because this is the way I want it, and I don't want to give the studio any way out." That was how he went about making sure he got final cut on that scene, because they would have had to call five actors back in to reshoot it. The scene was nonstop, five minutes long, and it was going to *remain* exactly as filmed on the set.

You have to sometimes go around the higher-ups. In a film I once made, there was a lighting problem. I didn't put gel on the florescent lights in a scene I was shooting in the morgue because I wanted an eerie green tone. The gel would have gotten rid of that tone. Word got back to the producer, who held to the going orthodoxy that gel had to be used with fluorescence and insisted that I continue in that way. What I did was get a *fake* gel and ask the DP to use it, and I let the producers think they're getting their way.

Robert Altman has said that he sometimes writes "fake scripts" to hustle financial supporters along—giving them something on paper they will buy, while keeping in his head the version of the film he actually will shoot.[4] But sometimes nothing works and directors feel that they have to throw their cards on the table and leave the room. That's drastic and dramatic—nothing foreign to Hollywood—and at least gets someone's attention. Sometimes the tactic can be a ploy rather than an endgame.

> You can have a tantrum and walk off the set if nothing else is working. The fact is that studios don't want to fire directors. It gives the studio a bad name, it's disruptive, and it costs extra money. That can give the director some elbowroom. It may also make it harder for him to get a job next time around. But studios can be intimidated by big-name directors in a way that they are never intimidated by writers. I've been both, and I know that for a fact.
>
> The ultimate solution we have is to take our name off the product when it's an intolerable situation. Before that, beg, cajole, discuss, write memos, send faxes, and negotiate the hell out of them. I once had an Alan Smithee experience, where I wouldn't put my name on the picture and the studio used that generic substitute credit. They took the movie away and made it a *totally* different one. It had been a "Saturday Night Live" sketch originally, and they removed what little heart and soul there was in it. The Guild has to rule in this kind of situation. They can say that you made a piece of shit and now you want your name taken off it. Or they can say that it *was* changed, but it's *still* your basic concept. The company has to agree to the Smithee name change, and you must agree not to belittle the film. I can tell you, it's nothing anyone in his right mind should look forward to going through.

Moral Rights Also

We've been dealing with rights that focus on guaranteeing a director's cut of the film. But the film critics notwithstanding, there are also assaults on the director's artistic integrity *after* final cut and the release of the movie. In that connection, the Directors Guild makes a distinction between creative rights and moral rights.[5]

Moral rights kick in when a work is completed and has to be protected against actions to alter or abridge it without the permission of the artist. In filmmaking, this means guarding against coloration, the "panning and scanning" of films for television, compressing time, or transforming one subject into another through morphing. It also involves film preservation, to assure that the artist's work can be shown *at all* in the future. In 1991, the Directors Guild established the Artists Rights Foundation—now the Film Foundation—to pursue those goals. The foundation has prevented the coloration of films like *Asphalt Jungle* (1950) and *The Seventh Cross* (1944), carries on a vigorous public-education program through audience awareness films and videos, and has instituted targeted legal actions. On a yearly basis, the foundation grants the John Huston Award to a filmmaker who has exhibited outstanding courage and service in working for these rights—honoring directors like Milos Forman, Martin Scorsese, Sydney Pollack, and Fred Zinnemann, and actor Tom Cruise for his fight to see that his work remains unaltered. The foundation leans heavily on the Berne treaty for supporting its position on moral rights.

One of the directors I interviewed, Elliot Silverstein, was instrumental in founding the Artists Rights Foundation and has served as its president. In a release issued by the foundation, he states the moral rights case in a cogent voice.

> Film artists have a long struggle to see that what is distributed is an accurate quote of what was originally created and released. That is their moral right. During over 200 years of American history human rights have on occasion been subordinated to property rights and that problem rises again as we seek the legal means of discouraging material alteration of films after their release, and the consequent damage to the reputations of filmmakers. Congress and society should allow film artists to enjoy what those in other countries enjoy, the human right to earn reputations based on what they themselves have created and to which they have signed their names, not based on what has been done to their work by others—who remain anonymous.[6]

In some other countries, filmmakers have greater copyright protection, for example, being able legally to prevent their films from being given over to television without their consent. The position of the Film Foundation and the Directors Guild is that owners of the work, studios and networks, have a responsibility to safeguard the work while making financial gains from it. They are essentially its custodians. The view is that artists should not be expected to have what they create changed by others, including the likeness and image of actors and the material content of films, and also suffer the indignity of having their names attached to what they consider counterfeit work. Among other things, that kind of alteration is a perversion of truth in advertising.

Ivy Tower Time

As a test, I examined ten prominent books on directing (written by working directors and academics—well-known and respected authors like Harold Clurman, Steven D. Katz, David Mamet, and Ken Russell) and discovered that all of them, as you probably would have thought, gave tremendous emphasis to the craft of filmmaking. But they also virtually ignore the organizational and political skills needed to bring to fruition the kinds of films committed directors wish to create in the environments of studio bureaucracies.[7] In no instance is there a chapter tucked away, larger or smaller, geared to coping with the organizational impediments that everyone acknowledges are ubiquitous and crippling to artistic intentions. Exceptionally good technical material is obviously there on the pages, but there is also an almost total void for finding out about organizational tactics. The books talked a lot about "defining your vision," but very little about "defending your vision." Film students apparently are expected on their own to absorb the skills of getting over the hurdles placed by studio executives—without formal instruction.

As I went over this collection of stratagems and machinations accrued from the thirty-two directors I interviewed, what intrigued me was how well they connected up with theories of social influence that some of my academic colleagues have formulated and tested. Researchers who have studied how people win concessions speak of *bases of power*, by which they mean personal resources that an individual uses to induce compliance or win commitment from others. Theorists have identified eight such influence resources.[8] Like me, you might marvel at their transparency in the director interviews.

Reward power is the ability to seduce people by way of things that they would like to have. In the interviews, I was told that directors who can deliver bountiful box-office returns for executives accomplish that and thereby boost their creative control. The counterpart to this is *coercive power*, the ability to punish or sanction people who don't behave in ways you want. Leaving the set or taking your name off a film both fall into this category.

When you are perceived as someone who is close to known influential people, that's an example of *connection power*. The respondents talked about exploiting their relationships with high-profile actors or with well-placed lawyers or agents to gain leverage. And you sometimes get your way by being someone people like and want to be with; that's *referent power*. Along those lines, some respondents talked about not rubbing important people the wrong way and keeping their personal comportment pleasant. You've got *information power* if you have, at hand, useful information that people want, perhaps preliminary audience reaction results. Broadly speaking, the most important information directors have is the footage they've shot, and they tell us they try to control that information through the amount of coverage they produce.

Expert power is based on the perception that you have a substantial amount of capability and experience. This came out in directors presenting themselves as important and capable operators. Also, directors mentioned that the stars they worked with previously and the pictures they had made conferred expertise.

With regard to *legitimate power*, people think you are entitled to make decisions because of your title or role. Respondents stated that only directors are in the position of having the whole picture in their heads, knowing how all the pieces fit together. No one else is expected to master the overall concept, and because of that, the much-flaunted "vision thing" of directors works to their advantage. Finally, there is *charismatic power*, which flows from a person's magnetic or commanding personality, described in terms of the "star power" some directors possess.

Researchers say that no one of these influence gambits is best; it's situational—based on how the pieces of the whole puzzle hang together at the time. When people are fairly receptive to what you are aiming at, then expert power works well, followed by information and referent power. When they are dug in against your position, then you should try coercive power, followed by connection and reward power—depending on which of these options are available to you to use. In the end, getting decision makers to accept your art is as much of an art, in some ways, as conceiving your art in the first place.

This all has an academic feel, I know, but consider that it does provide a way of imposing some order on the potpourri of battle techniques my respondents say they use. It doesn't cover everything, but it covers a good bit. And, I would argue, it could serve as a handy-dandy pocket checklist of action tools directors can refer to as they maneuver the studio trenches, fighting for their creative rights.

A Couple of Half-Smiles

I'd like to end the chapter with a happy face, or at least a half-smile. Contrary to the perceived stream of daunting obstacles facing today's directors, things actually have been looking up in the last few years. The concept of a director's cut has been experiencing an afterlife, or second life. Through DVD and new theatrical releases, pieces of footage from films like *Apocalypse Now* (1979) and *Amadeus* (1984) are being rescued from the cutting-room floor and reinserted the way the director originally intended. DVD was introduced in 1997, and at last count there were 25 million DVD buyers on the scene, and growing in number.[9] This has become a prime means of disseminating reconstituted films. The film restoration movement has joined DVD technology as a spur to reinstating directors' versions of their movies.

These select films have had their run financially, and so the studios see an advantage to giving them a rebirth and a new market through a director's-cut spin. The trend is encouraging but limited thus far, benefiting only a few directors who have a strong following or films that were much loved.

As a final word, I want to report one director's slant on creative freedom, a positive way of seeing things that might be of benefit to others. She said that directors often lose their perspective on what's important in the process. Making a movie requires raising huge amounts of money, mobilizing a legion of people with special talents and technical abilities, commandeering expensive and sometimes exquisite equipment, finding sites for shooting, and orchestrating the complicated logistics of carrying all this through.

For this director, it's a miracle that any film gets made at all, or at least a wonder. In her opinion, what's really important is that directors are able to work through this labyrinth and get to tell the story they want told. The details and the fine points aren't nearly as significant as getting your basic story on film and out there to be seen by millions of people. Is the overriding objective to get the picture right—or *out*?

Fair enough. The underside, though, is that directors who see things this way could come to relax their standards on artistic excellence and creative integrity (which is in the detail and fine points). The situation they find themselves in is, for many directors, certainly stressful and chilling. Most would welcome relief through a different cognitive take. It may be, though, that while this mellower perception has "feel good" value, it could deflect filmmakers from advancing the struggle for their full rights.

Which way to go on this? I can't rightly say. I'll have to leave that decision, of course, for others far more engaged in moviemaking skirmishes than I am. But I'm tempted to think that directors ought to stand their ground. The power balance is such that they're going to have to make concessions to the studio honchos in the long run. The less they concede up front, even psychologically, the more they can hold on to down the line, and the better for American film.

CHAPTER SIX

~

Women and Minorities in the Director's Chair

We have right now in Hollywood a very small group of people, basically from the same culture, background, same education—Harvard business and law schools—who determine what film is. Until that opens up, American film will be what it is.

—Julie Dash

"A woman's place is in the stove!" As a weekend closet comedian myself, I remember that classic stand-up line from way back. So I assume that's why there are so many hot movies coming out years later by women directors—Nora Ephron, Jane Campion, Penny Marshall, Nancy Meyers, Kathryn Bigelow, to name a few. But a better analogy would be a slow cooker. That's because outsider groups—women and minorities—have had a long trek to the director's chair, and the timer on the crockpot is still a long way from buzzing finis. To borrow another comic saw, progress hasn't been totally slow, and it hasn't been lightning fast; it's been half-fast.

From its very beginnings, filmmaking hasn't been a venue where those in charge were bent on portraying marginal and unpopular American groups glowingly—let alone giving them a major place in the movies, including the making of them. This was show biz, after all, and the aim was to give the public what it wanted, or what the financiers and managers thought it wanted: women and minorities in stereotyped roles—think ZaSu Pitts, Stepin Fetchit, and the Charlie Chan character—which allowed mainstream audiences to feel content, comfortable, and superior.

Throughout the history of motion pictures, there have been, from time to time, social breakthrough films like *To Kill a Mockingbird*, *The Grapes of Wrath*, and *All Quiet on the Western Front*, which forced presumably uncomfortable audiences to reconsider social mores, the transparent class system, race, and man's inhumanity to man. But taken in the aggregate, film has hardly been an art form with a broad commitment to challenging the status quo by calling into question commonly held prejudices and prodding ingrained ways of thinking. If moviegoers weren't at ease and happy with what was on the screen, they might not make as many return trips to the box office. Unlike art museums, the theater, and the opera, the film industry has always required a mass attendance to maintain operations and keep viable the economic calculus that it has contrived for itself.

For a majority of cinematic history, this general mindset played out differently for women and minorities, and among different minorities. Women like Madame Curie or Ma Joad could be heroines, but African Americans pretty much had to be obsequious or jolly and Mexicans invariably lazy.[1] But as the still-young nation made its way through the twentieth century, past the Great Depression and the liberalizing New Deal, and later into post–World War II global leadership and responsibility, biased attitudes softened and barriers to creative opportunity receded. The feminist and civil rights movements of the 1960s and 1970s threw open barricaded doors for women and minorities, particularly African Americans. Taking a long view, we are looking at a phenomenon that's in flux and elastic rather than one that's tightly rigidified. African Americans now win Academy Awards, and women head major studios and influential guilds. Film content has dared to peer into new areas like gay and lesbian love, abuses by religious sects, and incest. To illustrate relatively recent breakthroughs that have shaken the Hollywood system, let me depict the situation for women directors.

Female Flashback

From the beginning, filmmaking was a man's game. But in its dawning, when the industry was small and not yet crystallized, women directors were a visible element of the cinema enterprise and made important contributions.[2] Lois Weber, Alice Guy-Blaché, and Lillian Gish (a celebrated actress with one filmmaking credit) exercised a strong directorial hand, and screenwriters such as Frances Marion were highly influential. In the 1920s, as the studios gained big-business status, these women were phased out, together with their protégés, and men monopolized the game.

During the studio era that followed, access was narrow and only a few women carried the directing mantle. Dorothy Azner worked with high-profile stars like Katharine Hepburn and Joan Crawford from the late 1920s through the early 1940s. The feisty actress Ida Lupino transitioned into directing small movies with then-daring themes like rape and unwed motherhood (mainly in the late 1940s and early 1950s.) Women's work in film during that era was in front of the camera and in giving creative support as writers, editors, costumers, hairdressers, and makeup artists. Out on the fringe, though, a few women filmmakers were doing experimental and avant-garde independent cinema, including Mary Ellen Bute (*Rhythm in Light*, 1934) and Maya Deren (*Ritual in Transfigured Time*, 1946).

The societal bombshell that was the feminist movement of the 1960s and 1970s discharged shrapnel over the industry, changing the established order, probably forever. Mollie Gregory describes this development in *Women Who Run the Show*, conveying the flavor of her argument in the subtitle *How a Brilliant and Creative New Generation of Women Stormed Hollywood.*[3] Gregory begins with the 1970s, which she calls "The Beachhead." My own take starts with Elaine May launching the landing with *A New Leaf* in 1971, following through quickly with *The Heartbreak Kid* (1972) and *Mikey and Nicky* (1976). No doubt, her long-term success as an actress/comedienne in tandem with Mike Nichols and her offbeat quirky humor as a writer helped give her traction. Barbara Loden, wife of Elia Kazan, created a critical stir with the low-budget *Wanda* (1970). Coming right behind was Joan Micklin Silver, offering the well-received *Hester Street* (1975) and *Between the Lines* (1977). Toward the end of the decade, *Girlfriends* (1978) brought Claudia Weil's name forward and led to a prompt riposte with *It's My Turn* (1980). In 1979, Joan Tewkesbury released *Old Boyfriends* (fleeing immediately thereafter to TV).

Because the feminist movement was exerting ongoing pressure for better portrayals of women and of their concerns on the screen, a spate of "women's pictures" surfaced at this time. Ironically, they were directed by men; still, they gave increased prominence to women's concerns and struggles in films like *Alice Doesn't Live Here Anymore, Julia, An Unmarried Woman, The Turning Point, Norma Rae,* and *Looking for Mr. Goodbar.*

At that same time, women were beginning to move into executive positions in the studios, grooming themselves to climb the corporate ladder. Dawn Steel started work at Paramount and soon bedazzled her bosses with her merchandising campaign for *Star Trek—The Motion Picture.* Riding this tide, new recruits to directing fanned out along the beachhead through the 1980s: Jodie Foster, Penny Marshall, Amy Heckerling, Susan Seidelman, Barbra Streisand, Joan Micklin Silver, Amy Jones, Marisa Silver, Penelope Spheeris, Randa Haines, Joyce Chopra, Martha Coolidge, Kathryn Bigelow—to name some. This was astonishing—never before was there more than a small handful of women directors working at the same time. Sherry Lansing joined Dawn Steel high up the studio executive ranks, and they were further joined by a crowd of female producers who included the Midge Sanford/Sarah Pillsbury team (*River's Edge*, 1987), Gale Anne Hurd (*The Terminator*, 1984), and Debra Hill (*The Dead Zone*, 1983). From Mollie Gregory's standpoint, I assume, by now the beachhead was taken, the perimeter was secured, and Hollywood was into a new day.

Questions remain and abound. How far did the invasion penetrate and how firm are the front lines? What difference did this make in the content and themes of movies and in the operation of the Hollywood behemoth? What advances were other marginal groups making concurrently, particularly minorities of color? And there's an intriguing question that will dominate the discussion ahead: what were directors—men, women, and minorities—making of all this upheaval roiling the filmmaking field?

The Glass Is Murky

In my interviews, I tried to get at that last question by asking filmmakers to consider "How widely do women and minorities participate as directors?" In general, the replies gave neither a totally rosy nor totally bleak picture of participation by the emerging groups. The glass wasn't full or empty but was hovering in some broad halfway zone. However, most thought that the glass is filling.

I realized I was asking for perceptions and opinions about a complex issue that was somewhat subjective in character and hard to pin down concretely. As you'll see, I'll go on to look at how their answers jibe with factual studies that give us hard data on the subject. Keep in mind as we proceed that the quotes are a composite of voices; when the gender or ethnicity of the speaker is relevant, you will receive that information.

One group of directors, well over half, felt there is a serious problem in the degree of participation of women and minorities as directors. They thought this ought to be an urgent concern of the industry and of directors specifically.

> One of the most noticeable things in this work is how few women and minorities there are—there's low representation. It's *minuscule*. Women and minorities just don't get their share of directing work. It's a shame. Hey, the field is still too lily-white, and people of color just have more difficulties—particularly, from my experience, Asians.
>
> I've seen that the studios have been shutting down their mid-range budget features in the recent period. With fewer features being made, and in the face of enormous competition from so many people vying for directors' jobs, women and minorities have had *tough sledding*. If we mainstream directors think that the new conglomerate Hollywood is a closed corporation and we have a struggle breaking into it from deal to deal, women and minorities have to contend with that *in spades*.
>
> There are great women and minority directors, and I wish there were more of them. But I see more opportunities for women directors than there are for minorities. You know, I don't think there's as clear a case of resistance to hiring women. Things are difficult for them, but there are also a lot of women on the job, especially as producers, and that means more women will be getting all kinds of jobs. Minorities are really behind in making advances, even though the civil rights push started earlier than the women's movement.

A small number of directors thought the solution to the problem was in sight. They took a long view, and from that vantage point they saw a definite upswing for all groups. Things are getting better, they seemed to be saying; we can tone down the volume.

> I think there's an awareness of the issue in the industry and a commitment to improve things. Beyond that, who runs Paramount? Well, a woman. There's Sherry Lansing and a lot of other women in power in Hollywood. I can't talk about everyone, but I know for a fact there are a lot of Asian Americans not heading studios but in influential positions in studios. There has been a lot done to open doors; more can be done, but I think this will evolve as it should evolve. I don't think it is a *huge* problem anymore, not like fifty years ago.

Add in a very small cluster of directors (consisting entirely of Caucasian men) who came across as removed or uninformed. All of this seemed to be something going on in the background, maybe a distraction, as they were concentrating on trying to do their job.

> I'm not exposed to this issue myself very much. I just hear about it. Are there a lot of brilliant women and minority directors out there who are beating at the door and can't get an opportunity? I don't know. *I really don't know.* I know a lot of women directors and I know some black directors, and their ranks are increasing. I just haven't thought about this a lot. I can tell you, though, that when I was in film school at USC, we had a few women in the program and most of them wanted to be *producers*, not directors. It's not like with firemen, but there's a perception in society, including among women, that film is a guy's medium.

Whatever else the directors thought, there was wide consensus that things are in transition. All agreed that there have been major improvements and that the situation is on an upward track. (Some female directors demurred on that last point.)

> I think it has opened up. Women and blacks are getting a shot. There are women who are filmmakers, and there are women filmmakers who specialize in women's themes. Same with blacks. *Both* possibilities exist, and that expands the options.
>
> Say, you have to realize that just a short time ago it was considered *bizarre* to even imagine a woman could possibly carry out the job of directing a film. Now they have a strong foothold. It's just amazing how the business has embraced feminism!
>
> I think of this like I think about civil rights more generally. Is there still prejudice in our country? *Of course.* Are blacks still treated differently? *Of course.* But has a lot changed? *Yes.* There are a lot of laws there to protect people of color. We are moving in the right direction.

Just the Facts, Sir

Optimists among the directors thought things are definitely on the upswing and then added a *but* as in "But more needs to be done to have real equity." The more somber observers focused on the serious nature of the problem and then added their own *buts*: "But the situation clearly is improving and becoming less serious." These ricocheting "buts" create a Rashomon sort of reality. The glass is obviously half-murky.

To the Stats
What am I to make of this? When most people face incongruities and confusion of this kind, they head for the hills. Social scientists head for the data. They either do original research or forage for existing empirical information on the subject. I discovered that kind of information in studies conducted by the Directors Guild and at San Diego State University. I'm going to confine my academic stirrings in this chapter to giving those research studies their due.

The DGA has issued a series of reports going back to 1986 documenting yearly employment of women and minorities as filmmakers.[4] The figures are based on number of days worked by DGA-member women and minorities as a percent of the total number of days worked by all DGA members. I'm going to discuss the situation for women across the board first and then go on to minorities.

The percentage of overall employment time held by women is:

1986–1990	1991–1995	1996–2000	2001–2002
6.2%	7.7%	8.2%	8.1%

The figures show that employment of women was climbing during these years and reached a high point between 1996 and the turn of the century. There's a hint of a downturn more recently (we'll look into that further in a moment). This table tells us that women were able to claim around 8 percent of directing jobs at maximum (their peak *single year* was 1996 at 9.3). Considering that they make up 50.1 percent of the population, they are clearly underrepresented.

We get further insight on this from research conducted at California State University, San Diego, by Professor Martha M. Lauzen, who concentrates exclusively on film industry women.[5] Lauzen examined the 250 top grossing films in 2001 and discovered that women directed only 6 percent of them. (This was a sizable drop from an 11 percent figure just one year before.) Examining the 100 top grossing pictures in 2001, she found that women directed a meager 4 percent of them (a drop from the previous year's 7 percent). Take note that this doesn't give as broad a picture of employment as the DGA figures, which cut across all films rather than only the high moneymakers. However, the rollbacks here confirm the dip in women directors intimated in the DGA data. Lauzen titles her study "The Celluloid Ceiling," and the results show why.

What's clear is that women are directing only a small proportion of the most commercially successful films. Why the poor showing of women directors in high grossing films? These are films that typically demand enormous expenditures for production, marketing, and distribution. Are women being excluded from work on these big-money projects because they're not considered qualified for large, complex productions? Do they add another risk factor to these already uncertain high-stakes ventures? Or are women excluding themselves, steering away from dash-and-splash flicks and going for stories with human relations interest and higher quality? These data don't tell us, but talk around the industry conjectures that it's all of the above.

Here's how the DGA data break down for the percentage of overall employment time held by three minority groups:

	African American	Latino	Asian American
1986–1990	2.4	0.8	0.3
1991–1995	2.8	1.3	0.5
1996–2000	4.5	1.7	1.2
2001–2002	5.1	1.9	1.2

African Americans have moved up in a steady climb to claim 5.1 percent of employment time (from a fairly low starting line). Actually, they are doing relatively better than women, considering they make up only 12 plus percent of the population. Latinos have a low number, 1+ percent, and a static one, even though they are by far the fastest-growing group in the United States and stand at 13 percent of the population. Asian Americans have the lowest employment rates, just below Latinos, which is not radically out of line with their 3.6 percent share of the general population.[6]

Women and minority directors are also doing badly in the TV medium. DGA tracked the top 40 prime-time drama and comedy series in 2000–2001, with 826 total episodes. Women directed 11 percent of them, with minorities far behind: African Americans at 3 percent, Latinos at 2 percent, and Asian Americans at 1 percent. Nine of the series had no women directors at all, and nine included not one of the minority groups.

Listening to the Data

Reviewing all this data, I have to conclude that the overall employment situation for women and minority directors borders on deplorable. Women peaked at an unimpressive level, which is now dipping. Latinos and Asian Americans, their heads just above ground, are either in a holding pattern or making barely perceptible gains in numbers. Relatively, Latinos are in the poorest position of all. Because outsider groups started at close to zero, their numbers among the ranks of directors seem spectacular. In absolute numbers, the story is very different. It's diversity and perversity: entrenched patterns cling.

African Americans, we can see, are progressing up a moderate slope at a constant pace. Within the black group, though, there's a real difference by gender. Talented male directors have made their mark; women directors are a handful and have hardly made a dent. When we think of outstanding black male filmmakers like Spike Lee, John Singleton, Forest Whitaker, the Hughes brothers, soon a flood of others come to mind—Carl Franklin, Charles Burnett, Robert Townsend, the Hudlins, Van Peebles, and others, including Bill Duke and Michael Schultz, whose voices run through these pages. The list goes on.

When we think of women like Julie Dash, Kasi Lemmons, Gina Prince-Bythewood, Darnell Martin, and Cheryl Dunye, just about then we feel we are reaching some limit, as though this is an exclusive sorority (ironically, struggling for new members). For me, it's still surprising to realize that the first film by an African American woman filmmaker to receive national distribution was Julie Dash's *Daughters of the Dust* in 1992. The first studio-sponsored, studio-financed film by a black woman was Darnell Martin's *I Like It Like That* in 1994.

If we look at the stats, this time through Mollie Gregory's imagery, we have to deduce that the heralded invasion by these alien filmmakers hasn't penetrated very deeply into the directorship mainland. The front lines for women, rather than holding, seem to be falling back. Blacks are advancing on a fairly small patch of beach. Meanwhile, Latinos and Asian Americans have hardly gotten out of the water.

I know that other people who study this data may come to different conclusions—there is leeway for varying interpretations. Be that as it may, I do hope this analysis will lead to additional dialogue and scrutiny—and, if the stars are appropriately aligned (as well as the studio executives), to a push to elevate the level of diversity in the industry.

The payoffs from this move toward inclusiveness are real and important. The most immediate one is practical—more filmmaking jobs for women and people of color, which speaks to fairness and democratic norms in the industry. But the public potentially gains enormously also: from the many new and different stories these filmmakers will tell; from the exposure to the lives and experiences of other people in those stories; from a better understanding of others growing out of that kind of exposure; and hopefully, from the audience's increased capacity to relate to and work with people of other backgrounds. Universities make the case that affirmative action yields a gain for all students because it enriches the campus atmosphere for learning and living together. By analogy, the point can be made that this wider band of artistic exposure will enrich American culture. Nobody can predict that those results will come to pass. But the potential surely invites a try. And the moral imperative for fairness stands apart from those more utilitarian calculations.

Inventorying the Obstacle Course

As you've seen, the informants were frank in expressing their views on directorial diversity, but they went beyond that. They named and illustrated the kinds of obstacles to employment emerging directors experience—what and who gets in the way. These were some of the most interesting insights from the interviews.

No Change Is Good Change

One of the blocks that was named most frequently was *fear of change*. Everyone knows that Hollywood and money are joined at the hip, and that the cost of making films keeps rising to ever new astronomical heights, in tandem with costly innovative technology and the swelling price tags of top stars. Decision makers are terrified of losing enormous investments and, paralyzed by fear of failure in off-center ventures, they reject the new and hug awesomely to the familiar.

If this is true generally, it is particularly applicable, and pernicious, for traditionally outsider groups who embody the new. Women and minority directors, in the historical Hollywood context, *are* "the new." The directors I spoke with drove home this point. An African American director commented:

> I can see what's operating with executives when they turn down my films. In terms of their jobs, there's no guarantee that they'll make a good return on investment. You know, when executives are making decisions, they don't want to put their jobs in jeopardy. Say you take on a Tom Cruise film and the movie doesn't play well at the box office. No one would blame you for thinking that a Tom Cruise film could be a hit; *they always make money.* One turkey would be just a fluke. People don't get fired for putting

a hundred million dollars into a Tom Cruise film, even if it doesn't succeed. If an executive takes a risk on something that hasn't been tried before, that's a kind of decision that people *do* lose their jobs over.

So I think it's that nobody wants to break the ice, say, and do a *Boyz N the Hood*. But once *Boyz N the Hood* is successful, they only want to do that. I have a script now that has Alfre Woodard and Whoopie Goldberg attached. It's based on a short film I made that people loved, universally. Executives tell me "Gosh, if the story had white people, we would have made this already."

In their nervousness about change, executives have an aversion to new faces in the director's chair and to new themes that these interlopers might throw on the screen. First, the faces. This remark is from a film director with a longtime commitment to opening up opportunities for unrepresented people, and who currently produces a TV series. His experience in the TV area parallels what goes on in film.

I try to promote as much diversity in directors as possible in my television series, but it's very hard to get the people above me to agree to this. They agree in general, everyone agrees in the abstract, but it's a *constant battle*. I can't get anyone to take any real chances, so you basically see the same suspects over and over again.

I've brought new minority people in, looked over what they've done, brought them down to the set, gone with my instincts. Yet you're ultimately up against someone in an office saying, "Well, what are their credits?" Well, they don't have any credits; that's the point. There's no insurance policy for this person doing a great job. There is no such thing.

If you have a good feeling about a person and your instincts are giving off positive vibes, and if you're confident this person can direct, *that this is a director*, that's how they should get started.

Nothing New = Ignorance

By rejecting minority themes as too novel or unfamiliar, these fear-driven execs have become (*or remain*) unsophisticated about minority life and culture.

We run into roadblocks as minorities because top people are afraid to tell different stories in this industry. They judge mainstream American films individually, but they lump all the stories about people of color into a small pot, as if they're the same story. "Oh, we've done our black woman story already this decade." Yeah, but that wasn't *this* story. At one point I was pitching my screenplay, which is about a woman in her forties, and it was a fun and zany plot, a feel-good kind of story. And an executive said to me, "But *Stella Got Her Groove Back* didn't make any money." And I said, "Yeah, but that was a *bad book*. It shouldn't have been a movie in the first place. And it doesn't have anything to do with my movie." Both stories had black women, and that's all that was necessary for it to be a similar movie in that executive's mind. This whole thing is a big burden also because if one of us gets a chance and messes up, no studio is going to touch that black subject for a long, long time.

Minority directors told me that they come up against pressures on the set to distort or rearrange their stories of minority life even after a project is OK'd. That's dramatized in this outrageous experience of a director making a biographical film (for cable) about Rosa Parks, the eminent civil rights leader. Network executives were all too willing to drain the meaning out of Rosa Parks's inspirational role in spearheading the Montgomery bus boycott.

> I can't track the logic of *neutering* Rosa Parks and playing down her leadership. We've all known for years that Rosa Parks was a political activist. Before being arrested on the bus, she was closely connected with the NAACP and she attended the Highlander School, which was a training ground for civil rights workers and other activists. She was very much aware of society, of everything around her, *the whole Jim Crow thing.*
>
> As recently as last week a network executive demanded that we add what's called a loop line, a dubbing in after the fact of the movie, having Rosa Park saying, "I didn't stand up and get off the bus like I was ordered because my feet were tired." The executives are afraid that white America will not like her if they know she is educated and combative. And it's better if she's *liked.* Then people will supposedly stay tuned in. So she just happened to be on the bus and because her feet were hurting her she didn't get up. They didn't want to put in anything about her being a student at Highlander School, because that might get her tagged as a Communist.
>
> For me, leaving out Rosa's work together with the NAACP to end bus segregation before her arrest is a big mistake. It reduces her to a *foot-weary woman* who simply did not know what she was doing when she refused to give up her seat on the bus. I can't be part of this dumbing-down of America. But for whose purpose?

Of course, executives are generally gun-shy about controversial elements in any production. But knowing the place of Rosa Parks in black consciousness, why would they take on a project with the intent of reducing her as a symbol? Either they were not aware, or they were and were willing to disregard, and affront, the perspectives of the black community (and of history) to cater to a wider audience.

I'm Not That Type

The *typecasting of directors* by the studios was named a serious obstacle to women and minority employment. Just as actors are typecast, directors are shoehorned into slots that match their backgrounds and assumed proclivities. Directors told me it's restrictive and based on erroneous thinking.

> Hollywood has a tendency to look at minority directors and think that they can only do a film related to *that minority.* Blacks do black film, Latinos a Latino movie. The notion is, "How can a black person direct a mainstream film when they don't live in the same world as whites." There's a mistaken belief that people can't understand the life and struggles of others of a different background. This marginalizes directors, puts them in a niche market, and makes it difficult for them to get other assignments.

Black directors told me that African Americans and other minorities grow up and live in a mostly white world, which is the world of American culture. They are as fully prepared to portray broad social themes as they are minority themes. It's much easier for minorities to tell mainstream stories than it is for white directors to tell minority-oriented stories. But most directors argue against being straightjacketed in any way. They believe that storytelling and moviemaking should transcend the boundaries of a person's particular ethnic or gender classification.

> Stories about human experiences and endeavors basically are the same; the culture texture differs. Creative people, like writers and directors, can understand the soul of another person; it's their business to be able to do that. Look, it's common for British directors to do American stories, and there's no big outcry about authenticity.

Some directors lamented that once classified a minority filmmaker, a director is marginalized, since studios assume that minority-themed films will only appeal to minority audiences. The studios make relatively few of these ethnic-themed films, believing that mainstream audiences will stay away—which results in tightly confined opportunities for these directors.

> The prevailing wisdom is that white audiences will not respond to any black themes, that we can't sell those flicks to Europe or the rest of the world, and at the same time that the domestic black audience itself isn't big enough or consistent enough. The presumed result: even if we do a good project, we won't be able to make any money on it.
>
> Those are *myths*. The reality is that black culture in this country is the single most powerful cultural influence. Just think of music, dress, language, dance. It's reflected in white kids knowing every word of every lyric in rap music. It's *black kids* who determine what's *cool* and what's not. Gospel music, blues, jazz have all infused black culture into the American mainstream. And to some extent we see this even more in places like England and Japan. Record execs realize this. Movie execs haven't seen the light as yet, at least not very much of it.

Some directors threw out the notion of *self-imposed* typecasting, whereby directors decide to work exclusively on in-group themes, or are pushed in that direction by their fellow ethnics. Clearly, there are women and minority directors with a powerful commitment to telling the story of the life and struggles of their group. But some directors feel pressured to take that path as a result of external intimidation rather than internal motivation.

> Sometimes Latino filmmakers think they have to detach themselves from the common culture to do good work. There's a sense that you should tell the *barrio story* if you're worth your salt. Your people, your neighborhood, *your* situation. There's an internally propelled tendency in some of these people to be, what should I say, exclusive. And some implicit code about how these things should be dealt with. The Latino film should feel and sound and look a *certain way*. Certain spokespersons seem to want to set a mold for all Latino filmmakers. Why? There's no way we should be pigeonholing ourselves like that. There are as many different stories as there are people who want to tell stories.

Do women executives, by background part of an "outsider" group, do less typecasting and more hiring of women directors? Do they use their authority as studio heads to make a difference in work life for women in Hollywood? The answers are not definitive, and they are also not heartening. Patrick Goldstein, an analyst and critic who writes a weekly column on the film industry for the *Los Angeles Times*, concludes that studios run by women executives have a record on the hiring of female directors that is virtually identical to those headed by men and no better.[7] He took as his point of reference five studios with women as top creative decision makers—serving in the positions of either studio chair or head of production.

When Goldstein interviewed among this group, he was told that the scarcity of women directors is not a function of discrimination but an aversion to risk. The average film costs $60 million, and the mega-systems in which decision makers are embedded won't let them deviate from bankable directors who have a record of big box-office hits. At the same time, women directors aren't keen to make those action-saturated, comic-book-inspired flicks. Amy Pascal, who chairs Columbia Pictures, and was shepherding *Men in Black 2* and Adam Sandler vehicles at the time, said that she just doesn't have the kind of material that women directors want to sink their teeth into.

These women executives point to another factor that ties their hands in hiring. Male superstars, who hold sway in the business (when not going off to be the governor of California), tend to feel squeamish about a woman holding authority over them, so they give the edge to men. More on this later.

To this point, the obstacles to diversity to which directors spoke centered on the impact of attitudes: decision makers' dread of the new, their ignorance of minority life and concerns, and stereotypical thinking about who directs what. Following behind that type of hurdle—with a slightly lower number of mentions—were two structural ones: decision making in the industry, *formal* and *informal*, that works to the disadvantage of minorities and women. Specifically, the problems turn on *who* makes formal decisions and *how* informal decisions are made. I'll start with the who question first.

Who's in Charge of the Traffic Lights?

Projects that don't get green-lighted don't fly. At the crux of getting a film made is approval from a small coterie of executives with the authority to signal "go." I was told recurrently that women and minorities by and large don't inhabit the top decision-making circle. *L.A. Times* Hollywood reporter Lorenza Muñoz has estimated that fifteen executives at the major studios have ultimate green-lighting power: all of them are white, and only three of those are women.[8] Some observers, and I put myself among them, think that this decision-making group is *the* crucial pressure point for expanding diversity. Directors—minorities, women, and white males alike—were clear about this.

> It really comes down to one factor: there haven't been blacks in the executive level of Hollywood. They've been pretty much *nonexistent*. You've heard of the invisible man. There's no African American, *none*, on the inside with the authority to green-light a film. I'm convinced minorities and more women have to be added to the decision-making circle. Sure, there are some minority development staffers and executives, but they only have the power to say "No."

I want to do films dealing with African Americans, black women—and white male executives couldn't care less. Who decreed that mainly white men should decide on what movies women see and who makes them? The narrow group of decision people in control now is ignorant of literature, and even of film, and they're out of touch with Boise, Idaho, and Harlem.

There's no minority infrastructure with clout either on the creative side or in marketing and distribution that supports culturally diverse content. I think distribution is a crucial element in this because if you can't get the work out, *it dies*. And the distribution companies are predominantly white, predominately male, predominately Jewish. Sure, there have always been exceptions and champions who plugged diverse content, but they have to fight battles all the way down the line.

Getting into the Loop

All of that deals with decision making inside the studio bureaucracy, but decisions and deals and negotiations famously take place outside the official structure, in the notorious "Old Boy's Club" schmoozefests.[9] These informal tête-à-têtes among players build momentum for a project and pave a road into the green-light inner sanctum. If you can find your way to this network, you've got a leg up toward accessing that power set. If you can't, you probably won't get your foot in the door. Women and minorities ordinarily don't have solid buddy-buddy connections in this informal system.

> From a personal standpoint, I'm an outsider in Hollywood—my father was a chemist in the Midwest. My biggest problem is not that I'm a minority, it's that I'm not Francis Ford Coppola's son. That's my biggest problem.
>
> I think that people hire who they know—I do it, we all do it. We want to be around the people we know and trust, maybe people we grew up with, we went to college with, whose neighborhood we live in. That's very natural—people can't be blamed for that. But it disadvantages us people of color. Given where I came from, there's *no way* I was going to be related to the president of a studio, or have a neighbor or godfather in the system. I wasn't at the same country club.
>
> Family and connections, that's what opens doors in this town, regardless of your background. Hollywood is a game board of cliques and overlapping circles. The politics and social entanglements in the industry are probably more interesting than most movies.

There's an additional obstacle, this one affecting women directors specifically, and returning us to the old chestnut about "women's place." It's in the realm of attitudes again, but this time involving opinions about how strong and decisive women can be or ought to be in executing the "command" components of the director's job. And how men feel about it if they *are* able to do the "be in charge" thing. The reality seems to be this: many men just don't want to take direction from a woman.

> One of the director's roles is a *daddy role*, a sergeant role, and the assumption of many men is that women can't take on that kind of authority. When women do, though, there's resentment from men who do not know how to take orders from women. I think the director is the closest thing to an absolute dictator in our democratic culture. You

have to have control over everything. You can order the police force in, ask for anything you need, and everyone is there to be of service to your vision.

Men in our society are not trained to accept that kind of authority from women. So they stand in the way of hiring women to do that work. It will take more time for that to come about. The trick for women is to keep hammering away, without losing the special humanity that women can bring to film, and without totally becoming one of the boys.

Nixing the Mixing

Another obstacle goes to where movies are shown, rather than where they are made. Audience responses and interactions in the hinterlands find their way back to decision makers at the studios. Input from movie exhibitors is a component of that process. Exhibitors who are ill at ease about racially mixed audiences in their theaters can be a block to minority themes in movies. Listen to what this experienced African American director says about how movie theater owners can skew the ethnic content of film.

> Film execs have some hang-ups in latching on to black-themed film because of their concerns about mixed audiences. Film is a social experience. People gather together in a darkened hall. It's like going to a place of worship. And you see images conveyed to your conscious and unconscious mind in a hushed, shared experience for an hour and a half, two hours.
>
> Because of the racist way people are raised in our country, bringing black and white audiences together in close contact in the same space has been a terrifying experience for some theater owners. They have believed that the mixture would be volatile, or a black presence would simply *drive white people away*. Remember, theaters used to be Jim Crow, and black audiences had to sit separately upstairs—maybe you would get *contaminated* or whatever if you sat together. So over many years there was the notion of not doing films that would encourage the mixing of audiences.
>
> Richard Pryor was someone who, because of his honesty and his ability to make people laugh their way around very painful situations, had huge crossover white and black audiences. He could bring out both groups, and nobody had a problem because of the laughter. I directed an early Pryor movie mixing comedy and politics, and it was first shown in St. Louis in a downtown theater. I went there at the time to observe the opening. The theater owner did not expect a black audience to show up, and when they did he stood outside the theater perspiring and turning red—very anxious about what might happen.
>
> Another time, at an opening of one of my other Pryor films in a mall theater, I saw fifty, a hundred black kids line up for tickets. The owner of the mall, not the theater owner, watched this happening, and he walked over and *had the theater shut down*. The kids weren't disorderly or noisy, and when the show was cancelled out from under them they became upset. The mall owner, you know, could have combusted the very disturbance he was worried might happen.
>
> This social interaction around movies is something that I've watched and seen as an important factor in putting a clamp on the production of good black-themed films and on work for black directors. Good black film *results* in mixed-race audiences. Some dis-

tributors and exhibitors perceive of this mixture as running counter to audience comfort, audience decorum and control, and the loss of potential white audience box-office. But the anxiety around this isn't in sync with the reality.

The last point was verified later when films like *Barber Shop* (2003) and *Drum Line* (2003) opened, movies that had minority-group stars and stories but attracted large crossover audiences, especially younger ones. One movie features a barbershop in the inner city (run by Ice Cube); the other featured black college marching bands. About 40 percent of the audience for these films was not African American, which means a spreading out of theatergoers and a respectable gross from low production costs. Those minority-themed movies, of course, followed white-themed films like *Beverly Hills Cop* and other Eddie Murphy blockbusters, which produced mixed audiences and millions for Murphy but provided few minority jobs, either behind or in front of the camera.

That's the inventory. Those are the kinds of problems off-mainstream directors are up against, at least according to the filmmakers who informed me. But these informants also suggested ways of stepping back and understanding these problems, of gaining a perspective that clarifies and edifies the issue of diversity. That involves perceiving how prejudice plays into all of this. How money does also. And the question of individual merit and drive.

Everybody's Doing It

Diversity issues are not all confined to the movie studio milieu. Larger forces external to the movie industry bear on this problem. In American society, women and minorities generally have trouble entering the job market: they are excluded from certain types of jobs and do not move up as fast in jobs they are given or snare. It's hard to say offhand how the film industry stands in comparison to other fields. I believe that in my own field of academia, the university system is doing better, especially for women in certain disciplines.

I would add another external factor: the substantial international financing of American films today, with foreign investors convinced that white actors attract larger foreign audiences and produce greater profits overseas. These financiers exert muscle toward featuring the European–American faces of bankable stars like Leonardo DiCaprio, Mel Gibson, Tom Cruise, and Arnold Schwarzenegger.

To what degree is prejudice a significant factor? There was pretty strong consensus, including from women and minority directors, that prejudice doesn't count for that much. Other factors, which contribute an aura of prejudice, are much more potent. For example, money.

> There's no doubt that this is a bottom-line industry that puts a much greater emphasis on profits than prejudice. If you make money at the box office, *you will work*. It doesn't matter about your background. If you have the right material that promises commercial success, there's a good chance your picture will be made. You could be Charles Manson. You could be a ninety-year-old-woman *mass murderer* and you made *Titanic*, they would

hire you again. Yes, it's hard to get a break, but once you are in, raking in dollars for the company will keep you going.

Earlier I spoke of cliques and the informal power-lunch set and how they impeded diversity. But directors, regardless of background, told me that *deliberate* exclusion or conscious discrimination was not a big part of this problem.

> People like to cluster together, they socialize and work with people they are comfortable with, maybe are similar to. But I don't think there's a *master plan* by anyone to keep people out. It's just a natural way society functions, not bigotry or racism. People have to work their way into the film culture—women kind of have to become "one of the boys"—and white women have been able to do that better than minorities, whether male or female.
>
> I think there's always going to be these problems because filmmaking is a club. It's like a little fraternity, and the people in power are going to favor like-minded people. You've heard the word *nepotism*, right? That being said, there are opportunities available. I think Hollywood is as fair as you can expect it to be.

Early "No's" Woes

Some directors said that these problems can be overcome through merit, perseverance, and the "right stuff." America, they feel, is an open society where everything is possible. One director put forward this upbeat point of view in ebullient and semi-patriotic language:

> I believe Hollywood is the last outpost of the Wild West; it's the "American Dream" all over again. That's why people gravitate out here. Hard work and the image you can conjure up turn the trick. See, if you can put your imagination to something commercially attractive, you can attain great riches—go from *rags to riches* overnight. You know, cream rises to the top—it ignores background. Also, the people who hire keep changing, so there isn't a dug-in group of Neanderthals who can keep rejecting people.

Not everyone agreed with this optimism. An instructive exchange between directors took place when I related a mainstream male director's comments along these lines to a minority female filmmaker. (I withheld names in these conversations.)

First the comment:

> This is really a *non-issue*. You have to be driven and crazy to be in this business, no matter who you are. It's always tough sledding, but only if you are driven and passionate in forging ahead can you succeed. You have to be able to take rejection after rejection and keep going, without dropping out or getting up on a soapbox. Eventually you get there. But it takes laser-beam perseverance, whatever background you come from.

Now the response:

> Sure, I know it's difficult for everyone to get a movie made, and as difficult as it is for everyone, it's more difficult for people of color and for women. Just look at the numbers.

I think people who believe race is not an issue are very rarely people of color. It's easy to say there's no racism when you've never personally been on the receiving end.

My experience has not been the same as his. He gets a lot of "No's," but his is a level of "No" that I have not had the option of getting because *I won't even get into the room* where the decisions are made. As soon as I attach actors of color to my film, that puts it in another category, and I don't even get into that room to hear the "No." I get plenty of other no's that stop me much sooner in the process.

From his point of view, he's struggling so hard that he can't imagine anyone is struggling more, but we *are*. For us to even get into the room is an earthshaking event.

And, OK, there's another angle to this. From day one in your life, if you're a white male in this country, you have a certain sense of entitlement. You can become Steven Spielberg or you can be George Bush. You're an American and can be whatever you *want*. If you're a woman or a person of color, you learn that you don't have entitlement. You have to give yourself an extra psychological push to go after what you want. And you don't even have many examples, people *who look like you*, to emulate. There's nothing about the way those who are holding the jobs you aspire to have come up in the world that you can follow. You don't even have a relevant road map.

This comment brings home to me that there are powerful deterrents for emerging filmmakers that are both external and internal. External factors tell them, "Hey, reality dictates that you won't get into the room." Internal factors lodge in the mind and signal psychologically from within, "Hey, you're different and I bet you won't have a chance to get in the room. None of your brothers or sisters are in there." This minority director couldn't call up any role models to follow and couldn't visualize a well-trod pathway forward. So much for cream naturally rising to the top.

In one of my conversations with a director, a rejoinder of sorts came to the fore. I think it highlights the complexity of this subject and the feelings it evokes.

Do I believe we should have affirmative action in filmmaking? I don't know; I really don't know. For example, I lost out on directing a movie with a very well-known black actor, who said to me, "I'm going to hire a black director to do this picture, because I need to give a black filmmaker work." He was very up-front about that. It's a true story. Is that reverse racism: because I'm white, I can't direct this movie? Or am I obligated to help out a minority at my own expense? How do you answer that?

Breaking through the Clouds

As a skeptical scholar (and occasional carping comic), I was never a big fan of Pollyanna. To make ultimate sense of the part-wretched, part-exhilarating mosaic of women and minority filmmakers, and prognosticate prospects for the future, would be a bafflement even for a Theseus, who could decode the most tangled of labyrinths. But I'm going to go against my own tide and tilt the prism so I can see some bright sparkles in the conundrum that might signal progress ahead. Cassandra would be unhappy, but she always is anyway.

Ascent of Black Film

One of the directors told me that there's a forward-moving dynamic in the history of black film. There comes an advance, then a plateauing-off for a time, and then an advance to a new plateau. He felt confident about the continuity of that pattern.

Good things in the industry come in waves, and they're based on timing. The 1960s stimulated a breakthrough for black film when the social fabric was beginning to burst at the seams, and there were street demonstrations and the bus boycott and the demands for voting rights.[10]

That was one element in the opening for blacks. Another one, which started earlier, was that business was going down the tube in Hollywood. The introduction of television had deflected a big portion of the movie audience to the small screen in the living room.

So in the early 1970s the blaxploitiation movie appeared, introduced by Melvin Van Peebles with *Sweet Sweetback's Baad Asssss Song* [1971]. It was wholly unexpected from Hollywood's point of view. This was one of the first big independent films, financed totally with outside money. The industry turned down distribution, so it was distributed independently, with Peebles using the "four-walling" technique of simply renting a theater and throwing the movie up on the screen.

Peebles's group found a way to do their own advertising. Because he was snubbed by Hollywood, he retained all the rights, and made a ton of money. Peebles insisted on releasing the film both in mainstream neighborhoods and in black neighborhoods, Harlem. He was a *revolutionary* genius; the film and the handling of the film were so unique.

The movie dealt with the black experience, even though it showed a bizarre black experience. The central character was a brazen black man who wasn't reluctant to stand up in defiance of the police. The timing was right, and the film had tremendous success with black audiences—and also with some white audiences who were ready for that content.

It *stunned* Hollywood bigwigs, who said, "Wow, there's an audience for this stuff that we never catered to. Let's make more movies like this and bring in this hungry audience." A move was set afoot in Hollywood to involve blacks in making essentially B movies, peopling them with black actors to tap into this newfound gold mine called the *black audience*.

But the momentum wasn't sustained. The newfound black audience soon grew weary of the basically negative portrayal of blacks as gangsters and goons. There's a tendency of Hollywood to play out a vein of gold until it is totally consumed, and then they go on and look for the next big thing. Keep an eye out; *it'll be coming down the pike.*

This history prods me to branch off with an extended comment. For black filmmakers the next "big thing" was a second breakthrough in the late 1980s, early 1990s, after the crash of the first. I've spoken of this before in the context of male-female differences. In 1986, two independently made surprise hits opened: Spike Lee's *She's Gotta Have It* and Robert Townsend's *Hollywood Shuffle*. These very low-cost box-office bonanzas opened a wedge for black directors. Lee followed through with *School Daze* in 1988 and *Do the Right Thing* in 1989, and Reginald Hudlin added a raucous

House Party in 1990. By 1991, when twenty-three-year-old John Singleton released *Boyz N The Hood*, some twenty of these black-directed pictures were in production. That was a historical tipping point for black filmmakers.

A set of other in-the-moment factors drove the tipping-over. A group of young, dynamic, talented black filmmakers appeared on the scene. They had received training at film schools, thanks in part to affirmative action, and were serious, determined students. The influential Los Angeles Black Independent Film-Making Movement, started by Charles Burnett at UCLA and energized by other students like Julie Dash, is symbolic of the wave.

These fledgling directors were battle-scarred by the rich/perplexing/challenging experience of inner-city living and were ready to tell stories that America, particularly black America, was eager to hear. They presented fresh, raw material, told in new and energetic ways about urban violence, the gang culture, rap music, the projects, and drug dealing—and about the resilient and tattered black family, with father figures more often absent than present.

On the economic side, a profitable black film audience was coalescing. Studios saw that blacks were spending a disproportionate amount of their income on movies as compared to whites, and that a higher proportion of blacks than whites were attending movies. Studios decided to go after that audience in new ways, and that contributed to the tipping process.

We've seen that to get where they are, women directors forged a single breakthrough in the 1970s. Blacks had two breakthroughs (though mostly involving men). There's another historical difference between the two groups. Women were heavily involved in the Hollywood system right from the beginning. They were excluded from the executive suite and, except in the earliest years, from directing. But they were prominent in substantial numbers in creative jobs as actors and writers and in a slew of craft positions—set designers, hairdressers, costume designers, etc.

Blacks were basically closed out of the industry. On rare occasions, a Hattie McDaniel, Paul Robeson, or Bojangles Robinson came before the camera, but almost nobody worked behind the camera in either craft or trade areas. African American entrepreneurs like Oscar Micheaux and George and Noble Johnson established their own black cinema production and distribution companies, raising funds however they could to keep them running. These production companies were separate, and their audiences were separate.

When directing chances opened up for outsider groups, women had a launching pad from which to spring. Blacks had a blank slate. They had to come from nowhere. That helps explain why women have been more light-footed than blacks in moving into executive and producer positions as well as into director slots.

Some details round this out. A few black filmmakers directed before the first wave (Gordon Parks, *The Learning Tree*, 1969; Ozzie Davis, *Cotton Comes to Harlem*, 1970) and between the first and the second (Michael Schulz, *Cooley High*, 1975; *Bustin' Loose*, 1981; *Krush Groove*, 1985, etc.). But the broad strokes are pretty much as I presented them.

A Turn to the Bright

I'm branching back into my main line of thought after setting out what I think is a significant and interesting part of the story. Recall, we were told that there are hopeful elements embedded in the current diversity situation. The first one mentioned was a historical forward-motion dynamic for blacks. Another director now adds to that the intermingling of cultures currently taking place in American society. Cutting-edge culture in each group is overlapping with cutting-edge culture in other groups. New receptivity and new openness to difference is, in fact, percolating.

> Now, things are going to open up for minority directors. It's just *going to happen*. The interest in film of young people from all races, male and female, it's the same as in music, and in the music business nothing is shocking. Nothing is shocking in terms of who's a star. The same will ultimately be true in the movie business. It won't be an issue. It won't even be noticed that this is an Asian woman, this is a Latino guy. It's going to explode!

Boom! And here goes another one. Women executives at present are interlaced throughout the studio structure, poised at crucial levers of decision making, including studio heads Sherry Lansing at Paramount, Stacey Snider at Universal Pictures, and Amy Pascal at Columbia. Concurrently, the number of women producers has risen dramatically (as documented by the San Diego State research studies).

Suddenly, we saw women running Hollywood's major guilds, including the three most important ones: Martha Coolidge at the Directors Guild of America; Victoria Riskin at the Writers Guild of America, West; and Melissa Gilbert at the Screen Actors Guild. Fanning out from there, Kathleen Kennedy officiating at the Producers Guild and Lisa Zeno Churgin at the Motion Picture Editors Guild. Besides, female hands have been steering the uppermost tillers at the entertainment divisions of ABC, CBS, Fox, and UPN.

There's even a perceived positive side to the slide in the number of women filmmakers. Some people around town see this as a voluntary choice, a rejecting of the frenetically driven environment of directing and an embracing of a higher quality lifestyle, where work and family life are kept in better, more fulfilling balance. (There are of course other employment blocks, though, where women have no choice.) The peak career-making years coincide with the peak childbearing time of life, so there's an inherent conflict, or at least tension. Directors like Mary Harron (*American Psycho*), Rebecca Miller (*Personal Velocity*), and Gina Prince-Bythewood (*Love and Basketball*) have elected to have children in mid-career and potentially slow down their trajectories.

Producer Lynda Obst isn't buying any of this post-feminism. Writing in the *Los Angeles Times*, she declares this to be exhaustion and a female-driven backlash, with some women now striving for traditional homebound status and the safety umbrella of a well-bankrolled husband. To Obst, these dropouts are making a statement against the Big Career and Superwoman, and chickening out of the good fight.[11] Perhaps, though, they simply think that the *Good Career* is better than the *Big Career*.

Of late, African Americans have been on a roll of sorts. The 2002 Academy Award's top acting honors went to Denzel Washington and Halle Berry—a historical first for African Americans in capturing both these Oscars. At the same ceremony, the Academy bestowed an Oscar on Sidney Poitier for a lifetime of achievement, which has included both acting and directing. As we have seen, the ranks of first-rate African American directors are expanding steadily, particularly for men. Spike Lee is out there in the spotlight, but others are catching some glow.

Ang Lee has fired up Asian American filmmakers through his Academy Award that recognized his innovative cinematic work in *Crouching Tiger, Hidden Dragon*. Some may be even more impressed by his entry into the big-time movie circle, symbolized by *The Hulk*.

It's harder to spot signs of progress among Latino filmmakers, but some markers are there. Latino filmmakers are receiving a boost from the striking successes of recent Mexican films like *Amores Perros* and *Y Tu Mama Tambien*. Well-known, well-respected actors like Edward James Olmos and Andy Garcia are transitioning and bolstering the ranks of Latino directors. Alfonso Arau created some waves recently with *Zapata*.

I could probably shift gears and draw up longer and stronger lists of dismal elements in the mixed bag that is diversity in Hollywood, and I may do that somewhere else— maybe a personal letter to Jack Valenti, or his successor? But, on a final positive note, one of the minority directors I spoke with told me that minority status could actually serve as a real advantage rather than a thumb in the eye for a struggling filmmaker. Minorities generally lose access because of who they are, but they can also gain a different kind of access that's valuable.

> The upside in being off-center is that people really *remember me*. You know, you can't mix me up, because I'm *different*, there's nobody else to mix me up with. I enjoy that. It's an advantage, because in this industry, where there's so much competition, everybody is trying to stand out. And that's the benefit of not belonging to the mainstream demographic.
>
> People remember you. I see people I met *ten years ago*, and they know who I am. I have met executives at meetings who are so glad to talk to me because they are tired of hearing the same old thing. They enjoy talking to someone who has something *else* to say, who has a different slant on the same shit.

I'm tempted to say that if we could only go further and find a way to turn all the advantages of mainstream directors into disadvantages, we would be well on our way to solving this problem. Or creating a new one. So it is better to stick to our national commitment to equity and equal opportunity, linked to affirmative action, as the way to forge ahead.

Looking back, there's been a litany of painful roadblocks to diversity in these pages. But we've also come upon estimable proposals for giving diversity new life. These are exciting and pivotal days in the filmmaking community, days of change in technology and in how the system is organized and financed. Things are always changing in Hollywood, but now it's in totally different ways than before. Stand and take a breath. Something new, surely, will be appearing down the pike.

CHAPTER SEVEN

~

Writers in the Scene?

Writers provide the map that allows everything else to happen. When I read a script that is so compelling I can't put it down, it gives me all the elements of the movie—characters, message, essence of the scenes, ambiance. To me the story is the beginning of everything. But script making is not filmmaking.

—Bill Duke

If it's true that authors open a vein and bleed, screenwriters must endure a virtual bloodbath. Screenwriters I have spoken with all agree that directors hold the upper hand in their common work, that the balance of status and power falls disproportionately in their direction. Yet, writers claim, it is they who deliver the critical and prerequisite element for making a film, calling up the old adage: "If it ain't on the page, it ain't on the stage." But the reality is that once the script—and its vision—are locked in, writers are locked out. At that point, directors take over big time. Together with producers, stars, and executives, directors use the script as molding clay for sculpting a new vision—the director's.

Almost everyone in the business has heard the story of young Herman Mankiewicz, who in the mid-1920s summoned his pal Ben Hecht from New York to Hollywood to rake in easy bucks going against competitors who were "idiots." In his now-fabled telegram, "Manky" told Hecht that it would be wise not to "let this get around." Less well known is that thirty years later in an obituary for his friend, Hecht declared that decades of writing scenarios in Hollywood had throttled and fried Manckiewicz's nimble mind. He lamented a life withered in writing screenplays, which "all of them put together won him an early death." The notion of deep pockets and wasted talents is a dominant theme among observers of and participants in the screenwriting trade.[1]

For many of these early screenwriters, movie work was frivolous and even laughable. It was a way to make big bucks, which would ostensibly support more authentic authorial endeavors. But this has changed. New York used to be the single magnet drawing bright English majors who wanted to write books or become journalists, but today Hollywood is a strong rival, luring once and future novelists into the realm of the 112-page set. An Academy Award–winning film is as big an aspiration as the Great American Novel: budding authors are as interested in scripting *American Beauty* as in penning *An American Tragedy*. Screenwriting is a pathway to reach a vastly larger audience and have a staggering impact on the public psyche—while earning infinitely more money.

But for every *American Beauty* there are thirty *Scooby-Doos*, so the deep-pockets-cum-wasted-talents motif continues unabated. Anthropologist Hortense Powdermaker observed that, over the long run, writers absorb the values of executives and producers to a far greater extent than front-office people take on the artistic and cultural goals of writers.[2]

Late Arrivals Go to the End of the Line

Compared to directors, screenwriters are Johnny-come-lately appendages to moviemaking. It wasn't until 1927, about thirty years after the first film played at the first Bijou, when Al Jolson jump-started talkies with *The Jazz Singer*, that studios suddenly opened their doors to writers. The studios desperately needed wordsmiths to thread dialogue into moving pictures. East Coast playwrights, novelists, and journalists followed a cross-continental rainbow westward to cash in on the Hollywood pot of gold. The word got around after all, and Manky and Ben were joined by the likes of F. Scott Fitzgerald, Raymond Chandler, Dorothy Parker, Clifford Odets, Ernest Hemingway, and William Faulkner. But these writers weren't suited to establishing themselves within the fraternity of Hollywood old-timers. Studio executives pretty much treated all writers like hired hands, essentially hacks and rewrite men for scripts fabricated by other hacks.

It's no surprise that writers formed the Screen Writers Guild (a precursor of the Writers Guild of America) back in the 1920s.[3] But the organization received zero encouragement from the studios and basically functioned as little more than a social club and place to exchange information. The Wall Street crash in 1929, together with an eruption of social activism, changed that picture. In 1935, the National Labor Relations Act was passed, and the guild petitioned for an election to establish its authority as a union to represent writers in collective bargaining. The studios, used to a malleable collection of scribes, fought this move, countering through a Screen Playwrights group that they could keep under wraps. But the guild won the election and in 1939 began negotiating for a collective-bargaining agreement. The agreement was finally forged in 1941.

That agreement was the guild's achievement and its Achilles heel. The guild won crucial union representation rights, but the contract ceded the privileges of copyright to the studios. To my thinking, it gave away the store. And that has made all the difference in defining the authority and status of writers. The critical clause stipulated, "The studio, hereinafter referred to as the author." The author is not the *writer*; it is

Nandi Bowe. *Courtesy of Bowe*

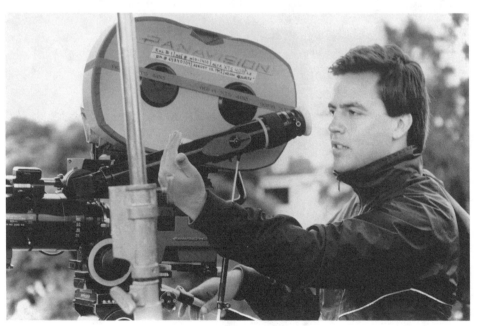

Salvador Carrasco. *Photo by Andrea Sanderson, courtesy of Carrasco*

Gilbert Cates. *Courtesy of Cates*

Martha Coolidge on the set of *The Prince and Me. Courtesy of Paramount Pictures*

Christopher Coppola. *Courtesy of Coppola*

Joe Dante on the set of *The Second Civil War. Photo courtesy of Dante*

Julie Dash. *Courtesy of Dash*

Andrew Davis on the set of *The Fugitive. Courtesy of Davis*

Bill Duke. *Courtesy of Duke*

Gary Fleder on the set of *Runaway Jury* with John Cusack. *Courtesy of Fleder*

Bob Gale. *Courtesy of Gale*

Monte Hellman.
Courtesy of Hellman

George Hickenlooper. *Courtesy of Hickenlooper*

Walter Hill. *Courtesy of Hill*

Arthur Hiller. *Courtesy of Hiller*

Henry Jaglom. *Courtesy of Jaglom*

Jonathan Kaplan. *Courtesy of Kaplan*

Irvin Kershner.
Courtesy of Kershner

Randal Kleiser. *Courtesy of Kleiser*

John Landis. *Courtesy of Landis*

Delbert Mann. *Courtesy of Mann*

Nancy Meyers.
Courtesy of Meyers

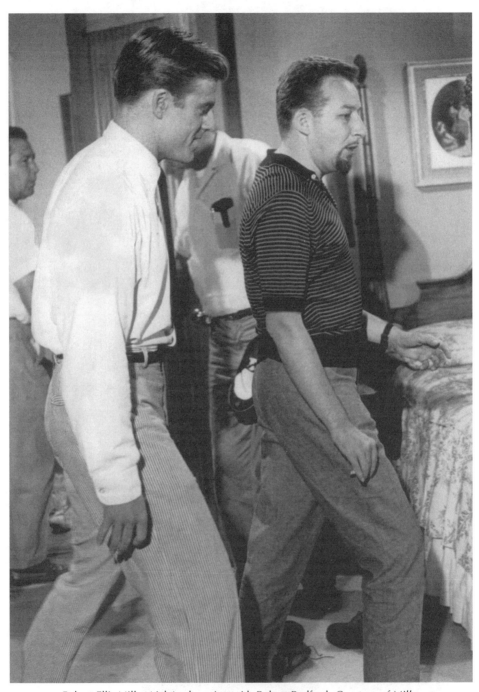

Robert Ellis Miller (right) rehearsing with Robert Redford. *Courtesy of Miller*

Sylvia Morales.
Courtesy of Morales

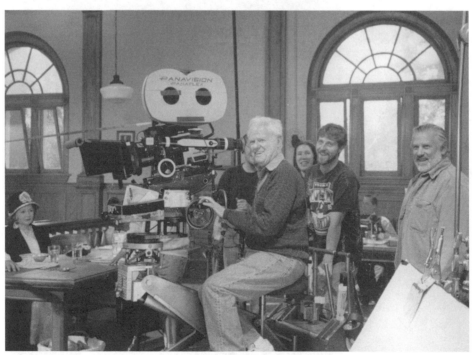

Daniel Petrie. *Courtesy of Petrie*

Myrl Schreibman. *Courtesy of Schreibman*

Michael Schultz.
Courtesy of Schultz

Krishna Shah. *Courtesy of Shah*

Charles Shyer. *Courtesy of Shyer*

Elliot Silverstein.
Courtesy of Silverstein

Sandy Tung. *Courtesy of Tung*

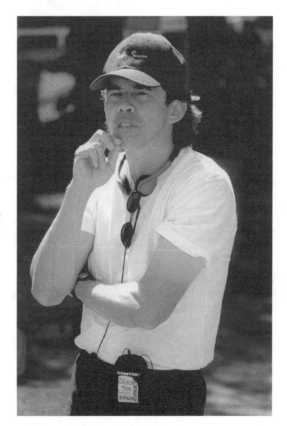

the *studio*. The property, namely the script, belongs not to the writer but to the studio—which is free to do with it whatever it wishes. Writers had signed on to a position of chronic subservience.

Contrast that with playwrights in New York, who hammered out their basic contract with theater owners in 1919 through the Dramatists Guild. There, the writer is the acknowledged creator and owner of the play, with full retention of the copyright. Playwrights license their plays to producers—essentially lease it to them temporarily—and producers can't change a word of the script without getting clear approval of the playwright. Playwrights also have a hand in selecting the cast and the director and participating in the rehearsal process.

None of this artistic possession holds for screenwriters, who forfeit control, absolutely, upon receiving payment for the script. From that moment, it's good-bye Charlie—they have no further formal say in what happens to their script on the way to becoming a film, if it ever becomes a film. It doesn't belong to them anymore.

Development as Disembowelment

Producing a script in the studio context is a dicey business that draws many people beyond the writer into a convoluted process called *development*—or, after a few Dirty Martinis at Musso and Frank's, "development hell."[4] The original story concept can spring from novels, news articles or public events, the stage, biography or history books—just about anywhere. Even the rantings of the local deli guy. Producers and development executives typically seize on these nuggets and engage a writer or several different writers on assignment to work up outlines, treatments, first drafts, rewrites, polished scripts, and all points between. Producers orchestrate a set of "step deals" with built-in milestones that allow them to change and rearrange writers or bail out altogether anywhere along the way.

So-called creative meetings that chop away at the script can go on for months or years, with notes for changes coming from a squad of producers, executives, creative department staffers, stars, and whoever else manages to get a foot in the door. "Script doctors" get called in to spice up the dialogue, juice up the action scenes, and add romance or jokes. John Gregory Dunne titled his book describing this arcane procedure *Monster*. A director I spoke with described the process this way:

> This is the writers' big problem, trying to preserve some sense of authorship for the script. It's because so many scripts are being developed by committees, which means you just keep throwing new writers into the pot. It's just a bunch of ideas and ripped off things from other movies. Add a chase scene like that, put a woman in it, and she should look like Jennifer Lopez. It's all tossed into this hopper, and these writers are supposed to make it into something. Some kind of "high concept" gimmick is supposed to help them organize it.

But the torture doesn't let up, and for most writers the next phase gets even more excruciating.

How Do I Get to the Set?

Writers have less say during filming than in development. Writers I have known who created their own original scripts on spec, or who were the principal author in development, bitterly resent the alteration—read *desecration*—of their scripts as they are carried forward into production. They equally resent their near impotency in being able to do anything about it.

Through the Writers Guild of America (WGA), writers have been politicking for a greater say in the mechanics of actually making movies from their scripts. They want to be on the set, review dailies, sit in on casting, attend rehearsals. As writers go after these goals, directors push back with a vengeance through their own guild (DGA) because, as we've seen, they feel the studios are already strangling their creative rights. The last thing the directors want is further infringement on their authority from players who historically have been given a back seat.[5]

During contentious contract negotiations with the studios in 2001, both guilds clashed on this "soft" issue with a ferocity that matched struggles over tough money matters. In the end, money demands were settled, but skirmishes around artistic control and how to apportion it continue at full tilt. These two parties continue to circle warily around one another, and I suspect that the abrasive quality of the relationship is a mixture of psychological and substantive components. What we have here is a war between different professional groups for power and turf and prestige, waged resolutely through the advocacy organizations representing them. We'll praise the guilds and pass the ammunition a little later.

I Love You, Honey, but Please Stay in the Kitchen

When I broached writer-director relationships with the filmmakers I interviewed, especially the question of writers on the set, they staunchly expressed two views. They say they respect and admire writers for what they do—but they also don't want them staying the director's hand in putting a script to celluloid. First, an appreciation:

> I drop to my knees before writers. Writers create the story from nowhere, from the air, sitting alone in front of a computer. The writer's is the most original and basic contribution to the making of a movie. Everyone else has something to start with, *a floor plan*—which the writer dreamed up and made into a screenplay.

Most of my respondents believe that this contribution isn't given weight and that writers don't get the regard they merit. That opinion mirrors the going view in Hollywood—one that hasn't changed in decades. Writers have been called stepchildren, bastard children, battered wives, and low man on the totem pole. Frances Marion was the highest paid writer in the 1920s and early 1930s yet still lamented that "Screenwriting is like writing in the sand with the wind blowing."[6] A colleague of mine at UCLA, Jorja Prover, interviewed a sample of screenwriters to document their attitudes toward their work. The title of her 1994 book, *No One Knows Their Names*, sums up most writers' overriding perception of themselves—unrecognized, unrewarded, and undervalued.

I can remember the gag making the rounds in L.A. a few years ago about the totally ditzy starlet who would do anything to get her first part in a picture—so she goes to bed with the *writer*. And I recall the movie portraits of downtrodden scribes like Joe Gillis, the unfortunate fellow floating in the pool in *Sunset Blvd.*, and the pathetically earnest Barton Fink. In viewing the Oscars on TV, I've seen writers neglect thanking fellow scribes who contributed to award-winning scripts. And I know of writers who believe that screenwriting isn't actually writing at all, because it isn't created to be seen by an audience of readers.

The average income of writers isn't anything to crow about. According to the year 2000 report of the Writers Guild of America, the median earnings of a writer was just over $87,000 a year—meaning that half the members brought home less than that figure, if they had any work that year. The Writers Guild claims that a quarter of its members earn under $30,000 a year, and not even half earn enough income from their writing alone.[7] Some writers like M. Night Shyamalan and Shane Black make $2 million or more for writing a script, and others $150,000 a week for giving a back rub to someone else's. We hear a lot about them, but they are a small exception. And even the highest-paid writers never share in profits through first-dollar gross. Directors are well aware of this unhappy plight of their fellow artists and are troubled by it.

I am a member of the Writers Guild as well as a director. I have worn both hats. So do writers get the credit they deserve? Probably not, *probably not*. There has always been that attitude toward the "lowly writer," jokes and all. I've often seen actors making fun of the writer on the set, and I wonder where that came from. To me, it's amazing how badly writers are treated. In the New York theater they are like God; here they are like *Kleenex.*

You see, when writers came into filmmaking, directors and producers had already carved out territories and they weren't going to give them up easily. Writers became second-class citizens. They've been treated shabbily by the ignorant producers. Bright people, which writers have traditionally been, have had to subvert their intelligence and their talent to far less bright people, which producers have traditionally been. Everyone around writers *thinks* they can write, and they can't. This means that for writers, there's been a constant struggle for dignity. They are justifiably resentful of their status, and they should get more respect, but it's hard to say how to accomplish that.

Embraceable You—Replaceable You

Directors were hard put to tell me the path to higher status for writers, but they could spell out reasons for writers being at the bottom of the heap.

Writers Are Interchangeable

Studios will treat people as bad as they can. Writers get the brunt of that, mainly because they can be replaced. There is often a gaggle of writers working on a script, and one can substitute for another. The studio can fire a writer at no risk because another all-too-willing writer can spell a writer easily. And that has no effect on marketing a movie because a writer's name in the credits usually has a *zilch* impact on ticket sales.

They Have Low Visibility

The writer is hidden, off to a side doing lonely and solitary work. They are not center-stage stars (nor are the majority of directors anymore; only big stars are big stars). The more hidden you are, the more you are unimportant, because this is a celebrity-driven town in a celebrity-driven society.

Writers Aren't Very Sexy

Writers crave being at press junkets, but nobody in the press wants to interview them. They are *not very interesting*. Look, which pictures would a newspaper want to print: a photo of a director on the set pointing fingers, telling a bunch of people what to do, or a shot of a writer just sitting there at a word processor.

They Can Get in the Way and Drive Up Costs

It's natural for writers to want to be in on the shoot and see their scripts come to life. But they can interfere and hold up the works. Producers often worry about an economic disaster from having them around, so they keep them at arm's length from everybody.

Writers Don't Own the Script

In film, many times the writer is hired and paid to do specific piecework involving the preparation of a script, like writing a treatment or a story line or maybe polishing someone else's work. They are for-hire functionaries of the studios. With Hollywood writers, the script isn't theirs legally and often isn't theirs artistically. Playwrights in New York write and complete the full play *before* they bring it to the producer. They own it, and they control it.

As you see, the directors I interviewed, to a greater or lesser extent, give homage to the input of screenwriters and appreciate their all-too-humiliating standing. Further, they know that the Writers Guild has been pressing for writers to gain a stronger foothold during production. But these directors—to a man and a woman—reject the idea of writers being on the set routinely during the shooting of a movie. They believe that kind of participation should not be obligatory; rather it should be conditional and under the discretion of the director. This view was unanimous and verbalized with from-the-gut intensity.

A DGA executive told me an anecdote that confirms what I found in my interviews. When writers recently ratcheted up the rhetoric on creative rights issues, the DGA held a series of meetings with A-List feature directors. There were nineteen directors at the first meeting, and at one point one of them asked the others, "How many of you belong to the WGA?" The executive counted seventeen hands in the air. The next question was, "How many of you prefer to have the writer on the set?" This time eighteen hands went up. Finally the inquiring director asked, "How many of you think the writer should have the *right* to be on the set?" Now zero hands went up.

I Need to Make the Music My Own Way

A declaration by filmmaker David Lean seems to be virtual scripture in the directors' community. It was contained in his 1967 cable to a DGA action committee embroiled in a high-stakes dispute with the Writers Guild on possessory credits. For a long time writers have been fighting the "a film by" designation at the top of film credits. Directors feel they earn it and that writers should stop trying to undercut them.

Lean's declaration used his *Doctor Zhivago* movie as a reference point for laying out the commanding domain of the director: "I worked one year with the writer. Unlike him, I directed not only the actors but the cameraman, set designer, costume designer, soundmen, editor, composer and even the laboratory in their final print. Unlike him, I chose the actors, the technicians, the subject and him to write it. I staged it. I filmed it. It was my film of his script which I shot when he was not there."[8] Echoes of this far-reaching conception of the director's role sounded throughout my interviews.

Directors told me they need undivided authority to shoot the script as they understand it *cinematically* and to change the story line as the production process unfolds in all its untidy volatility on the set. From the directorial standpoint, filmmakers are to a script as singers are to a song—imaginative interpreters rather than mechanistic transcribers (along with actors). Directors believe that writers often do not grasp the reasons for necessary adaptations. When writers are there in the filming situation, many will stand guard over the sanctity of their specific words and interfere with the process.

The Split Vision

This is a medium that doesn't take well to groupthink at the helm. You know, the director is already orchestrating a thousand people and doesn't need the writer there as a distraction and thorn in the side. A film needs one voice, and two chiefs can muffle that. It's antithetical to the creative process. You can't have actors taking sides on who has the right concept. My position is: "One picture, one director." And that can come down to taste, just taste, which is not negotiable.

The Process

I had a scene that was supposed to be shot in a barbershop, but we couldn't get to it on the scheduled day and had to move to a new location. That site required us to do the scene in a *bedroom*. A writer has to be able to take account of time, logistics, and the will of God in changing the weather, having the sun go down, or making actors sick.

A movie evolves. It can't be stuck in the blueprint that's the screenplay. The directors have to move out of and beyond the writer's concept if they are going to achieve something. The reality of making a movie is that you shape the action based on what actors have done in critical scenes, how the cast has jelled as an ensemble, and how much money you have available to devise scenes, not on what was put down on the page *a year ago*. Other people just can't see the film in their head the way the filmmaker can—shooting a certain way, with certain kinds of coverage, and certain lighting— people just can't see it until they see the finished product. It's very subjective, and intangible, with a kind of *alchemy*.

Oh, Those Words

Writers are focused intently on the words themselves in a way that actually can be either helpful or dysfunctional. I remember working with the writer James Costigan on the TV movie *Eleanor and Franklin* and experiencing how words can have the subtlest of nuances.

An actor speaking to the Eleanor Roosevelt and Louis Howe characters said, "You two *are* really a pair, aren't you?" The writer objected to the order of two words. He wanted the phrase to come out as "You two *really are* a pair." That's more arch, and it's what he wanted to convey. It's a tricky business.

The script is an assemblage of words, and that's the foundation for the film. The screenwriter is an engineer who lays that foundation down. But the director is the architect who designs and constructs the building from it—which is, after all, what people come to see. They don't go to visit the basement. If people are coming to the movie theater to see the script, why not just flash the script up on the screen. That's not what they want; it's the visual representation. If two words are left out, that's OK, if the *intent* and *tone* are there. The actor is supposed to make the words come to life, and there are some words that some actors *can't say*. The point is not the words and sentences, but what they convey and how they get translated into images and actions.

The Interference

The more writers are on the set, the more the actors turn and look at them, and say, "Oh, oh, did I hurt the writer's feelings the way I said the lines?" You find you're getting bad work from the actor, and you wonder *why*, and you see that the writer is making bad faces at the video monitor. This comes out to be a loss of time and money, and a schizophrenic movie. See, you can't have a writer looking over the dailies and telling the director everything he did wrong in misinterpreting the script. I once had a writer who complained to the head of the studio the way the movie was being shot, and another who talked to the actors, telling them how to say the lines. That makes for chaos on the set.

All directors sometimes do something that seems to run against the intent of the script, but it's meant in a roundabout way to draw out from the actor a response that brings out the intent. A writer on the set who's not familiar with the psychology of actors may hit his head or groan and befuddle the actor. As I see it, writers wouldn't like directors looking over their shoulder at the word processor, and directors don't want writers looking over their shoulder on the set.

Scribes and Vibes

Yes, it's a process. Yes, writers can interfere. But in the end all of these comments are only prelude to the crucial question: "Should writers actually be on the set, or will that stay directors' hands in making their music?" The consensus of these directors was, "It depends." Generally, they believe the writer's skills can be a godsend during shooting, but then they pause and speak about the significance of the relationship between the director and the writer—how they communicate, how well they understand each other's expectations. And then they add that the writer's presence shouldn't be de rigueur.

The answer to a writer's involvement, these directors agree, hinges on whether or not the writer is tuned in to the complex intricacies of shooting a film, and, in particular, shooting a film from the director's standpoint. Those directors I spoke with all believe that's the director's call. At the end of the day, it comes down to the director's judgment about whether placing a writer on the scene is going to benefit and speed the creation of the movie or create a nightmare.

There were clues about which writers are more likely to be good collaborators during shooting. Among the bad bets are bright writers who think that directing is easy enough to master and go right ahead getting their hands into it. Or those who see screenwriting as a stepping-stone toward directing and naturally slide on beyond the bounds. Those writers who want to control the specifics of how the story is told can be a disaster and are invited to consider going into directing or into writing novels, where they are free to create their mental world and keep it intact.

All my respondents shared this view: writers have had their turn, sometimes sitting unimpeded in solitude with absolute control over their scripts while writing them—a luxury nobody else in the industry has. Filmmakers want to work with writers who recognize that and are now willing to give directors their turn.

There's also the difficult problem of a mélange of writers working on the script. Which one or subcollectivity should be in on the shoot? Directors think it helps collaboration when there is a single writer, including in rewrite, who has branded the script with a consistent point of view that the writer can communicate coherently. If there isn't a single voice in the script, the *director* has to provide it, not some also-ran writer.

Directors believe that some writers don't crave at all to be on the set. They went into writing because they don't relish talking with people. And they're not as creative and productive there, or making as much money around the camera, as they would be at their word processor punching out a new script. Add in writers who simply despise the hassle of making a movie. To them, it's torture to be out in some outlandish place and up and running at 4:30 in the morning. Let them sleep.

Writer on the Set? How It Sums Up
Given all these dilemmas and qualifications, I'd like to crystallize, in their own words, the main points the directors made about the writer-on-the-set issue. They were in agreement that writers can be useful—they can help the director bring out his or her music. That said, the relationship between the director and writer is a critical factor in whether that occurs. Ergo, there should be no strict requirements about writers occupying space on the set.

The Scribe as Right-hand Man
> I myself love having a writer on the set. When an actor can't do a line, I love being able to turn to the writer and ask whether we can use another line. You see, I prefer not having the responsibility of making new words. Say I'm rehearsing a scene and a beat is missing, or something is not working in the story: it's good to have a writer *right there* to fix it or jump in with me and the actors in fixing it—that's just another part of the collaborative process. I start out wanting to be faithful to the original impulse of the writer because *that's what attracted me to the piece in the first place*, so I like being able to check things out with him or her. As I see it, most directors want the input of writers—the welcome mat is out—when the chances are there'll be a cooperative interplay on the set.

Personal Chemistry Counts

It's obvious to me that everything depends so much on the matchup between the direc-tor and the writer, on the give and take and the personalities of the two people. If writ-ers really want to attach themselves to the director and the film and work at it being a good match, *it can be terrific*. A smart writer will try to cultivate good relations with the director and become savvy about how things work during a shoot. Also, in my experi-ence, a lot of potential hang-ups can be solved *beforehand*, in pre-production, by direc-tors and writers having a good, thorough exchange about what the writer intended and how the director wants to bring it to the screen.

Mandated Rules Not Allowed

No director I know of wants to be ordered to have writers on the set and have a *shotgun marriage*. If our egos clash, I don't want that writer in on filming. If it's a Paul Shrader and Martin Scorsese doing *Taxi Driver*, yes, the writer should be around and in the process. In fact, one time I cast the writer John Sayles in a part so that he would be at my side to consult with me—but I don't want that happening with everyone. The writer's participation really ought to be optional and at the discretion of the director. See, the relationship is very individual, and except when there's been a long-term part-nership, it has to be negotiated *case-by-case, movie-by-movie*. I myself will accept any-one's suggestion, on or off the set, but I have to have the prerogative to have the final say, and to have a writer who goes along with that.

A few directors spoke in a statesman-like voice that worked at playing down the antagonism and viewing writers as close allies in film industry combat.

I think that generally this whole argument over writers is overblown, because there's much more *in common* and more potential for wonderful collaboration between writers and directors than there is between directors and studio executives. Most studio execu-tives have done hardly any thinking about the movie. Beyond buying the movie and at-taching some actors to it to sell it to audiences . . . beyond that, why are they qualified to say what the content should be, who can be the DP [director of photography] and who can't, who can do the editing, who can be the production designer? That is a far more destructive intrusion into the process than the writer. I don't see the writer as the en-emy; I see the writer as my *colleague*, my fellow storyteller, a co-combatant in upholding creative values in the industry.

At the guild level, the view isn't as sanguine. There are organizational interests to up-hold and members to mobilize for a cause.

My Organization Can Lick Your Organization

"Creative rights" is the terminology directors and writers use to address these matters, and they address them collectively through their respective guilds. What we have is a conflict between two professional groups for power and control, with their respec-tive unions giving voice and muscle to the arguments of both sides. The rather fuzzy and esoteric talk about relationships and creative concerns can be codified in legal form through official contracts between the studios and the guilds. Tough negotiations set out salary, residuals, and health benefits with one hand, and can tie down creative and artistic prerogatives with the other.

My interviews often focused on creative arrangements for making a movie, but the back story involved who has control of the cinematic tiller on the set and who has the organizational power outside the set to decide that issue. Don't assume my respondents were unaware of the back story.

> The Writers Guild and the Directors Guild are adversaries, and they have *always been*. There's an unstable and conflictual situation between them—a power struggle. The whole thing about the guilds is to protect their creative turfs. When writers came along, directors weren't going to say, "Oh, why don't you come onto the set, take the better screen credits, decide on casting?"

The two guilds are close in membership, with the Directors Guild having about 12,500 members and the Writers Guild (West and East branches) coming in at about 11,500. Compared to the 135,000 Screen Actors Guild/American Federation of Television and Radio Artists, the two are fairly small and pretty even in numbers.

The Writers Guild has had a history of militancy, with strikes in 1960, 1973, 1981, 1985, and 1988. During the 1930s, many writers had progressive and left-wing leanings, so the guild later bore the brunt of the horrendous blacklist boycott of "subversives" in Hollywood. The decimated Screen Writers Guild, a predecessor organization of writers, was forced to dissolve and merge into a newly formed Writers Guild of America (West and East).

The DGA, in contrast, doesn't want to hear the word "strike" and, if you will permit me an oxymoron, is exceedingly moderate. It has had fairly stable leadership, whereas the writers' organization had a contentious flip-flop at the top in the mid-1980s and late 1990s. Also, the WGA has a division between high-paid "hyphenate" television producer-writers and other writers who stick strictly to putting words on the page. The TV producer types carry significant managerial responsibilities that, in the uproar of labor disputes, pit them against more radical writers who are free of those binds.

Say Uncle

In general, I see the DGA as the stronger of the two because of its stability and the elevated standing of directors in the industry. For example, newspapers often refer to the DGA as an "elite" organization. But it's a close call. It's clear that directors are the ones who run the machinery of actually making movies. During the heyday of the studio system, towering producers like David O. Selznick and executives like Darryl Zanuck ruled production with an iron hand. With the demise of the studios and of these titans, directors, to some degree, slipped in to pick up the slack—especially during the auteur spurt of the 1970s. But writers feed the entire picture-making apparatus of Hollywood at the front end by inserting scripts into machinery. They can bring everything to a halt by holding back their words.

The militancy of the writers is a potential strength for their union, but it frequently backfires—as, for example, in the 1988 strike where the guild held out too long for too much. They had to accept a humiliating compromise settlement after a twenty-two-week work stoppage that shut down Hollywood and antagonized everyone.

The directors I interviewed generally saw directors as the stronger force.

> For me, the reality is that directors can close down the industry and it's harder for writers to do that. So when push comes to shove, *directors* have more clout. Also, directors have power not just because they have taken it. They hold the combination to the safe because they alone have the key to synchronizing an amazing number of different talents to create a compelling vision on the screen. But in coverage of writer-director disputes, the media favors writers. Reporters are writers, and so they slant their coverage toward the writers' point of view. That makes the Directors Guild seem weaker, and some directors are apprehensive about that.

The complex and shifting landscape of union alliances in filmmaking makes me proceed with caution in assessing power authoritatively. You've got a plethora of different skills in filmmaking, both in the art and the craft of the process, and there's a tangle of different unions representing each of these groups. There can be people from more then twenty guilds and unions on the set for any movie—and jurisdictional disputes among all of them abound. During the 2001 writer negotiations with the studios—who bargain in unity through the Alliance of Motion Picture and Television Producers (AMPTP)—writers allied themselves with the actors' union around upping the artists' share of residuals, and actors were signaling that they would throw their weight in support of a writers' strike.

The DGA joined with the blue-collar International Alliance of Theatrical Stage Employees, with its tens of thousands of workers, to push for early negotiations aimed at reducing the likelihood of a strike action. Those groups were more interested in protecting themselves against the loss of income from a work stoppage than in promoting trade union solidarity. These alliances rise and then re-form unpredictably at different times, making it hard to determine who holds the upper hand.

Down to Cases

In connection with their 2001 negotiations with the AMPTP, writers made a strong pitch for more visibility in the whole filmmaking process (beyond their economic demands on salary, residuals, and health benefits). They brought out a whole gamut of creative rights: to be present on the set; to watch the dailies; to have their names on the cast and crew lists; to participate in casting, cast readings, and rehearsals; and to attend test screenings, premiers, junkets, festivals, and trade shows. They also continued their uphill battle to eliminate the "a film by" possessory credit (what they call a "vanity" credit), which is a third-rail inflammatory issue for directors.

This stance continued the recent spats of these groups, like the 1970s tiff about control over script changes and the 1980s gambit of the writers to have a say on the hiring of directors. As I see it, the opening gun in the most recent encounter began in 1999 with a fiery candidacy statement by TV writer-producer John Wells (who earns more than $35 million a year) when he ran for, and later won, the WGA presidency. He wrote that the creative rights limitations on writers were "intolerable," " a disgrace," "unpardonable," and "unconscionable." Wells skyrocketed the level of rhetoric on matters that writers had been grousing about for a very long time. He added, vaguely, that these creative issues should "be fully addressed" in upcoming negotiations with the AMPTP on the MBA (Minimum Basic Agreement—which is the mutually accepted WGA-studios contract). And he added ominously that if these aims cannot be achieved in negotiations, they would be achieved "on the picket line."

The Directors Guild was provoked and responded by drafting a set of "preferred practices" on creative issues in place of the WGA's "pattern of demands"—practices that would be agreed upon voluntarily through the two guilds, rather than officially through the AMPTP. In this formula, writers would be able to participate on the set, but with the approval of the director. *DGA Magazine* laid out the rejoinder of the directors by stating bluntly that what writers want are "new contractual rights . . . mandating that a writer . . . be allowed on the set." They said that this would "strip directors of decision-making power," and also jack up production costs and cause chaos. They declared the mandatory feature a scheme by writers to "reinvent the movie business" by putting production control in their own hands.[9]

In a return-fire article in the WGA magazine, *Written By*, WGA officers Phil Alden Robinson and Tom Schulman insisted that they were offering voluntary proposals that "encourage, but not mandate" participation by screenwriters. Concretely, the language specified that the writer participates, "absent an objection" by the director or the company. The authors insisted that these proposals are "moderate" and "reasonable" and don't saddle directors with anything of which they don't approve.[10]

So what's going on here? The WGA is adamant that its provisions are essentially voluntary, and the DGA counters that they are bluntly mandatory. Every director I spoke with, without exception, believed the WGA was out to set mandatory rules, which the directors resented bitterly. For them, this is a first-order issue and one that at least some are willing to go out on strike over. They see the writers' campaign, in part, as a power grab, led by guild TV producer-writers, who are dominating "show runners" on episodic TV series with total control there—like David E. Kelley (*Ally McBeal*) and Dick Wolf (*Law and Order*). Many directors believe that show runners have tasted power and want to establish the same kind of model for writers in the feature-film business, using creative rights as a way in. With two-thirds of the WGA members as TV writers, these people have real influence in the writers' group.

Hollywood mavens I spoke to thought the writers started out by asking for mandatory requirements but retreated to accepting voluntary guidelines or "preferred practices." Some cynics were of the view that the WGA tried to put one over on their members by claiming they had negotiated something they hadn't. As best I can tell, the WGA current language does have a voluntary caste. But directors I spoke with see that as a guise, a sly foot in the door. Once the language of participation on the set and elsewhere is officially in writing in the contract, it can be built on, expanded, and argued through the AMPTP and in the courts.

So when the WGA says "voluntary," the DGA *hears* "mandatory." Using the WGA formula, writers have automatic right of entrance to the set, except when there are specific objections from the director or studio (and it's clear which of the two and under what circumstances). Directors want right of entrance to the set to be pre-negotiated between director and writer on a picture-by-picture basis.

From the directors' point of view, the prevailing open interplay between professional organizations would become defunct in favor of more legalistic mechanisms with outside organizations calling some of the shots. For directors, this is a serious backslide, because in the going relationship between the guilds, they have the upper hand and are in much better control of their standing and status.

One of the directors I interviewed thought there is an irrational element in this whole entanglement, carrying psychological rather than political baggage. He believes that because of a history of past grievances, writers are angrily overstepping the bounds of the possible in their try for unattainable rules.

> I think there's a core of people at the Writers Guild who really don't want to come to some conclusion with this. They're really mad about something that happened to them in the past and they want revenge. I can't do anything about how they've been treated by some other directors in the past. They were treated much, much more badly by the studios. We can't rectify that background for all these writers; we can just try to make a better environment for the future. But their approach—they're going to *legislate this* . . . it's never going to happen.

Sizing It Up, Peering Ahead

The upshot of the recent negotiations was that writers made respectable gains on economic issues but got nowhere on the creative front. AMPTP just didn't want to take on this hot potato and play the heavy with the writers. They shifted the problem right back to the two guilds to battle through between themselves.

The guilds agreed to set up joint creative rights committees to work out solutions and committed themselves to publishing an annual article on successful collaborations (one in film and one in TV) in their respective house organs. Also, symposia on creative partnerships were instituted. But the meetings have gone on haltingly with the sound of grinding machinery and the smell of pro-forma in the air. Ominously, the ground rules specify that either party (think DGA—they insisted on the clause) has the right to exit the joint meetings.

This drawn-out match between directors and writers is labeled "inter-professional competition" by sociologists who study these matters. For a long time, sociologists analyzed professions by focusing on their social structures and viewing professions, more or less, as benign public interest groups serving a particular need of society (like physicians healing the sick). Andrew Abbott, a professor at the University of Chicago, turned that notion around abruptly and virtually single-handedly in the 1980s. In his ground-breaking book *The System of Professions*, Abbott argued that professions are about claiming a monopoly in their area of activity in the workplace.[11] They aim to control the important conditions of work, including the labor process and the labor market, and in that way increase their occupational power and status.

In the language of the theory, professions regularly strive for jurisdictional dominance through claims of singular expertise and knowledge, and consequently the study of professions is actually the study of jurisdictional disputes (what the rest of us typically call "turf battles"). The director-writer fracas is an obvious case in point falling under Abbott's theory.

Conflict theory gives us some handles for understanding this dispute at a deeper level.[12] Disputes in formal organizations (like the studios) come to the forefront when three conditions exist.

- First, there's a breakout of functions, such as sales, manufacturing, and accounting in industry. In film, in the early days, directors were like three-handed painters carrying out almost all the functions; then the talkies arrived and screenwriters were imported to take on the function of writing the scripts.
- Second, tasks of different working groups rub up against each other and lead to role conflict. That leads people in the different functions (or divisions) to declare authority over the same work. Both writers and directors think they're responsible for the telling of the story,
- Third, a scarcity of resources inflames the conflict. There is a limited pot of money for making a movie. Paying writers to be on the set and expanding the time for production (so writers and directors can work through their differences) devours money that can be directed elsewhere, like for set design, special effects, and marketing. The studios balk at that, and so do directors.

Conflict theorists tell us that disputes can be substantive in origin—related to ends (what kind of picture to make) or means (who should do what in making the picture). Disputes can also have an emotional component—anger, resentment, or fear. It's obvious that writers are gushing pent-up anger and resentment, and directors are in abject fear of losing a portion of what they believe is rightly theirs.

In a classic book called *The Functions of Social Conflict*, sociologist Lewis Coser turns up some surprises about how conflict operates (including in the director-writer imbroglio).[13] Conflict may have purposes that are totally out of the awareness of adversaries. An example is the group-bonding elements of conflict. John Wells may well have thought that his high-octane declaration before negotiations would be the opening volley of a march toward real gains for the WGA. But I think that backfired. His statements put the DGA on guard and just caused them to dig in—and drag out their big cannons. Mainly, Wells's pronouncements brought WGA members closer together in their discontent, but it didn't change their concrete situation for the better.

Another point Coser makes is that when relationships among people are relatively close, conflict is relatively intense. It may be that because directors and writers, cinematic co-professionals in the same work environment in the same town, have formal and informal contacts in pre-production, on the set, and in the filmmaking community generally, there is a level of familiarity between them that heightens disappointment and antagonism when disagreements come to the surface. There's an analogy here to the heated emotional flare-ups that we see in close families.

Conflict theory lays out a set of different options for dealing with conflict. Competition, or fighting it out, is the main MO we've seen operating here. There's also "authoritative command," which turns the dispute over to some legally constituted entity to decide. The writers tried that unsuccessfully with the AMPTP. The parties also can enter into bargaining or negotiation—which they did. Add avoidance—the option of looking the other way—which I think the directors, with the status and power advantage they have and don't want to lose, would really prefer. Finally, there's the rare and super-idealistic problem-solving approach, where the parties rely strictly on objective factfinding and impartial analysis to resolve the issue. That's a more likely script for a Mr. Deeds movie than for this wrangle.

My bet is that this process will move from bargaining, where it is now, to avoidance (or withdrawal) by the directors, and back into competition through WGA pressure. Then, whenever new cycles of contract negotiations come up, the writers will try to latch on to the authority of the AMPTP again to advance their cause.

I want to interject here that directors are not lockstep in castigating writers alone for generating this dispute. Some directors are more conciliatory, acknowledging that directors share blame for the acrimonious climate of the conflict.

> I believe it's a bit of a tempest in a teapot and this latest rhubarb is being pushed by certain people in the Writers Guild whose careers it helps. But, look, on the directors' side also this whole issue is being inflamed way, way beyond where it should be. I can't see any objection to writers wanting some more say in what's going on. A bunch of us directors know that this keeping them on a leash is nonsense. I'm a director, but I'm not going to defend the pretentious auteurs who come on the set with their hands on their brow saying, "It's my vision, get out of my way." That's just *crap*. It's a collaborative medium, and we all know that.

Hearing this director made me cheer internally, "Hooray for voices of moderation." But the issue is tangled and tortured and, alas, won't be solved alone by virtuous straight thinking and good will.

If the Hairdressers Can Do It

The reality in contemporary filmmaking for me is that a balance of power, a kind of détente, has evolved whereby producer-writers take charge of episodic television and directors control feature films. Is this the best arrangement artistically and commercially? That's hard to say. Arguably, it would advance the quality of film if writers were co-equal with directors on the movie set. I've heard it said that the writer is the only truly original artist on the filmmaking team, all others, including directors and actors, being derivative and interpretive. Be that as it may, the truth is that someone has to be in creative charge; ultimately and historically, directors have had that role. I think the growing number of upcoming talented writer-directors like M. Night Shyamalan, Wes Anderson, Paul Thomas Anderson, James Mangold, and respondent Nancy Meyers serve as a hopeful bridging development.[14]

Writers like to bring up Louis Malle's comment that if there can be someone on the set for the hair, why not screenwriters for the words. Actually, I sense that many directors would love to have writers on the set if they behaved more like hairdressers. That means respectfully following the wishes of directors, working within a bounded scope—and not constantly broadcasting that they gave birth to the spine of the film and jousting to keep it as originally conceived at all costs.

But that kind of supine role for writers is not in the cards. The writer-director relationship involves inherent friction and creative tension, and from my vantage point, that's inherently a big plus for filmmaking. But there have to be ways of fomenting the interplay, on the one hand, and on the other, containing the friction and resolving the differences. We can wonder whether the going arrangement in film, which puts the control lever squarely in the director's hands, is fair to writers, and that's a disquieting question.

But this is the way the system has evolved, and it is not going to change soon. Directors are passionate about not wanting writers on the set *automatically*, and writers' low status in the Hollywood culture will make it possible for directors to keep them off if they want, at least in the short term.

Nonetheless, these things shift historically. In the 1930s and 1940s, film was an actors' and producers' medium, and the director's name was often smaller in the credits than actors, producers, and even writers. These definitions of relative position change over time. That hasn't been the case for writers so far; they've been stuck near the bottom. But we've seen flunky computer nerds rise up to become instant billionaire CEOs during the dot-com craze, so the salad days of screenwriters may yet come.

CHAPTER EIGHT

~

A New Take

The media ought to get over their infatuation with box-office returns every single week. The obsession with box-office stats should go away. There should be less talk about the quantity of tickets that were sold and more talk about the quality of the movies that are made.

—George Hickenlooper

We should do away with talking pictures and rely entirely on music to get across the feelings that speech conveys. Well, that's what pioneer filmmaker D. W. Griffith proposed in 1924. Writing in *Collier's* magazine, in an article titled "The Movies 100 Years From Now," he went on to press his point: "We do not want now and we shall never want the human voice with our films. . . . no voice can speak so beautifully as music."[1] To Griffith, storytelling was an act of imagination, and he felt that music delivered the depth and nuance of imagination much more eloquently than human speech ever could. Ergo, to his way of thinking, first-class movie houses should have on board orchestras, string quartets, guitar players, and "thumpety banjos." History, of course, was paying heed. And history wanted voices.

Though off-base on this one, Griffith was a soothsayer par excellence (not to say a budding business consultant) in advocating movie screenings on airline flights and foreseeing what many years later we now call home entertainment centers. As he looked ahead almost a full century, his batting average wasn't bad. He foresaw and endorsed color photography and home movies to supplement photo albums. On the other hand, and ironically, although he invented the close-up technique, he thought it was disconcerting and a mere "mechanical trick" that mostly should be discarded.

From the start, other industry people proposed far-reaching changes in the techniques and organization of filmmaking—changes they believed would elevate the level of the business and the art: censor unacceptable film content, let directors be auteurs with sweeping authority, go all out for Cinerama or 3D. These are risky and unpredictable kinds of choices because side effects, unintended consequences, and quirky reversals scramble the course of events and play tricks on careful plans to change it.

Among other unforeseen outcomes, studio moguls never imagined that anyone (including the Supreme Court) would overturn their lucrative little vertical scheme of production-distribution-exhibition. And who would have thought that the availability of videocassettes rather than dismantling the studios would create a gigantic cash cow at millions of neighborhood stores? In most instances, it was scientists and technicians, not the strategic-planning mavens, who took the industry out of its doldrums at crucial moments by coming up with sound, color, and widescreen technologies.

Despite the perils of being upended by potholes along the way, there are strivers who have an unalterable drive to make things better. The status quo can be cozy but flawed; still, those who seek change take upon themselves the risk of folly. And I will admit that I, too, have not been able to escape that foible. My last interview question to directors probed for their ideas and recommendations for upgrading the quality of American film. My thought was that perhaps a wide cross section of sophisticated filmmakers like this would give birth to interesting and noteworthy proposals for cinematic improvement. It was worth a try. And you will be able to judge the results.

Incidentally, I did not define "quality," and nobody asked for a definition. Directors had a tacit understanding of which films leaned toward quality and which leaned the other way. If they did ask, my inclination would have been to define quality films as intelligent films, with the likelihood that artistic expression will thrive, to a greater or lesser degree, through an intelligent and sophisticated approach to filmmaking— whether drama, mystery, or slapstick comedy.

Mixed Reviews—Boosters, Qualifiers, and Critics

The directors I interviewed came up with a mélange of noteworthy ideas for improvements, large and small, well-trod and novel. These ideas should provoke dialogue among people who care about film. Before detailing them, I ought to tell you that not everyone in the group shared the assumption behind the question I put to them about raising the quality of American filmmaking. You see, at the front end of my interviews I typically asked about problems facing directors, and the volume of troubles that gushed forth—together with the strong feelings behind them—led me to believe that filmmakers had real qualms about the quality of the products their labors begat. Actually, many did, but others wanted me to know right away that they believed the quality of American film was high.

That view came from two different groups: the Boosters (American films are straight-out the best), and the Qualifiers (taking into account the context of the Hollywood system, we have a laudable record of excellence.) About a half-dozen directors were in each of these groups, while the rest, by and large, simply accepted at face value the need for improvement.

Here's what the Boosters had to say:

I believe that the best of our filmmaking is top drawer. We are capable of doing wonders: *Norma Rae* fifteen years ago and *Traffic* yesterday. We have a wide range of types and attitudes in film nowadays and in different venues—movie houses, cable, video—and that's the way it should be. Over the long haul Hollywood has delivered *mightily well*. I don't put down foreign filmmakers, but Hollywood compares with and even surpasses the best of what's done anywhere in the world. We ought to let this continue and flourish.

As I see it, the American film industry is set up to develop a certain product, and it's successful in developing that product. In that sense, we have the highest quality of *any* product on Earth. It infuses culture and politics *everywhere*—the vast majority of people in every country watch American films. From the standpoint of what the American film system defines as its goals, it succeeds at that phenomenally. What other industry can we say has a 75 to 80 percent market share in many countries—and might have more if there weren't government regulations elsewhere trying to whittle down our share.

The caliber of writing and directing is the best it has ever been, and new technology is moving things toward higher achievement.

All That Glitters Is Gold

The Qualifiers had reservations, but they also saw bright spots. Despite the limitations of the Hollywood system, with its bottom-line mentality that shoves everything toward a maudlin middle, they believe pictures of distinction do get to the movie screens.

Sure, studios repeat things that have happened before pretty slavishly. But there's a natural homeostasis in the complexity of the industry, allowing a huge wave of a film to crash on the shore at any time. Strangely enough, as I see it, the quality of American films is getting better, even though the budgets are going up and the pressures toward mass appeal are increasing correspondingly.

Look, as long as every year a movie like *The Full Monty* comes out, a Fox Searchlight Picture that was a blockbuster hit, as long as every year you can have a film like *Cider House Rules* that is profitable and wins an Oscar, and *Moulin Rouge*, an inexpensive art movie and not a standard, conventional piece of filmmaking . . . as long as those movies can survive and make money, there'll be more like them. I believe that there really is some *good stuff* out there, but let's face it; things are all over the ballpark.

One director succinctly summed up the core attitude underlying the qualifier position.

I guess I take a philosophical view of this that lets me live with the situation. There are certain parameters of life you have to accept, and in this industry there are certain realities that are set in stone. You're not going to change them. Within that setup, it's possible for wonderful work to happen.

Some of the directors who agreed with the question's premise, the majority view, that there are fundamental quality deficits to address—let's call these folks the Critics

—paused to describe that problem in their own terms before going on with their proposed solutions.

> Our system truly doesn't encourage the making of high-level cinema. I find that the best films made outside of the United States are better than the best films made here. Maybe those exceptional foreign films will influence cinema here, maybe not. Maybe they will just be there for our aficionados to discover and make us nostalgic for what we wish we could do. We will never reach that level. *We're just not allowed to.*
>
> In any given year, 95 percent of our films are *garbage.* That remains a pretty constant proportion. When you consider the number of films that are produced, and that's less than before, maybe 400 or 450—India does 600, you know—the number of good-quality films in a year you can almost count on your fingers, *maybe twenty at most.* And every year people moan that this is the worst year. Actually it's the same as the last year and the one before that. There are a few exceptional years, like 1939, but by and large things remain pretty bleak.

How does this add up? Apparently, looking at the same phenomenon, the American movie product as a whole, there was a difference in what was catching the eye of the observers and registering on their consciousness: the trickle of outstanding films—or the sea of schlock and mediocrity.

Maybe this is another example of the remarkable capacity of directors to absorb complexity and juggle contradictions, artfully balancing dissimilar buckets on their shoulders. Or are the Qualifiers actually *Deniers,* who blot out the unacceptable as a way to justify a professional existence that otherwise they would find painful to sustain? Let's leave this conundrum hanging for another time and go on to look at the proposals that all the directors—the handful of Boosters, the handful of Qualifiers, and the cross section of Critics—brought forth for making movies more worth the trip to the mall.

Menu for a New Meal

The directors' ideas for improvement constitute a menu of possibilities resembling a smorgasbord more than a set table d'hôte. There won't be a recipe—or should I say a blueprint—at the end, like a Roosevelt New Deal strategy. I think it would be useful to let you have a snapshot of the mixed set of proposals at the outset. I have grouped them by the frequency with which directors mentioned the proposals.

Higher Frequency
- Reduce the prominence of money in moviemaking.
- Educate the audience toward higher cinematic sophistication.

Intermediate Frequency
- Encourage directors to push the limits of creativity.
- Make procedural changes in the filmmaking process.
- Produce more and smaller films for specialized audiences.
- Provide subsidies and grants to promote quality film.

Lower Frequency
- Enhance film school practices that foster film quality.

Take note that both of the higher-frequency proposals deal with systemic issues, which are macro-scaled and have broad policy ramifications. I'll have more to say about that as we continue.

Money, Money, Money

The first proposal under Higher Frequency that I'll report, a systemic one, was a re-action to the pervasive place of finance and profit-making in the industry—an issue directors highlighted when they identified problems in chapter 1. Directors proposed this: *there should be an effort to reduce the role of money in filmmaking.* They saw all kinds of downward pressures on film integrity caused by the enormous expense of making a movie: the need to recover large investments by reducing risk, to have a mass audi-ence for each movie, to test market the movie to death, to spend exorbitant sums on marketing, to attract high-appeal/outlandish-cost stars, and on and on.

The respondents, as a whole, were saying that *as pictures get bigger and costlier, they get smaller and emptier.* A symptom of this trend in studio productions is that Academy Awards are going to independent studios like Miramax and Focus Films and bypassing the puffed-up majors. Someone has described film as the sleeping giant of the arts—a medium of gigantic artistic power whose potential is curtailed through the cheapening effect of overwhelming commercial pursuit. Directors were on board with that.

> Cinema has the potential of being the richest art form. It combines sight and sound to present fine art in three dimensions. But it's evolved so little because it depends on huge amounts of money to capitalize it. *It's all economics.* American film is so money driven, profit driven. If getting a movie made weren't dependent on mass marketing of mindless, thrill-seeking adventures aimed at young male adolescents, things would look up. Studios think that a film geared to teenage girls can't work, but didn't they come out to see *Crouching Tiger?* The studios should do more of that. If less up-front money were required, investors would take more chances on offbeat themes and go less for copies and sequels.
>
>   We should try to lower the stakes in producing film by encouraging lower-cost films, maybe through digital technology, streamlined distributing, and other cost-cutting means. The going belief is that a top star is needed to open a weekend; otherwise the movie is dead. A film that should cost 10 million will cost 30 million, with 20 million going to the actor and entourage. There has got to be a drastic reduction of money paid to stars and their agents.

At a university lecture I attended, I heard some other approaches to reducing the detrimental consequences of big money on film production from Arthur De Vany, au-thor of *Hollywood Economics: How Extreme Uncertainty Shapes the Film Industry*, an important new book on the workings of high finance on filmdom.[2] When I asked Pro-fessor De Vany how he thought the quality of American film could rise, given the prominence and volatility of the economic forces he uncovered in his studies of Hol-lywood, he came back with two ideas.

Theater owners, who are in direct contact with audiences, should have more of a say about the movie business. The Paramount Decision of 1948, breaking the monopoly of the studios by amputating their theater chains, pretty much put exhibitors out of the loop. Right now, they can decide on which movies that studios have produced should be shown in the venues they control, and how long the runs should be extended. But they do not have a direct voice on what movies should be made. Of course, theater owners would add still another commercial point of view in green-lighting decisions, but it would be informed through close and continuing contact with the moviegoing public.

De Vany also believes the green-lighting process ought to be changed. As it is, a circle of decision-making elites with blinders on takes action on one movie at a time, sitting in isolation within the studio inner sanctum. What is needed, he believes, is a portfolio concept, where executives program a rounded set of films of various types and at various levels of artistic and commercial appeal. The portfolio notion was used in the old studio days, with good results, and De Vany advocates that it be reinstated. This approach suggests the targeted inclusion of at least some high-quality movies in the studios' menu of movie fare. One of the directors I interviewed alluded to this:

> The studios in the old days were making films for everybody. They made the mature films, the immature B films, the kid films—they made *film*. And they knew they always had an outlet for every film and knew what every film should cost.

Some directors thought there ought to be a turnover in the people who manage studios. (We heard this before in chapter 6.) To them, this group, homogeneous in background, has common training (business and law) centering on the bottom line; therefore, it's fundamentally out of touch with what it means to create first-class cinema.

> There really should be an effort to democratize the film industry, so there are divergent points of view in decision making—you know, women, minorities, young people. From an artistic point of view, it would be wonderful if some newer filmmakers were given a voice to help shape decisions, even if the voice wasn't a commercial one, wasn't necessarily the voice of popular America.
>
> I've had two different heads of studios say to me that a movie doesn't have to be good, it just has to be *good enough*. The guys up there just don't seem to care. That's the prevailing attitude. It used to be the attitude for only a certain category of movie, the B pictures; now it's for practically every movie.
>
> You can't have the kinds of conversations with executives the same as you used to. You could walk in and see a poster on the wall and say, "God, *I loved that movie*," and you were into it together. You can't really mention movies to most of the development and studio executives now, the younger ones; you can't mention the old standby movies to them. They *haven't seen them*.
>
> I would make a case for corporate balancing through giving people with show-business experience more of a place in running things. And it would be a good thing, too, to disaffiliate from conglomerate corporations that see moviemaking exclusively as profit making.

The idea of changing the composition of management is appealing. It has a "throw the rascals out" ring to it. Mark Litwak makes the same point in his book *Reel Power*. He holds that the industry "must recruit executives who understand and love movies and encourage them to take risks. . . . Otherwise Hollywood will become a monument to past glory—and present folly."[3] But the appeal of this notion is checkmated by the overriding weight of system forces. It's the system that put the present cast of administrative characters in place, and it is the system that will not long tolerate new "rascals" marching to a discordant tune. The turnover approach involves passing the buck through the revolving door to a series of hapless initiates, who are likely to fall by the wayside.

I remember vividly the late poet Joseph Brodsky saying at a gathering at my Ann Arbor home shortly after his arrival in the United States that it was inevitable for the Soviet Union to expel him. He observed that ruling commissars perceived his relentless pursuit of freedom of expression as a cancer to that system that had to be purged for the system to survive. Brodsky seemed to accept this with resignation; it was only natural and predictable.

A classic example of this expunging in filmland is the case of David Puttnam. After he produced such Oscar-acknowledged smashes as *Chariots of Fire* and *The Killing Fields*, Columbia Pictures hired him in 1986 to head that studio, with a mission precisely to deliver quality films at reasonable cost. His effort to accomplish that was thwarted at every turn by, yes, the system (and also his direct, no-nonsense approach), and after thirteen months he resigned in frustration and defeat.[4] My point in recounting this horror story is not (God save me) to throw cold water on putting inventive executives in place, but to bring out the limitations of shifting individuals about to make significant change without also reconstructing some features of the overarching system.

Is There a Reader in the House? The Audience for Film

The first proposal by directors—putting restraints on money mania—deals with the *producers* of film, and the next one they put forward focuses on the *audience*. Without people to produce movies and without audiences to watch them, there can't be film. Those groupings are essential partners in a perpetual cycle of input and feedback. Many in my interview group thought that the tastes and preferences of moviegoers are a block to substance in cinema. A frequent proposal of theirs to raise film quality: *educate the general public to increase the level of understanding of filmgoers.*

When movie executives are pressed as to why they don't improve cinematic fare, they invariably respond that they are giving the audience what it wants and will pay to see. According to their reasoning, they have no choice but to tailor picture content to the entertain-me interests of moviegoers who most often frequent theaters.

Attendance figures seem to support their contentions. A study of 2002 moviegoers by MPA Worldwide Market Research reveals that the twelve to twenty-nine age group makes up 50 percent of moviegoers and includes a high percentage of *frequent* moviegoers and people who see movies during opening weekend.[5] This group impacts the initial box-office sales and, therefore, the longer-term prospects for a film.

Clearly, if these audiences register a preference for the shallow and diverting, Hollywood isn't likely to become a citadel of high art. Social critic Dwight Macdonald observed that there's a *Gresham's Law* in culture as well as in economics: the bad drives out the good because it is easier to understand and enjoy.[6] When serious ideas have to compete with commercial formulas, the advantage is all on one side. (We can probably say the same thing about politics, can't we?)

Mad Cows?

Interviewees spoke eloquently about blocks to serious cinema emanating from the viewing public.

> If you look at the general quality of recent film, it's been about as bad as I can recall. I like doing comedy, and what do you have a lot of there? You've got a glut of pushing-the-envelope comedies, pictures where people can ejaculate into hair, they can belch, they can fart, any kind of disgusting bodily functions—*things that would never have been acceptable before* and for good reason. When Mel Brooks had those cowboys farting around a campfire, he had *no idea* what he was creating!
>
> Look, we have a film with Jim Carey shooting a cow over and over again because he somehow can't kill it. The humor level is pitched very low, the lowest we ever had, because they're catering to a crew of teenagers and to a market that is debased. And that's not going to change soon; we're not going to go back and have lots of Noël Coward movies suddenly. This is the way things are.
>
> I think the world of film is just a reflection of our society, of how we have educated our people. As an example, when there are educational cuts, the first things to get squeezed out are the art and music appreciation courses because they are considered nonessential. Because we're a young culture, maybe our society hasn't gotten its educational priorities and values in order yet. To me, if the public doesn't want and doesn't appreciate good film, I don't know how we get to higher ground. It all ties in with what and how much students read, how much television they watch, and the dumbing-down of the country that we've seen.
>
> You know, to say that movies have gotten worse is another way of saying that the popular culture is reflecting simply a *breakdown in taste*. And this is true in television. The things that are shown on television wouldn't have been attempted in feature films when we were kids. I'm not advocating censorship and saying these films shouldn't be shown, but look, my parents were just high school graduates; nevertheless they knew good literature and enjoyed it. *I can't say the same about people now.* The studios pathetically seek to mirror American popular culture and to cater to a huge world market of semi-illiterates. If the public demanded better, the studios would deliver that.

Now, to borrow from Lenin's timeless query, *What Is to Be Done?* Directors agreed that educational approaches are key. But they gave few details on how to bring this about. And they identified stumbling blocks.

> So how do you deal with this? A godlike thunderbolt could hit the town like in Sodom and Gomorrah. Ruling that out, I would say that to improve the depth of film, we have to improve the depth of our education. If the American people become *smarter*, movies

will be *better*. We are embarrassingly undereducated as a people; we're missing a world-view. We don't know there is a world to know and relate to outside our experience in the United States, that Africa is three times the size of America.

I think something that would help would be teaching the arts, including film appreciation, in a substantial way in elementary school. Kids would see how much they can get from quality films and, as they grow up, would relate to films that have more to them and demand to see that kind of fare. Kids nowadays not only don't learn how to appreciate good movies; by and large, they just don't even get *to see them*.

And as to the stumbling blocks:

We can hope that this kind of education will happen, but for the time being, the traditional cultural sensitivity subjects in music and art are being cut way back in elementary schools. And I myself found that it's really hard to reach young people with good movies that have relevance. I showed *Grapes of Wrath* to high school kids, and they laughed at the wrong places. They couldn't relate to black and white. They couldn't relate to the past, to things outside of their own here-and-now existence. They want to have a rapid-fire pace with lots of pyrotechnics. It will be tough to get to them.

There is a bright spot here. Motion Picture Association of America statistics show that attendance by all age categories dropped or fluctuated between 1990 and 2000, except for the over-fifty group. The fifty to fifty-nine category doubled from 5 to 10 percent.[7] Moreover, the baby-boomer horde going into retirement soon, with increased leisure time to use, might be a large market of more mature people for more mature cinema. Support for that view comes from *Something's Gotta Give*, a sophisticated romantic comedy by Nancy Meyers that was released at the end of 2003 and portrays a love affair between Diane Keaton and Jack Nicholson as an over-the-age-of-fifty couple. The movie took in top box-office on the opening weekend, with its estimated $7.1 million gross intake nosing out Tom Cruise in *The Last Samurai*. The movie attracted an audience that was mainly thirty and above.

You Have to Love Me 'Cause I'm All You're Gonna Get

A fault in this line of thought is that it blames the victim and takes movie executives off the hook. Moviegoers are educated not solely by the schools but also by the movie theaters they go to. And that education, in my view, is largely failing. Basically it's miseducation, and the onus then gets put on audiences for the miseducation given to them. They are fed a diet of junk food, both at the refreshment stand and on the screen, so that most become unable to tell the difference, cinematically speaking, between a meal of Coke and popcorn and one of coq au vin. If studios do have a sense of responsibility to sensitize the audience's taste and discernment in some way, it's pretty hidden. Several directors talked to these points. I'll report what they said and then expand on the discussion.

People go to see movies that they see because they're *told to*—there's so much money spent in promoting those films. It's like people become robots, shuffling in automatically to see big, splashy blockbusters. You're programmed to see them, and the executives are happy with thinking that works. So audiences nowadays are preconditioned. They want action and speed. The audiences have seen big movies with big stars, where studios spend a lot to make a lot. And they've also seen lots of MTV.

Executives and producers should trust the audience more. I think the public eventually tires of dreck movies all the time and seeks out more substantial fare and is rewarded. Time after time the formulas and the handed-down truisms have been proven wrong. *Traffic* is an example of a strong but outside-of-the-mold movie that's gotten an enthusiastic reception. *The Thin Red Line* is another offbeat movie I liked that managed somehow to get produced. Executives ought to be more open-minded and flexible about what people will see. You go to a pitch meeting and it's like an exercise in pushing the same buttons. You're told, "Nobody would go to see a movie about grief, or sacrifice." *But they do.*

Jonathan Rosenbaum, film critic of the *Chicago Review*, in his book *Movie Wars* expands on this.[8] Rosenbaum doesn't buy the cry of executives that they are simply meeting the demands of audiences, and he demolishes their argument rhetorically. His subtitle spells out his rejoinder: *How Hollywood and the Media Conspire to Limit What Films We Can See.* To him, the audience is a mixed quantity and overlapping, not one thing. It can't be defined as demanding just one thing. Executives presume audience demands and hand them those presumptions. Rosenbaum illustrates by challenging the going dogma that the American public hates foreign movies with subtitles. He notes that most Americans have never seen a subtitled foreign-language movie, so it can't be known that they don't like them. Secondly, audiences have flocked to American movies using extensive subtitles, like *Schindler's List* and *Dances With Wolves.* Hard realities sometimes aren't able to checkmate doctrinaire studio beliefs. Since Rosenbaum's book, mainline films have continued using subtitles: for the Farsi spoken in *House of Sand and Fog*, for Chiricahua Apache in *The Missing*, and for Elvish, the chatter among the elf creatures in the *Lord of the Rings* trilogy. And what about Mel Gibson's *The Passion of the Christ*, with its Aramaic lingua franca?

But even assuming the public is hesitant, if executives had more of a long-term investment outlook, and were willing to give audiences some slack, the risk factor would shrink. As it stands, studio elites, with power to decide in advance what films to supply moviegoers, justify their decisions by essentially saying, "See, the public bought the one product that we gave them." There's an analogy to drugs: once people are habituated to a product, the product creates its own demand.

Rosenbaum lambastes the marketing research methods used to gauge the public's preferences for film. He believes the methods are nothing more than imprecise quasi-science as they are applied in the business field, often doctored and trumped up to yield desired results. In chapter 1, "Troubles in Mind," directors I interviewed reported the same thing.

Rosenbaum owns up to pushing the envelope in his thesis: audiences, in reality, have limitations, but the people who run the show in Hollywood have contributed mightily to the coarsening of the spectators. Raymond Chandler once wrote about gazing at a gathering of overdressed, overblown Tinseltown elites and thinking, "In these hands lie the destinies of the only original art the modern world has conceived."[9] In addition to noticing their hands, it would be good to hold their feet to the fire.

The largest number of proposals for change focused on the economic and viewer issues we've reviewed. Both are *system level* phenomena that implicate the whole studio-conglomerate complex and the audience of moviegoers—the producers and the consumers of film. These are wide-ranging and fateful areas, places where changes can reverberate and make a huge difference. In chapter 1, the most frequently mentioned problems were systemic ones. I wasn't surprised, then, to see that the most frequent solutions have the same focus.

Ordinarily, structural change involves formal policy shifts by top decision makers at the pinnacle of organizations. (Operational change generally takes place lower down the bureaucratic pyramid and can be set in motion informally by motivated individuals.) Because system conversions are large, they are hard to maneuver, like steering the proverbial aircraft carrier, or the Walt Disney Company, into reverse direction. Systems fight ferociously to maintain their equilibrium and repel attempts to make real alterations. I think that's why some of the suggestions and proposals made here have a hard-to-deal-with feel to them. They seem somewhat obvious in one sense and unattainable in another—"pie-in-the-sky" wishes. But they do spell out a long-range agenda.

We'll be looking at Intermediate Frequency proposals now, four in number, each of which was mentioned roughly the same number of times by the directors.

Pushing the Limits: Do Your Own Thing, or Nothing

If you can't get mammoth studios to shift gears, maybe the other option is to go it alone and go around them. Directors proposed: *filmmakers individually should engage in bold and persistent acts of creativity*. Committed filmmakers have always been able to make their distinctive mark on films they've directed, and are doing that now. This isn't changing the system; it's chipping away at it piecemeal in places where directors have a bit of leverage and the guts to use it. Orson Welles is the archetype of the creative rebel, triumphant and breathtaking when he succeeded, crestfallen when he often didn't. All of us can name our own band of exemplars and heroes. I'll nominate mine in just a little while. First, let's get the comments of the directors on taking these personal chances.

> I said it before, but we're facing it all the time. Violence is pervasive, and so is commercialism, and cynicism, and that is what seeps into our films. Certainly, executives are not going to step in the way of that if it makes money. So that leaves the higher ground to *individual artists* whose brilliance is such that they can cut through the substantial obstacle course in front of them and get their films made, one way or another, through the studios or independently, and there are a number of those artists. One can look toward the Coen brothers or the Hughes brothers, or a Jane Campion, or at some younger filmmakers with a distinctive voice who are still managing to make films pretty regularly.

I also put some faith in the occasional visionary name director who comes along, like a Jim Cameron, someone with clout who says, "This year, I'm going to make my quality Academy Award winner." Guys like him are so *big* and so *important* that they have the power to move things in the right direction, if they are determined to make a difference, even if the studios themselves aren't going to do it. I don't put myself in that category, but I move ahead by sticking to making films, independent ones, that I want to make and that I think have something of value to say. I make them one at a time, and *keep at it*, with high hope that there will be an audience out there to see it each time.

It's tough going, not a movement with power, no utopia. We have to just hope that enough good people keep emerging in the field to expand it and keep it fresh. But I don't think we're in any *Golden Age of filmmaking*; that's for sure.

There are those new voices emerging and tried-and-true old warhorses who keep plugging away. I would put in a pitch for Steven Soderbergh, who has mastered the knack of making unique pictures that combine the sensibilities of independent *and* studio traditions. Through films like *Traffic* and *Erin Brockovich*, Soderbergh is one of the few people keeping the term "intelligent popular entertainment" from falling into oblivion. But he can swing over to a cool mainstream flick like *Ocean's Eleven* or an idiosyncratic, experimental movie like *Schizopolis* with a twist of his wrist. Maybe he needs to continue practicing on both ends to gel the amalgam in the middle.

John Sayles goes right on with his politically tinged, humanistic films like *Lone Star*, *The Return of the Secaucus Seven*, and *Matewan*. Sayles is someone who earns his keep through acting, being a B-movie screenwriter, and writing novels—rather than switching over to more lucrative mainstream fare. Jim Jarmusch has created a stream of eccentric comedies, essentially works of cultural criticism, in quirky films like *Stranger Than Paradise* and *Night on Earth*. Ang Lee joined up with writer James Schamus to form a powerful team putting out classy fare like *Sense and Sensibility* and *Crouching Tiger, Hidden Dragon*.

To these directors I would add some of my favorites: the Andersons (Paul Thomas and Wes), Charles Burnett, Mike Figgis, Kimberly Pierce, Kenneth Lonergan, and Allison Anders. And it's easy to overlook Woody Allen; he's such an institution that we take him for granted. Or Martin Scorsese. And what about Robert Redford for multiple astonishing contributions?

See the Wall Bend

The path for these innovating filmmakers is not trouble free. When filming *A Star Is Born*, George Cukor is said to have told the crew that they could be as arty as they would like, *but not to get caught at it*. This signals to me that those who want to go beyond the commonplace have to be willing to take chances, but they also need to be wily.

In his book *My First Movie*, Stephen Lowenstein describes how twenty directors overcame immense terror and adversity to create their virgin films.[10] Lions of cinema like Oliver Stone, Ken Loach, and Joel Coen recount the youthful trials they had to endure to bring to life the vision that inhabited them. Struggle, passion, and courage are major themes running through the book.

Courage is indispensable. But I wouldn't underplay know-how. The director's mission requires individualized creativity, but it's carried out in an organizational context where there are bureaucratic rules, policies, and operational procedures of studios that set boundaries around how the work is performed. These regs strangle the director's freedom of action; venturesome directors walk a razor's edge.

Sociologically speaking, most organizations are inherently conservative; they want to keep themselves on track and they ward off changes to their MO. But organizational theory tells us that the boundaries imposed on or by these organizations are not totally rigid; they are relatively elastic here and there and at different times. Maybe after a financial crisis or a change of leadership the people at the top are distracted and there is a window open for doing something different (and sly). I guess sometimes it works for a director to be loud and obvious about doing something different, and sometimes it's better to keep it all under wraps (Orson Welles vs. George Cukor).

In his seminal theory of bureaucratic organizations, Max Weber described their unique combination of efficiency and rigidity stemming from tight control at the top and standardized rules.[11] These characteristics of hierarchy and formalization eventually make these organizations inflexible and insufferable. Ironically, as their ossification goes up, their effectiveness goes down. Among the research into how to work against this is a useful recent book by organizational theorist Edward E. Lawler and his associates: *Creating a Strategic Human Resources Organization* provides light on ways of opening up and altering these unaccommodating entities.[12]

Committed directors are in a constant cycle of boundary testing, pushing up against enstrangling walls of studio bureaucracies to search for expandable areas. In the end, they come to an outer wall that will give no further. But without testing boundaries in thought and in action, they can't know how far they can go. A core role of directors, I think, is to counteract the natural conservatizing inclination of the studios they work for to see how much they can get away with in the interest of cinematic creativity and quality.

Directors tell me that they have another option on the individual creativity issue, too. That's to pull out and just not play the game. There are costs, financial and career-wise, to taking that tack, but a few people seem driven to do that. Faced with those hardships, others resign themselves psychologically to playing along with things as they are.

> I would have worked for the studios more in the past five years if I hadn't gotten so many scripts that I couldn't get past page 10 on, and that I rejected, and that went on and were made into movies that made a fortune. That's not who I *am*. I just can't condone putting out that stuff. If it doesn't register for me, how can I make it register for anyone else? You know, some directors cop out by a kind of *self-censoring*, where they don't even take a chance on more interesting themes, just enlist projects that they believe will make it through the executive vetting process.

Procedures! Procedures!

Some recommendations the directors made don't involve individual acts of imagination or daring. They involve influencing procedures and policies where directors may have a say.[13] Filmmakers have some control over some of these and can negotiate with the studio on others. The proposal: *retool procedures in ways that induce creativity.*

Methods around the Madness

The directors' suggested changes are concrete and self-explanatory. I'll briefly set them out.

More Prep Time

> The movie has to have enough time for the director and other departments to set the groundwork before starting to shoot. You have to press for that time. Otherwise, you're rushed—at the cost of reflection and at the cost of the quality of the movie.

More Script Time

> You have to demand a working script to start with. You should insist that the script be well-developed before you begin to shoot a movie. I see them green-lighting movies nowadays without having anything *near* a working script.

More Development Work

> The development system has really changed over time. They don't develop much with producers anymore. They depend on the major agencies to deliver a script with sequel potentials and sometimes a package. They'll make that movie—often hiring a hotshot commercial director—and then preview it around. Then they'll spend a huge amount of extra money to reshoot, recut, and rescore. Why not develop it right in the first place?

More Respect for the Creative Process

> We should make sure that the studios and producers follow the Directors Guild creative rights provisions. Those provisions *do* set out proven ways to make good movies.[14]

More Respect for Writers

> We ought to cut out treating writers like a commodity, changing and discarding them after each draft. Studios have to allow writers to have experience in how to rewrite. We need to contribute to developing rounded writers who can stick with a project and produce a full script that's woven together and ready to go.

Less Middle Management

> There's too much middle-level bureaucracy and too many people making decisions along the way. There should be *fewer meddlers* in the process. These people feel they have to justify their existence by criticizing everything that passes by them. If they simply say "yes," they think they won't be justifying their existence and will be putting their job in jeopardy. I don't know how much we can really do about this.

Less High Concept

"High Concept" gimmicks ought to go; we should fight against them. I was told very specifically that if you can't sell something in a *sentence*, like you'd find in a newspaper ad or *TV Guide*, then you're never going to sell it. That forces the stuff to be shallow, contrived, and without any genuine resonance.

Fewer Movies/More Movies

Studios shouldn't make as many films. There's too much product out there. Spend less money on doing so many movies and focus on doing fewer ones of higher caliber. Studios, you know, don't have to put out a movie every month in a big rush; it impairs the judgment. We get caught up in shoveling out junk. *Less means better.*

But alternatively:

More films should be made, at lower cost for each film. In that way there could be more jobs for more people in film. Just looking at it from a probability standpoint, I think that would result in a greater number of good films.

"More" or "less" can be argued ad infinitum, and there wasn't much discussion or consensus on that point in the respondent group. Actually, only a few people made each of these comments, so they stand as a series of individual suggestions that are worth thinking about. What cumulates in the responses is the notion that executing various procedural changes (some with policy aspects) is a way to impact quality.

Let's Switch and Niche

Studios would love to fill up all the theaters in America, and around the globe, with one film, rather than coughing up the money to make a slew of them to draw in different audiences. Witness the *Matrix Revolutions*, the last of the trilogy, opening at the same hour in ninety-six countries, on eighteen thousand screens! It's not hard to figure that there's a maximum profit motive in that scheme. So the majors have undertaken to produce a limited number of powerhouse blockbuster movies, each geared to a mass audience of viewers. Directors were clear in perceiving this as death to quality filmmaking.

What they propose takes a different course: *stress diversity—make different movies and more smaller-budget movies for different audiences.* They see digital methods as the wedge that opens up this possibility. To some degree, this discussion overlaps chapter 4, "Digital Rising."

There are many people who are over thirty or over forty who would love to see a film that moved them, that didn't have guns and car chases and explosions and mega-star performers. We may be coming into an era where many people have big screens in their homes. The plasma screens, digital and plasma screens, and DVDs, which are real inexpensive to make, might give us an audience that starts to build and *makes demands*, and then we can get unusual and brilliant small productions that will rival in quality, if not outdo, what's coming out of foreign countries. Groups of people with special interests just may be able to decide what should be shown to them. With this, new filmmaking voices from unusual places will rise and be able to be heard.

More home viewing may be a thing of the future simply on the basis of economics. The theaters are closing up and becoming less important because it costs so much to keep a theater open and there's an oversupply of them. A half-empty theater doesn't sell a lot of popcorn, and that's how they make their rent. Anyway, if the viewing is good, people may be content with seeing movies at home.

It's possible with the advent of digital to make top-level film without stars, but with *good actors*. You see, every other country uses actors from the stage in film, and these actors do a wide variety of things, including commercials, documentaries, and TV. In this country, it's more specialized; the stars star in pictures. That's it. That could change if they become attracted to small pictures that exude excellence.

True, when people watch movies at home, we'll lose the communal feeling, and that's especially important for comedy. But there are also some good possibilities for more nonconventional films in the theaters. Digital projectors—Texas Instruments has a great one—will help in this. You can take one of the screens at a mall, install a digital projector, and show movies that are being made by independent filmmakers, who won't have to go to the expense of converting the stock to 35. The productions can be projected directly. That's going to make a difference.

What I am saying is that all the conventional wisdom *has to be turned upside down* and Hollywood people have to learn that what is *conventional* is not *wise*. Just compare the size of the audience needed for a successful novel and for a successful film. You don't need an enormous audience for the novel, and the same principle should apply to quality film. I think technology can save us by giving us the means to more creative filmmaking and giving a deserved demotion to formulaic filmmaking.

One concrete proposal was to *release films by subscriptions at certain movie houses for smaller markets that want high-quality movies* and don't lust for high production values. The legitimate theater sets a precedent for that, as do HBO and other cable ventures. It could be a flex plan, where moviegoers attend a certain number of films during the year, at their own discretion.

Rewarding Experiences, or Where Do I Apply for a Grant?

About a half-dozen directors thought that government subsidies would be a route to better cinema. They pointed to film subsidy programs in other countries around the world and to the precedent here with the National Endowment for the Arts. Since the barons of the industry are riveted, with narrow vision, on generating commercial rewards for themselves and their companies, ergo, *the federal government, with an obligation to promote the welfare of all the people, should provide rewards to cultural workers through subsidies to encourage the enrichment of American life through cinema.* In other countries, film is viewed as a culture-building enterprise, and their governments acknowledge a clear responsibility to aid that endeavor.

I wish the government was more proactive in giving money to cultural developments. *Christ*, we're the only society I know of that doesn't support a national theater. France, Britain, Russia do it. It's a disgrace that this country doesn't have a national theater. It's the negative aspect of pure capitalism that's rampant. There could be government subsidies specifically for film—most other countries do it—and tax incentives, given under set specifications.

The Canadian Film Board does a great job and so do the English. Those countries feel it is their job to promote film, whether commercial or not commercial. I wish we could do that here. That's a bit of a fantasy of mine, but I have no idea how to put the key in the lock to make that happen.

The proposal for subsidizing film is nothing new; industry people and cultural critics have promoted the notion over the years. One of the strongest statements I've come across was by William Fadiman, a special assistant to Howard Hughes at RKO and an executive at Columbia Pictures. Writing in 1972, Fadiman left no doubt about his position: "The only way to advance film art in America would be by some form of government subsidization. . . . If subsidization of some kind is not forthcoming, the portends for Hollywood are dim."[15]

Other countries have taken that admonition to heart. In his book *The Movie Game*, Martin Dale spells out a plethora of different programs and approaches to film subsidies in European nations, including France, England, Scotland, Spain, Italy, Germany, and the Scandinavian countries.[16] The number and forms of these subsidies stagger the imagination. There are direct money grants, guarantees to cover financial loss, taxes on movie tickets at the box office, allocations from the lottery, low-interest loans, awards, prizes, and donations.

Asian nations are also active in this, as are other countries around the world. There are lots of models for America to adopt if it decides to get around to the notion of government support of quality cinema. Awards could be made to individual artists, cinema groups, and production companies based on good ideas, demonstrated achievement, or promising potential. There's reticence to this kind of government support for film in this country. But the United States hasn't been gun-shy about extending subsidies in other fields—the airlines, the maritime, oil, minerals, munitions, the whole corporate welfare complex, as well as home ownership and farming, to name a few.

Some directors didn't go along with this notion. They had reservations about who would decide on merit and whether the approach would really be a spur to creativity.

This all means we're talking about a government situation. But is that the solution? Invariably, what happens is that you have some board or approving group that is *defining what artistic quality is*. And that sometimes works and oftentimes it doesn't, in my opinion. I don't think there's a simple answer. It's not clear. Because someone then is going to have to be in control, someone is going to be out there making the assessment of what quality is, and whether those folks will have the ability and the expertise to do that nobody knows. *It's problematic.*

Once some group has its own expectations of quality, by definition, that's not going to breed creativity. You see, because instead of making films to Hollywood standards, you'll be making them to the government's standards. And real creativity comes when people hold to nobody's standards, only *their own*. That's the way creative breakthroughs happen. There should be no control and no edicts about what is made. We can't control an enterprise as vast as American filmmaking, and thank God for that. The way things develop should be free and open.

Film subsidies have a lot going for them, but I want to chime in with some reservations. The idea clashes with the outlook of a segment, whether large or small, of American society. Individuality is embedded so deeply into the national consciousness that, as came across in the remarks of the naysayers, the idea of external judges of artistic merit runs against the grain of many people. We saw that up close in the volatile experiences of the National Endowment for the Arts, where grants were contested, some withdrawn, policies shifted about, and funds cut.

I believe art is a radical, if not revolutionary, exercise. Artists peer penetratingly at what *is* and dream of what *might be*. Those going into the arts are critics, explorers, idealists, malcontents, and exhibitionists. Many use their art as a means to advocate change and shake up the way people think.

These are the people who in large proportion would apply for grants and stipends in cinema. And we know there is a currently vociferous conservative/right-wing voice on the American political landscape that would rally against the projects of these supplicants. The result: an unstable situation, contentious and abrasive, that would be mired in political and bureaucratic bickering and stalemate.

While I agree philosophically and in principle with the intent of subsidies for film, I have to wonder about the feasibility of it as a viable option in the short run on the U.S. scene. I don't say no; I say, on this one, proceed with due caution.

The Hunt for Deep Pockets

If the government is nixed on funding film development, who else should do it? One of my informants had an ingenious idea: let rich directors do it. (I would dare to suggest including high-paid stars.) The proposal: *induce affluent filmmakers to volunteer funds to encourage quality filmmaking.* Here's how it would work.

Some of the film directors who have struck gold beyond anyone's wildest imagination could offer to finance ten movies at a budget of 2 million each; that's 20 million dollars. Twenty million dollars is the salary that some directors make, that some movie stars make, *per film*. It sounds like a lot of money, it *is* a lot of money, but it could probably be structured where it actually became a tax benefit for this person.

Pick ten interesting filmmakers and give them each 2 million—there is no more money, that's all the money there is—and let them make ten movies. And *leave them alone*, give them final cut. You're not going to get big productions. You're not going to get *Gladiator*. But you're going to get a couple of home runs. You're going to get a couple of very good movies.

And how do you pick these filmmakers? Well, the people who give the money pick the filmmakers. That's it. You don't make it a contest. You pick some veteran filmmakers whose work you know and admire, and you think they have something to say and they're worth backing; you pick some young filmmakers right out of film school, or maybe out of the theater. You mix it up, ten people with as much diversity as you can have. There doesn't need to be a committee, no application process, no pitch.

Even for a veteran director, getting that kind of backing would be a tempting opportunity and a challenge, to use the cost limitations to your advantage. As a filmmaker you're never not solving problems, so this would become a problem to solve: how can I create this thing that's been intriguing me without spending all that money?

The only standard for what gets funded is the taste of the people giving the money. They decide it. I believe this is a very practical suggestion about how to start to right the American film business. That's because the most interesting work is being done independently, but the independent films are so limited by economics, by budget constraints, by the requirements of casting. They have to get anybody who the distributor, the guy who is putting up the money, will take as an actor that will protect their investment. So you end up starting the movie where it's miscast.

Sure, if someone actually did what I suggest, there would be some terrible movies, some self-indulgent movies, but there could be some *great movies* that we're not getting now.

I'm waiting to see the line-up of well-heeled directors dispensing cash after this book hits the shelves! But there are also other possibilities for support that were not mentioned by the directors I interviewed. One is the studios themselves. Fadiman proposes this in his book: The film industry should channel a given proportion of dollar profits from successful commercial films to support more experimental film ventures. A system of self-taxation would be put in place for this purpose. Ironically, Hollywood's well-honed capability to produce the humdrum would be put to use instead to create the extraordinary.

The usual suspects high up in the hierarchy would object that the industry is set up to be a purely profit-seeking institution. True, but other corporations invest to upgrade their product, through R&D and other means. The pharmaceutical industry, for one, invests enormous sums to develop new medicines and promote better health for the public. Of course, they do this as shrewd managers with an eye on ultimate financial gain rather than as starry-eyed altruists. But who is to say that engaging in the R&D-like activity of nurturing ground-breaking creative filmmakers would not be a profitable investment for the industry, long-range?

More Pockets, Not So Deep

Still another approach for funding quality film occurs to me. *People* magazine, among other media and professional entities, asks the viewing public to vote on awards for outstanding performers and filmmakers. Why not ask the public to contribute financially also to promote excellence—in this instance, in filmmaking? The public makes donations from time to time at picture houses to aid infirm actors and for other causes. The public also contributes generally for research and service for health promotion and child development. They contribute as well to PBS and NPR. There may be film buffs out there who wouldn't resent, or might even relish, doing their part to bring into being distinguished film offerings. The proposal: *set up a means for the public to contribute funds expressly to support the production of quality films*. What about a discount ticket package for those who do?

Carnaby Films, a London-based company, carries the notion of public support forward in another direction. They make a direct mailing appeal to a spread of private individuals, asking them to invest in making film production by the company possible. The company raised $4.1 million to make the movie *Spivs* from eight hundred individual investors. Tax breaks for investing under England's Enterprise Investment Scheme help fuel the approach through write-offs and capital gain exclusions. But other incentives enter too: inviting investors down to the set, arranging contacts with actors, having them attend premiers and previews, and even giving them a chance to appear as extras. Carnaby has financed three films in this way. Are there portents here for advancing independent film?

Global Fertilization—or Let a Thousand Movies Grow

That takes us through the Intermediate-Frequency proposals for improving American filmmaking. There was one Lower-Frequency recommendation. A couple of directors thought that *film schools should do more to promote quality filmmaking*. Illustratively, the Directors Guild's academic committee is experimenting with interactive conferencing so that top-notch directors can lecture and dialogue electronically with students at small film schools in remote places. A director who participated in that program, thinks that it's a big plus for students to have these opportunities for contact with exceptional pros and that it should happen more often.

Another suggestion was to beef up the recruitment and training of women and minorities in film schools as a way of widening the content and style of film offerings. Chapter 6, "Women and Minorities in the Director's Chair," goes into this in detail. I assume that because film schools already emphasize creativity and substance, there weren't a larger number of suggestions aimed in this direction.

I'm going to add a proposal of my own here, and use it as an opportunity to sound off a bit. D. W. Griffith, in his aforementioned article, made another long-range prediction about what the twenty-first-century film world would be like. He envisioned the breakup of the concentrated film industry in Hollywood and its wide dispersal, with some clustering around New York City. He seemed not at all displeased with that turn of events. This leads me to conjecture that the overpowering global domination of filmmaking by Hollywood is a serious drag on cinema quality generally, and that greater evenness of film production internationally would be a happy occurrence for the art.

American supremacy in this field is astonishing and beyond challenge from any quarter. *The Economist* estimates that in 1996 the U.S. took 70 percent overall of the

European film market and even 50 percent in Japan. American films are uniquely the only ones that reach every market in the world. In urban centers internationally, the highest-grossing films locally are imported Hollywood blockbusters. Roughly 50 percent of Hollywood's revenue comes from overseas markets, and there isn't very much reverse traffic. Foreign films capture less than 3 percent of the American market.[17] Of course, there are foreign investments in the film industry, joint ventures, and substantial ownership of some studios by overseas investors, but financial gains don't revert back to building cinema in those countries in a substantial way. This economic elevator for U.S. cinema shows no signs of reaching the top; our market share keeps rising, and the situation for other major filmmaking countries keeps declining.

It wasn't ordained that this would be the pattern. The Pathé Company in France made a commanding start in film, setting up shop as far back as 1869 and by 1908 gathering in more than twice the market share in the United States than all the American companies put together. Before World War I, Pathé was the biggest producer of films internationally, without real competition. It pioneered in creating the film newsreel and the weekly adventure serial, and it was a dominant manufacturer of cameras, projectors, and film.[18]

It was World War I that stopped Pathé in its tracks. American companies, sheltered from the devastation of the conflict, were able to fill the void that was created, aided by the fact that American silent movies could travel to audiences anywhere without barriers of language. Also, Hollywood was aggressive in importing outstanding foreign talent, people like Chaplin, Stroheim, Hitchcock—who were not averse to joining the big show in California.

This massive Hollywood hegemony has overwhelmed film production in nations around the world, as their cinema industries shrivel and become appendages of Global Hollywood (India, China, and Hong Kong exempted).[19] In recent years, this has created a complex and intermeshed global system of production, copyright, promotion, distribution, and exhibition. Cries of economic domination and cultural imperialism come from every quarter.

Intimidated nations establish protective mechanisms to save their industries from the American juggernaut, either by defending local operations against foreign imports or lending support to local production. Their regulatory and legislative actions include such tactics as low-interest loans, remittances by foreign distributors, co-productions of various kinds, taxes on profits, the already mentioned box-office taxes, and subsidies and subversions. While decrying these national tactics of resistance as "protectionist," Jack Valenti and the Motion Picture Association of America (MPAA) carry out a forceful unofficial but government-supported program of international economic exploitation, prettied up as virtuous free enterprise.

There's a David-and-Goliath feel to this, as the American moviemaking machine rolls over these flimsy armaments of vulnerable nations. Rather than backing the MPAA assault on their survival program, using GATT (the General Agreement on Tariffs and Trade) as a club to destroy opposition, I see value in reinforcing the flowering of cinematic art everywhere.

As Hollywood relaxes its smothering reign over McMovieWorld, there may come to pass additional French New Waves, Italian Neo-Realisms, and Third Cinemas, as well as other Asian and African and South American variations and transmutations. That's another avenue potentially leading to an upsurge in film quality. Therefore, *we should support the development of strong and competitive motion picture industries in countries around the world (and drop policies that impede that)*. Increased investment, technical assistance, training, and targeted cultural exchange are ways of accomplishing this.

I suppose espousing that view puts me in the camp of those who favor optimizing cinema art at the expense of U.S. economic boosterism. I don't know whether members of my interview group would agree with me on this. But, given the existing circumstances, there really ought to be some balance. With the huge economic power, resiliency, and ingenuity of the United States, a loss of some strength in the area of film surely would be offset by growth in another area. And the amount of time such a development would consume would provide enough time, if it were necessary, for those in American cinema to revise and redirect their goals.

From Here to Nativity

Those are the proposals that came out of the interviews. So what happens to them now? I'm reminded of poet Kenneth Rexroth's lines:

> History would be so much simpler if you could just write it
> Without ever having to let it happen.

That's every author's pipe dream. There's a wide gap between putting forth a set of proposals, no matter how remarkable or worthy, and having them, in turn, give birth to programs and policies in the real world. Without clear political and organizational strategies, recommendations usually remain enticing thoughts and heartfelt wishes— essentially airy abstractions. What I would like to do is reflect on some theoretical approaches for moving across the gap between good ideas and programs that actually come to life. That means reaching for my tweed jacket with leather elbow patches.

Planned Change Theory gives us some handles for thinking this question through. Social scientists and community organizers have assembled guides to what's sometimes been called "the production of intended effects." This area has been a professional specialization of mine, and in the course of my work, I've discovered that there are basically three important approaches used by community "change agents": *social planning, social action,* and *community development*.[20]

In the *social planning* approach, you rely on data to make a case for a goal you're going after. Rationality rules: if you can prove there's a need for something or that it will solve a vexing problem, then a lot of people will be persuaded to go along. Typically, urban planning departments proceed this way when they want to convince citizens to put in a new road or rezone a neighborhood, and so do health planning organizations and federal departments dealing with delinquency or the environment. A couple of intellectual godfathers of data-based change are decision theorist Herbert Simon and political scientist Harold Lasswell.

Social action has a more confrontational style. It assumes you're dealing with some powerful adversary (like a studio or regulatory body), a force that has to be pressured if you're going to reach your goal (like scaling down runaway production). It isn't reason but pressure that will make the difference. We all know about unions leaning on corporations during tough negotiations—holding the possibility of strikes, picketing, and boycotts over their heads in the background. Community action groups, like the civil rights, feminist, and environmental movements, add marches and traffic disruptions to the pressure cocktail. For the intellectual roots for social action, look to thinkers and social activists like Jane Addams, Mikhail Bakunin, and Saul Alinsky.

I believe the *community development* approach is less familiar to most people. It has a more conciliatory tone; it proposes that people caught up in a problem basically get together and talk it over. You can think of the traditional New England "town hall" as a model. Participation is a key point. Solutions and self-education of the participants spring from an exchange of ideas. An assumption here is that as people get to understand and trust each other, they'll join in collaborative action. The adult education movement, the Peace Corps, and religious organizations are examples of this approach. John Dewey's philosophy was an important influence.

In *social action*, you assume the parties involved have strong basic differences and that you have to use a hammer to prod your opponent to move in the right direction. *Community development* has a consensus outlook—there's basically good will among people, so just talking it out will work it out. *Social planning* doesn't have prior assumptions about agreement—the facts will either convince people or turn up ammunition to use against them.

Since there has to be some group or organization to give life to an action campaign, I'll choose the Directors Guild to illustrate. As an alternative, it could be an interested group of directors getting together, a coalition of organizations like the American Film Institute, Women in Film, and American Cinematique (an unlikely combination), or an interest group like Independent Feature Project/West.

Let's deal with the recommendation to up the targeting of films to niche audiences, as it might be approached by the DGA. *Social planning* is the intervention strategy I suggest for this goal in this hypothetical. The research people at the DGA issue a report on different niche audiences, their interests, the best promotional media for reaching them, and a statement of financial gains to studios through the approach. The DGA releases the report to the media at a news conference, where high-profile directors and other film dignitaries give it their backing. A DGA team meets with studio executives to review the report and describes ways to implement the approach. The DGA assembles further facts if they seem needed. Other important groups—industry, political, and special interest—are given the information and asked to lend support.

Dealing with proposals for changing filmmaking procedures—such as beginning a shoot only with finished scripts or giving directors more preparation time—it seems to me would take a different tack. Studios would probably see this as cost trouble and dig in their heels. So *social action* would be the method of choice. This one goes to the DGA committee dealing with negotiations to be worked up as a demand for the next contract. It becomes part of the overall package on the bargaining table. The threat of a strike or other disruptions in the industry is always a component of that process.

The proposal for directors to push for maximum creativity for themselves, in this case by personally expanding the boundaries in their work, falls naturally under the *community development strategy*. The DGA announces a workshop/seminar on increasing the channels for creativity for a group of directors who volunteer to participate. A panel of directors who are respected by their colleagues for their accomplishments in doing this are invited to tell their stories. This is an open discussion, with directors frankly sharing their experiences—failures and successes—and trying to come up with ideas for the panel and members of the audience. At the conclusion, each member of the audience is asked to call together a group of friends and colleagues to carry out a similar event. These participants, in turn, are asked to call similar gatherings. Through this process, information, exchange of views, and a determination to act ripples out across a wide spectrum of the DGA membership. The end result, with luck, is a refueling of the motivation and fortitude of many directors to strike another blow for creativity.

These three examples I fabricated are an exercise in brainstorming, not a set of blueprints. Some of the bigger proposals, like taking Global Hollywood to task, are well beyond the scope of any advocacy group I can dream up. Mainly, the exercise demonstrates that different proposals need different strategies to carry them out. The three planned-change concepts I spelled out give a way to think about matching goals with the means—basing action plans on an understanding of the circumstances. That takes us at least a small step beyond simply putting meritorious objectives on the table.

I'll add, though, that lovers of the classic Hollywood movie style and ambiance need not alarm themselves or slip into a depression. I have high hopes but not great expectations for the banquet of proposals that the directors, with my amendments, put forward. If anything, these ideas may become part of the long-range and ongoing dialogue at Musso and Frank's and similar watering holes around town. Hollywood is a place that trumpets creativity and novelty but is hunkered down in do-the-same-thing continuity. Nothing I've reported here, I fear, will be jump cut tomorrow.

The Hollywood movie establishment has had a century to become what it is, and the system is solidly rooted. But it's an open system that is constantly bombarded from the outside—economically, artistically, politically, ethically. Despite the contour of the behemoth and its ferocity at self-protection, the beast relents when there is an undeniable need to make patch-ups. I suspect there are prospects for some kind of back-to-the-future pastiche of the old and the new ahead. If director Griffith were still with us, he could probably tell us what the changes will be.

CHAPTER NINE

~

Mapping Planet Hollywood
(Not the Restaurant)

All the studios are actually only pieces of huge conglomerates that are interested in a smorgasbord of products. You can no longer be in the business just to make a nice profit. They're only interested in a mega-smash, because a mega-smash impacts the next quarterly report of the parent company. It's changed totally, and it's very strange. Merchandising and marketing is everything.

—John Landis

Now I know what it's like to be an explorer. Taking notebook and tape recorder in hand, I left my snug (should I say smug?) UCLA campus office and made my way across town to peer into the Hollywood underbrush, a mysterious place masked in hyperbole and pretension and deception—Hortense Powdermaker's illusive "Dream Factory."

In the preview chapter, "The Ivy Tower Meets the Silver Screen," I spoke about the media conspiring against a realistic portrayal and assessment of the filmmaking industry, leaving an empirical black hole that bothered and intrigued me. I set out to provide some balance, trying to get the lay of the land by looking for sociological landmarks that would accurately identify and describe this curious "planet Hollywood" (that's what some of the inhabitants who are interested in culinary investments call it). An astronaut of social science, what would my university colleagues think? In these pages, I've described pieces of the landscape that I came upon. Now that I've completed the journey, I want to look back and draw a map that captures the essential features of that planet—what film folk and cinema analysts refer to as the *New Hollywood*.[1]

I was lucky to enlist the assistance of a team of scouts, natives who were familiar with the turf—feature film directors who gave me clues and solid intelligence. They told me that to know this terrain now I had to know how it came to be what it is; I had to be cognizant of the Old Hollywood to understand the characteristics of the

New Hollywood. In other words, I would have to be both a social surveyor and an archivist.

I surmise Hollywood veterans won't discern a great deal that's startling or unfamiliar, but they may gain some insights by seeing the familiar through fresh eyes—mine. What I've done is put the known pieces together (along with what is in previous chapters of this book) in a different way that I hope is interesting and synthesizing. An industry friend who read the manuscript said that what I came up with was for him (and I don't know whether to take this as compliment or its opposite) "innocent wisdom."

I need to say at the start that the vaunted studio system of Hollywood's Golden Age is no more. In its place is a more unbounded system—diffuse, tangled, expansive, and expensive. People working in film are shaped professionally by this illusory backdrop, with its real social and economic vectors. Or at least they have to contend with it if they want to hold on to their jobs, let alone achieve something like success—either artistic or commercial.

My observations led me to conclude that five core landmarks—social-structural constructs—chart the movie capital of the world in its present orbit. I'm going to set them out succinctly.

Congloms on the March

Conglomerates are the order of the day, and their tentacles spread outwardly in an ever widening arc. Studios have become an element in a vast, complex corporate intermesh. That wasn't always the case. The studios of yore were more localized and personal: you knew where Warner Bros. was based and you knew that Jack Warner ran it.

That "studio system" coincides with the zenith of Hollywood's exuberance and prosperity, the period between the 1920s and 1950s, when the studios were in full flower.[2] Five major studios dominated the scene—Paramount, Twentieth-Century Fox, MGM, Warner Bros., and RKO. Following behind were the Little Three—United Artists, Universal, and Columbia. And there was space remaining still for the smaller Republic and Monograph companies that cranked out low-budget B-pictures, mainly Westerns, to feed the double-feature bills shown at most theaters. Behind all this web of activity was an insatiable demand by the public for the still new and magical form of visual pleasure, a demand that, at that time, had little competition from other forms of mass entertainment.

The studios developed an assembly-line approach, mass-producing a profusion of cinematic commodities to satisfy the exuberant market. Starting as far back as 1912, there were the beginnings of a division of labor; the shooting of units of a film—the scenes out of order—to save money; designating a production head rather than directors to manage film projects; and using formulaic approaches to manufacture cheap and audience-friendly fare.

The following step was studio control of the distribution of films, and then on to ownership of the theaters themselves, a sure way to guarantee unimpeded access to audiences for the four to five hundred films that were eventually produced each year. In this way, studios had a vertical monopoly in the movie field, including production, distribution, and exhibition.

The costs of running this vast enterprise were enormous, and even more so when sound was introduced, requiring heavy financing from the East Coast money centers, primarily Wall Street. Financial policy decisions affecting film came from the East Coast, while the so-called moguls, the Louis B. Mayers and Samuel Goldwyns, ran production with an iron hand on the West Coast.

Studios were organized like a factory, with specialist departments of producers, directors, screenwriters, cinematographers, and the like. There was typically one person in charge of production, like Vice President Irving Thalberg at MGM, below whom were producers or associate producers assigned to different films. They, in turn, were in charge of a wide range of creative and technical people who were employees of the studios. I'll describe this arrangement more fully in a bit.

This lucrative apparatus began to fall apart with the 1948 Paramount Decision when the Supreme Count ruled that the studios had to give up their monopoly control—through vertical integration—by selling off their theater chains.[3] Economically, that was a devastating kick in the teeth. Soon after, television sets began filtering into living rooms throughout the nation, draining off a vast portion of the moviegoing public. That was the culminating one-two punch. Studios began selling off their overhead—sound studios, back lots, and costly equipment—to cope with these financial shock waves.

The revolt of movie stars and other creative artists against the suffocating long-term contract arrangement further propelled the demise of the studios—an aftermath of Olivia de Havilland's defeat of Warner Bros. on this issue in 1944. Without their stars, I'll deign to quip, the studios could not help but lose some of their luster.

To counter these developments, studios tried an assortment of initiatives: color cinematography, widescreens, selling off their back lots, renting out space to independent producers and television companies, and going into TV production themselves. None of these overtures could restore the grandeur and glamour of the past.

If I may fast-forward to the present, in contrast to the stand-alone studios of the Old Hollywood, today's eight major studios are mostly units of international conglomerates. These are diversified behemoths, multimedia and beyond in scope, but some have a particular signature line. Time Warner is heavily into the Internet and magazines. Viacom (Paramount) does the Internet but is also strong in books and live venues. Vivendi Universal (Universal Studios) ambidextrously ranges from financial and insurance services to railroad cargo, landfill sites, industrial cleaning, and miscellaneous others. Disney has put its stamp on theme parks, retail stores, and the ABC-TV network. Add other powerhouses like Fox-News Corp., Sony, Dreamworks, and the smaller minor-major MGM, which still deals mainly in film. These multifaceted and nondescript economic enormities gobble up more and more companies—each striving, as I imagine it, to become the one master corporation that manages it all. I think Orwell may have had it wrong: Big Brother may turn out to be a corporate overlord rather than a government honcho.

A catchword in this is "synergy," meaning that a company's scattered ventures will reinforce one another economically, one feeding into the other in domino-theory progression. Only 20 percent of the gross revenue of a movie nowadays comes from box-office receipts through exhibition at movie houses. For the bulk of their profits, studios rely on other venues like video and DVD sales, airline and cable TV viewings, and foreign distribution. The descending order of dispersal often proceeds from theaters to an afterlife in home video and pay-per-view TV channels, to cable programs, then to network showings, and, at last, to local programming, perhaps in the early hours of the morning.

Final Cut or Opening Card

Realize that a completed film is essentially a vehicle that provides entry into varied avenues of more lucrative profit making. A film is valuable to the degree that it can be exploited through a multiplicity of commercial outlets. Hardware and software are expected to reinforce each other, like film libraries feeding audio and DVD devices. A new film project will be reviewed—green-lighted or trashed—based on whether it will also generate aggregate sales in manifold venues.

"*Franchise*" is a related term, meaning that a product becomes a kind of brand name for the company. A prime example was Disney's *Lizzie McGuire*. An item aimed at consumers in the tween market, she was a spin-off from a cable show to a movie, and also appeared in the form of a fashion doll, a children's book series, Oscar Mayer Lunchables in supermarkets, and a gift line—with perhaps, who knows, a video game and fashion line of clothing planned to follow. But we will never know, for to Disney's ill fortune, the adorable moppet had a dispute with the company over salary and went off looking for a more lucrative sponsor.

Old-time studio moguls like Harry Cohn or Darryl Zanuck had a lifelong and singular attachment to the movie medium and how it fared. In the New Hollywood, for far-flung industrial potentates like Sumner Redstone or Rupert Murdoch, film is one commodity among a mass of others, and an expendable one whenever profits disappoint.

So, in my sightings, a first landmark is *conglomoratization*.

Global and Mobile

Global reach is another force on the march. A once notably American industry has gone worldwide. American film has been moving outward at a phenomenal clip to penetrate movie houses and video stores everywhere on the planet, so that our industry dominates the international film market. I discussed Hollywood's global preeminence in the previous chapter and will only emphasize a couple of high points. Overseas markets contribute as much as 50 percent of American total movie revenues, and the exchange is wildly off balance. Foreign film offerings make up less than 3 percent of the American market. The highest grossing films in foreign urban centers around the world are American mega-pictures. U.S. market share, worldwide, is on a trajectory that is on a ceaseless climb. Cries of cultural imperialism reverberate in countries like France and Italy, as they see their film industries dry up following years of Yankee invasion.

Since foreign distribution accounts for much of the box-office income from films made in the United States, the major studios create movies to appeal to mass audiences around the world, rather than catering exclusively to American audiences. This means playing down the language elements and playing up the visual shock-and-awe special effects. That's built-in strangulation for quality.

The volume of investments coming in the opposite direction from overseas sources has been on the rise also. These investors want to reap rich rewards from the communications revolution, and they see advantages in bellying up to the most powerful film industry in the world. Consider that a Japanese electronics giant owns the SONY studio; that the French Vivendi Corporation, which began as a water-bottling company, controls Universal (but at last count was considering a sell-off); that an Australian newspaper magnate runs Twentieth-Century Fox. Matsushita and other foreign companies have been in and out of the movie scene.

The making of American movies away from Hollywood and in foreign locations—runaway production—has been growing by leaps and bounds, inevitably affecting jobs and morale. Movie executives' attraction to other countries and states is driven by the spiraling costs of making films in California and elsewhere in the United States.

A big component of the upsurge, we know, is the astronomical fees demanded by and paid to superstars, supposedly to lure audiences to theaters in droves. When studios collapsed following the 1948 Paramount Decision mandating divestiture of theater chains, and actors' long-term studio contracts went out the window, setting fees for performers became a free-for-all. Agents rather than studio executives began calling the tune. Marlon Brando raised the bar in 1978 to an unprecedented high with his $4 million demand for four minutes of work in *Superman II*, a cool million dollars a minute. Another milestone was Jim Carrey's $20 million up-front deal for *The Cable Guy* in 1996.

This new fee scale blew the lid off above-the-line costs, causing dwindling expenditures for almost all other areas of filmmaking, and sending producers and executives scurrying in search of economies, including those in foreign locations. Canada has become a major production locale, based on its cheap dollar, the wage and tax credits offered, and proximity. The United Kingdom, Ireland, and Australia are following the Canadian pattern of incentives. Proximity, too, has made Mexico a draw. This phenomenon has resulted in such absurdities as Fox Network shooting its *Pasadena* series not just down the freeway a bit, but in Vancouver, B.C., 1,200 miles away. That's where NBC's movie *L.A. Law: Return to Justice* also was shot.

To illustrate the dimensions of this outbound migration, a U.S. Department of Commerce study issued in 2001 estimates that the loss to the American economy from runaway film and television production was $10.3 billion in 1998—a five-fold increase from the beginning of the decade. A study conducted by the Monitor Company, commissioned by the Directors Guild of America and the Screen Actors Guild, compared the runaway situation in 1998 with 1990, with similarly striking results. In 1998, 27 percent of film and television productions were shot out of the country, almost double the number in 1990. The figure for movies for television was especially high: a whopping 45 percent in 1998. All told, there was a cumulative loss of 125,100 jobs over the time period that was studied, with job losses rising 241 percent over the eight-year period. Canada captured 81 percent of the runaways, with Toronto getting the lion's share.[4]

That, then, is the second landmark of today's Hollywood—*globalization*.

Finding a Job among the Pieces

A fragmented, I could say chaotic, mode of operation characterizes the New Hollywood. It's occupational and it's geographic and it's pervasive. Working in film is like being in a floating crap game: no one knows when and where the next game will take place or who the players will be. The employment situation is ad hoc, and quirky.

To illustrate the difference in work life, let's look back again at the classic studio system. A studio operated then, to a greater or lesser degree, in the style of a formal bureaucracy, with a boss/president/mogul at the top who ruled through a chain-of-command flow. The studio hired everyone it needed to make movies: producers, writers, directors, stars, character actors, cinematographers, and all the other crafts and technical people. Regular employees were assigned to specific pictures and projects, one following another. Most competent directors, screenwriters, and skilled actors had contracts that assured them a job and a salary with a single studio for a protracted period of time, usually seven years. Certainly there was more flexibility and flux than in a typical Ford assembly plant, since filmmaking organizations include creative elements, but there was also a bureaucratic command structure.

In the 1960s, when the contract system really disintegrated, together with the old studio system, creative people became free agents. This happened, as we saw, because studios were being squeezed to death economically by the stampede of patrons to TV sets, so they shed overhead costs, including the contract format.

Pick-up Team, Anyone?

Michael Storper, a fellow faculty member at UCLA, researched this "vertical disintegration" development, as he calls it.[5] He documented the process whereby studios, instead of making contracts with individuals, shifted to picture-by-picture subcontracting ("flexible specialization") with a wide external network of production and post-production companies. The film industry is no longer several self-standing large studios, but rather a widespread patchwork of many organizations freckled about a sprawling region, each doing different pieces of film production work.

Each new movie now has a fresh pick-up team of freelancers (agents, producers, high-profile directors) gathered together by the studio or anyone else who has extensive contacts and can work out a deal. Every time a project is conceived, a negotiating process is launched to assemble a package that includes the freelance talent necessary to produce a film. The studios generally orchestrate the ingredients or buy a package from an agent, finance projects, and farm out projects to independent producers and production companies to turn into a film. Sometimes a studio will fund the entire film, or else put up some of the funding for a portion of the proceeds. The studio also manages the distribution of the product. After the film is put in the can, the project team is disbanded.

Capitalizing and *distributing* films have become the two cornerstones of the modern studio. *That's what the studios have become.* Making the movies is accomplished in a scatter of other places by production subcontractors like Revolution Studio (Joe Roth's company) linked to Sony Pictures, Icon Productions (Mel Gibson's company) linked to Paramount, and Jerry Bruckheimer Films linked to Walt Disney/Touchstone. Denise Mann, who co-heads UCLA's Producers' Program, tells me that there are about 1,750 production companies in and around Hollywood, and that 700 to 1,000 of them have deals with studios, TV studio production companies, cable networks, and other entities. (*The Hollywood Creative Directory* lays this out, cross-referenced by deal.)

Between the one-shot projects, directors, actors, and others are at liberty—meaning without a job or income (unless fortunate enough to have made a sweet multi-picture deal). Directors now have freedom from the restrictions placed on them by contracts: some, after all, had complained that the contracts put them into feudal bondage. However, they also now have the insecurity of temporary work that goes in tandem with their liberty. The numerous craft and skills guilds, such as the Directors Guild of America, the Screen Actors Guild, the Motion Picture Editors Guild, and the International Alliance of Theatrical Stage Employees (IATSE) are important in the downtimes between engagements, because the freelance workforce relies on them for continuity of health and pension benefit coverage.

The guilds are also a crucial instrument of collective bargaining for dispersed individuals vis-à-vis the powerful conglomerates. Compared to the Old Hollywood, there is no top dog with line authority to organize or assign creative people around projects. Thus, arranging film packages weirdly resembles maneuvering in a Middle Eastern street bazaar (floating crap game aside). Paradoxically, though finance and overall policy making take place globally through the multinationals, the production function of setting up movies occurs through local village-like personal contacts and informal networks. That is another way of describing the contorted deal-making process that directors decried in chapter 1.

Therefore, *fragmentation* is a third landmark we can use to map the industry. That includes ad hoc jobs and widely dispersed work sites.

Risky/Not Frisky

Everyone agrees that filmmaking is an economically uncertain undertaking that engenders enormous insecurity. There is no way to predict which films will make a bundle and which ones will bomb. William Goldman's Hollywood-inspired mantra, "Nobody knows

anything," has become an accepted doctrine in the industry. *Risky Business* is the title political scientist David Prindle gave his book that analyzes the political economy of Hollywood, and economist Arthur De Vany subtitles his recent book *How Extreme Uncertainty Shapes the Film Industry*.[6] De Vany shows that there is an only 0–4 percent return
on feature films at theaters and that just 6.3 percent of movies earned 80 percent of Hollywood's total profit over the past decade. He concludes that it's a winner-take-all setup.

This roulette wheel of a business involving colossal risks, costs, and gains results in
a revolving-door turnover of beleaguered studio executives. It also results in cautious
choices in the executive suites that rule out films that are venturesome, off the beaten
path, and potentially offensive to any slice of the moviegoing public. Modest movies
with small budgets, like *The Full Monty* and *Good Will Hunting*, have hit the jackpot,
while "sure" smashes, like *Pearl Harbor* and *Last Action Hero*, have hit the dust. And
history has shown that super-costly films that prove to be disastrous failures, such as
Heaven's Gate or *Cleopatra*, can kill an entire studio or put it in intensive care.

With the average cost of making a major film about $55 million (plus another $27
million for distribution) and top stars pulling down $20 million per feature, any mis-
calculation can be disastrous. With costs so high, studios have taken to making fewer
feature films. They also often do cost sharing with other studios and financiers to cushion the risks. But, on the upside, a box-office winner like *Titanic* scored a $601 million
gross, which led all the wobbly knees to do a jig when the $200 million blockbuster
first opened. And *Star Wars* came in at $451 million, after consuming about $10 million in production costs. You never can tell where the rainbow's pot of gold will be
found: *Blair Witch* cost only $100,000 to make but rolled up a $140 million return.

My colleagues in sociology have their own vernacular. They call a roller-coaster
situation like this a "turbulent environment."[7] Filmmaking is prototypical of that
kind of high-flying, low-dipping business enterprise with all of its casino-style chanci-
ness, its oil industry "boom or bust" volatility. Overall, most films disappoint in the
revenue they bring in, so the successful ones have to pay for the flops. Diversification
by going conglomerate is a way of balancing out the risks. So is the diligent exploitation of multiple vending venues through video and cable that extend beyond the
short lives of feature films in movie theaters.

The volatile environment generates a mentality of frozen caution and conven-
tionality, where successful parts of the past are repeated endlessly and executives
won't take a chance on the venturesome. Dorothy Parker was inspired to record in
verse her brush with this, for her, deadening milieu:

> Come grace this lotus-laden shore,
> This isle of do-what's-done-before.
> Come, curb the new, and watch the old win,
> Out where the streets are paved with Goldwyn.

Open Strong, and Damn the "Legs"
The high-risk environment is sparking ever more strident high-impact strategies. Historically, movies opened in a gradual pattern: first in large urban centers, then in

smaller cities and suburbs, and finally in rural locations. This long-established procedure changed dramatically in 1975 when *Jaws* opened in 409 theaters at once, grossing a jackpot, and beginning a new kind of distribution frenzy that was carried forward with flicks like *Return of the Jedi*, *Back to the Future*, and *Home Alone*. This
so-called saturation release marketing proceeded apace, with *Mission Impossible* breaking the 3,000-theater barrier in 1996.

The go-for-broke blockbuster approach has mushroomed in the past few years.
During the summer of 2001, studios dramatically upped the ante for opening weekend razzmatazz. The studios staged openings at megaplexes having multiple screens
that allowed 4,000 or 5,000 showings to erupt simultaneously. Everyone could get a
seat on the first weekend, with a wait of no more than a half-hour for anyone missing
a previous showing. This "front-loading" strategy resulted in gigantic ticket sales the
first weekend, followed by a plummeting of sales in equally gigantic proportions
the next.[8]

The gross for *Planet of the Apes* ($68.5 million) dived 60 percent after its opening
weekend, and *Jurassic Park III* fell 56 percent (from a $50.8 million gross). The aver-
age slide for blockbusters was about 50 percent as compared to a typical drop-off of 35
percent in prior years. Huge audiences were hopping from one blockbuster to another
in short spurts. The high-grossing films averaged about the same amount of money as
the hits of the previous year, but they made it in a shorter time interval, with lucrative results for the studios and headaches for the theater chains.

There's an underlying reason for this new way of introducing movies. For one
thing, you don't leave the uncertainties to the long run; you ratchet up your chances
in the short run. And you maximize all channels of immediate profit to the hilt. According to a time-sequenced scheme, the studios and the chains customarily split the
box-office take. Studios get a bigger percentage of the returns, about 70 to 80 percent
for the first weekend of blockbuster-type movies, dropping to about a 50/50 split over
time. Studios get more at the beginning to compensate for the high initial costs of
marketing the movie and manufacturing the film prints.

To the degree that studios bring in a bigger slice of the audience early, preferably
the first weekend, they pocket a greater proportion of the total profits for the film.
Counterwise, the theater chains, many of which are already operating under Chapter
11 of the U.S. Bankruptcy Code because of rapid overexpansion, dig themselves
deeper into a hole.

The studios, no longer having any use for long-running features with "legs," as
they once did, are on a campaign to narrow, more and more, the time window for
sweeping customers into the theaters. This means going after even more massive
audiences through increasingly gut-wrenching special effects, squeezing out of the
films anything that smacks of controversy or unfamiliarity, and generally accentu-
ating odious features of organized filmmaking that the directors in the survey found
objectionable. The oncoming movies are then promoted through supersaturated advertising in newspapers and magazines, on huge billboards, and in TV and radio
commercials. Stars are steered into appearing on the most-watched national network shows.

The *New York Times* noted on its editorial page on August 19, 2001, that democracy is becoming the supreme experience of seeing the same blockbuster movie the same weekend that everyone else in America sees it. *Editorial Notebook* writer Verlyn Klinkenborg believes that the age-old question of what is culture is being answered circularly: "Culture is to support the industry of culture. Entertainment is to support the industry of entertainment."[9]

That describes the fourth landmark, *a high-risk environment*, which is coupled with avoiding novelty or offense and unleashing bedazzling mass appeal movies.

What Makes You So Independent?

The Indie phenomenon wasn't around during the heyday of the studios. Studios did produce small B-movies on a regular basis, inexpensively made films that were often quirky and off-mainstream, but quality and seriousness were missing ingredients. The contemporary major studios, as we've noted, have become absorbed into huge corporations and typically mount a shrinking number of films that have astronomical budgets—sums that only their conglomerate sponsors have the wherewithal to finance. That leaves a hole in the film production spectrum that, together with the emergence of digital technology, partially explains the independent film movement. Digital methods of recording, storing, and transmitting visual data have bypassed traditional filmmaking and film processing and reduced the cost of making movies to the lower thousands. This has simplified the technology of making movies to the point that almost any neighborhood teenager or college sophomore can make a humble picture if so moved. From what I've seen, this is not a guarantee of film quality, but certainly of diversity and quantity. It leads to more options to choose from and to the probability of more good productions statistically emerging from the sheer volume of cinematic creations.

With the Sundance Institute as godfather, digital cameras as a tool, and film festivals as a distribution mechanism, the independent movement has become a serious force in the world of film. Sundance has as its mission the recruitment of young talent into creative filmmaking and the elevation of the art generally. Founded by Robert Redford in 1980 and based in Park City, Utah, Sundance offers training to aspiring independent filmmakers, drawing on leading personalities from the film world to lead seminars and workshops. It is a place where fledgling independent filmmakers can receive expert critique and modest funding for their works in progress.

Sundance sponsors the largest and most respected film festival in the Indie field, attracting filmmakers and distributors from far and wide. The festival, though, has been overwhelmed by the number of films that are being made and submitted by fresh talent, with the volume of submissions escalating dramatically each year. New film festival outlets for the Indies pop up regularly, though opportunities for widespread commercial distribution beyond are bottlenecked, except for all but a few aspirants and festival winners. That's because the major studios have close to a monopoly on what films get marketed and exhibited in the regular movie houses.

Old Hollywood was basically studios, with a tiny handful of isolated, iconoclastic souls like John Cassavetes marching to a different, and very distant, drummer. Cassavetes is acknowledged to have invented independent cinema virtually single-handedly when he came out with *Shadows* in 1960.[10] It took another decade or two for a more substantial Indie presence to make the scene.

Most independent filmmakers still function outside mainstream filmmaking, but talented people do move in and out across the two communities, and there is some— here's the word again—synergy. A Disney appendage like Miramax constitutes a hybrid form, and a Steven Soderbergh operates as a hybrid director. This contemporary Indie movement, growing in size and influence as a generator of some number of small films of quality and substance, serves as a cinematic conscience-prod to the larger film establishment.

So, a fifth landmark of modern Hollywood: *the existence of a parallel and vibrant independent film community.* It is a community in flux, with indistinct demarcations; therefore, it's hard to say exactly what it is and what it will become. But it's worth watching and nourishing.

Map Quest Accomplished

Based on interviews, observations, and reading other analysts, I would say those five landmarks are the core elements that describe the socio-structural environment of modern filmmaking. Certainly these characteristics are there to a greater or lesser extent in many other modern industries and businesses, but probably no other contains them in quite this same pattern and intensity.

As you may have noted, I didn't address how distant the Hollywood Planet is. That's something you can't pin down; Hollywood is a state of mind as much as it is geographical space. For a select few, it's a quick one hop away. For others, it requires a long and circuitous route to get there. Many have to make repeated return trips. And a lot never make it.

In my conversations, directors kept bringing up the question of "defining the Hollywood Beast." To them, like so many others, comprehending the film workplace is a distraction and a puzzle. I suppose they suggested an alternative metaphor I could have used for the mission of this chapter, bypassing the imagery of landmarks and substituting items of physiology—teeth, moles, hair color, and maybe DNA for describing the industry monster. But landmarks will do just as well—or better.

Other explorers setting out for the same space may have sighted additional landmarks or turned some of these aside as irrelevant. So be it. Explorers, after all, are individualistic, not to say eccentric, beings. Over time, accumulated sightings will produce an improved map. Meanwhile, I am not reluctant to recommend this one. If that causes you to get lost in Hollywood, alas, you won't be the first one. Nor the last.

Drop the Money and Run

Filmmaking is the only new art form of modern times, and it may be the most powerful and far-reaching art form of all times. Its development, I fear, is currently far too deep in the hands of avaricious commercial interests in Hollywood and in multinational corporations. The special power and excitement of film derives from the countless elements and talents that go into its fabrication, and that magnifies the cost of creating film. So the cinematic artist most often is dependent on providers of staggering sums to cover the expense—primarily studios and private financiers, although they also may be philanthropists, patrons, or friends and family.

The art of film, historically, has been locked into an embrace with large commercial organizations, whose fondness for the financial return is appreciably more than for the art. The popular throw-away phrase "It's only a movie" is an attitude accepted by all too many of the overseers of filmmaking, with its implied dismissal of aesthetic standards for appreciation or evaluation of the film product. These very people would disdain the words "It's only a symphony" or "It's only a novel" (I think a more exact analogy would be "It's only music" or "literature.")

Too many film critics contribute to that state of mind by letting their analytical sensibilities take a dive in the face of the morass of twaddle descending on them week after week. In his novel *Snow White*, Donald Barthelme brings out that when people live in a culture inundated by trash, after a time the question shifts from getting rid of all the rubbish to "appreciating its qualities . . . because it's all there is."[11] Certainly the great filmmakers of the past—from Griffith, to Eisenstein, to Renoir, to Fellini, to Satyajit Ray—who demonstrated through their craft what this medium could achieve, would decry from their graves the purging of artistic standards from film.

The digital revolution may just prove to be a way out of the dominating influence of big money. By driving down the cost of making and processing films and, eventually, their distribution, the way may be open for individual filmmakers and aficionados of the art to create film offerings relatively independently and relatively free from the overriding profit-accretion mentality.

There are many unknowns and blind alleys along that path, and also the practiced ability of the industry establishment to capture and co-opt whatever new directions arise. Still, many of the directors I interviewed voiced, with some passion, a hope for digital salvation. And I join them in that vision. Against all the awesome gravitational pulls, the planet may just somehow spin itself into a new orbit, or at least a big chunk of it might. So fortified, my fellow film lovers, let's not give up hope. Let's keep on turning to the movie page to see what brilliant new feature may be coming to the silver screen to astonish and transform us.

~

Appendix A: Directors' Credits

Awards and Nominations

List does not generally include TV series.

NANDI BOWE (1963, New York, New York)
One Flight Stand (2003) first assistant director
Funny Valentines (1999) (TV) first assistant director
Statistically Speaking (1995) director
Sister Act 2: Back in the Habit (1993) assistant director

SALVADOR CARRASCO (1967, Mexico City, Mexico)
La Otra Conquista (The Other Conquest) (1998) AFI Fest, nomination, Grand Jury Prize

GILBERT CATES (1934, New York, New York)
President, Directors Guild of America (DGA), 1983–1987
Dean, UCLA School of Theater, Film, and Television, 1990–1997
DGA Honorary Life Achievement Award, 1991
DGA Robert E. Aldrich Achievement Award, 1989
A Death in the Family (2002) (TV)
Collected Stories (2002) (TV)
Innocent Victims (1996) (TV)

Confessions: Two Faces of Evil (1994) (TV)
Absolute Strangers (1991) (TV) Emmy Award, nomination, Outstanding Directing in a Miniseries or a Special
Call Me Anna (1990) (TV) DGA Award, nomination, Outstanding Directorial Achievement in Dramatic Specials
Do You Know the Muffin Man? (1989) (TV)
My First Love (1988) (TV)
Fatal Judgement (1988) (TV)
Backfire (1987)
Child's Cry (1986) (TV)
Consenting Adult (1985) (TV)
Burning Rage (1984) (TV)
Hobson's Choice (1983) (TV)
Country Gold (1982) (TV)
The Last Married Couple in America (1980)
Oh, God! Book II (1980)
The Promise (1979)
Johnny, We Hardly Knew Ye (1977) (TV)
Dragonfly (1976)
After the Fall (1974) (TV)
The Affair (1973) (TV)
Summer Wishes, Winter Dreams (1973)
To All My Friends on Shore (1972) (TV)
I Never Sang for My Father (1970)
Rings Around the World (1966)
Also Emmy Award for Annual Academy Awards, 1991; Emmy Award, nominations, Academy Award Specials, 1993, 1994, 1995, 1997, 1998, 1999, 2001, 2003

MARTHA COOLIDGE (1946, New Haven, Connecticut)
First Woman President DGA, 2002–2003
DGA, Robert B. Aldridge Award, 1998
Women in Film, Crystal Award, 1992
The Prince and Me (2004)
The Ponder Heart (2001) (TV)
The Flamingo Rising (2001) (TV)
If These Walls Could Talk (2000) (TV) DGA Award, nomination, Outstanding Directorial Achievement for Movies in Television
Introducing Dorothy Dandridge (1999) (TV) Emmy Award, nomination, Outstanding Directing for a Miniseries, Movie or a Special; DGA Award, nomination, Outstanding Directorial Achievement for Movies for Television
Out to Sea (1997)
Three Wishes (1995)
Angie (1994)
Lost in Yonkers (1993)
Crazy in Love (1992) (TV)
Rambling Rose (1991) Independent Spirit Award, Best Director
Bare Essentials (1991) (TV)
Trenchcoat in Paradise (1989) (TV)
Plain Clothes (1988)
Real Genius (1985) Paris Film Festival, Grand Prix
Joy of Sex (1984)
City Girl (1984)
Valley Girl (1983)
Bimbo (1978)
Employment Discrimination: The Troubleshooters (1976)
Not a Pretty Picture (1975)
More Than a School (1974)
Old-Fashioned Woman (1974)
David: Off and On (1972)

CHRISTOPHER COPPOLA (1962, Los Angeles County, California)
Bloodhead (2003)
Bel Air (2000)
G-Men from Hell (2000)
Palmer's Pick Up (1999)
Gunfighter (1998)
Deadfall (1993)
Gunfight at Red Dog Corral (1993)
Dracula's Widow (1989)

JOE DANTE (1946, Morristown, New Jersey)
Chicago Film Festival, American Treasure Award, Emerging Artist Award, 2000
Locarno International Film Festival, Leopard of Honor, 1998
Looney Tunes: Back in Action (2003)
Haunted Lighthouse (2003)
Small Soldiers (1998) Catalonian International Film Festival, nomination, Best Film
The Warlord: Battle for the Galaxy (1998) (TV)
The Second Civil War (1997) (TV) Biarritz International Festival of Audiovisual Programming, Golden FIPA Award
Runaway Daughters (1994) (TV)
Matinee (1993) Brussels International Festival of Fantasy Film, Silver Raven Award
Gremlins 2: The New Batch (1990)
The "Burbs" (1989)
Innerspace (1987)
Explorers (1985)
Gremlins (1984) Academy of Science Fiction, Fantasy and Horror Films, Saturn Award
Twilight Zone: The Movie (1983) Fantasporto, nomination, International Fantasy Film Award, Best Film
The Howling (1981)
Rock 'n' Roll High School (1979) (uncredited)
Piranha (1978) Academy of Science Fiction, Fantasy and Horror Films, Saturn Award, Best Editing
Hollywood Boulevard (1976)
The Movie Orgy (1968)

JULIE DASH (1952, Long Island City, New York)
Maya Deren Independent Film and Video Artists Award, 1993
The Rosa Parks Story (2002) (TV) DGA, nomination, Outstanding Directorial Achievement in Movies for Television; Black Reel Award, nomination, Network/Cable, Best Director
Love Song (2000) (TV) Black Reel Award, nomination, Network/Cable, Best Director
Incognito (1999) (TV)
Funny Valentines (1999) (TV) Black Reel Award, nomination, Network Cable, Best Director

Praise House (1991)
Daughters of the Dust (1991) Sundance Film
    Festival, nomination, Grand Jury Prize,
    Dramatic
Illusions (1982)
Diary of an African Nun (1977)
Four Women (1975)
Working Models of Success (1973)

ANDREW DAVIS (1947, Chicago, Illinois)

Holes (2003)
Collateral Damage (2002)
A Perfect Murder (1998)
Chain Reaction (1996)
Steal Big, Steal Little (1995)
The Fugitive (1993) DGA, nomination,
    Outstanding Directorial Achievement in
    Motion Pictures; Golden Globes,
    nomination, Best Director, Motion
    Picture
Under Siege (1992)
The Package (1989)
Above the Law (1988)
Code of Silence (1985)
The Final Terror (1983)

BILL DUKE (1943, Poughkeepsie, New York)

Acapulco Black Film Festival, Career
    Achievement Award, 1997
Deacons for Defense (2003) (TV)
Angel: One More Road to Cross (2001)
    (Video)
The Golden Spiders: A Nero Wolfe Mystery
    (2000) (TV)
Hoodlum (1997) Acapulco Black Film
    Festival, nomination, Best Director
America's Dream (1997) (TV)
Sister Act 2: Back in the Habit (1993)
The Cemetery Club (1993)
Deep Cover (1992)
A Rage in Harlem (1991) Cannes Film
    Festival, nomination, Golden Palm
A Raisin in the Sun (1989) (TV)
Flag (1986)
Johnnie Mae Gibson: FBI (1986) (TV)
The Killing Floor (1985) (TV) Sundance
    Film Festival, Special Jury Prize,
    Dramatic, Nomination, Grand Jury Prize,
    Dramatic

GARY FLEDER (1965, Norfolk, Virginia)

Runaway Jury (2003)
Imposter (2002) *Fantasporto, nomination,*
    International Fantasy Film Award, Best Film
Don't Say a Word (2001)
Kiss the Girls (1997)
Things to Do in Denver When You're Dead
    (1995) Cognac Festival du Film Policier,
    Special Jury Prize, Critics Award
The Companion (1994) (TV)
Air Time (1992) (TV)

BOB GALE (1951, University City, Missouri)

St. Louis International Film Festival, Lifetime
    Achievement Award, 2001
Interstate 60 (2002) DVD Exclusive Awards,
    DVDX Award, Best Live Action DVD
    Premiere Movie, and nomination, Best
    Director of a DVD Premiere Movie
Mr. Payback: An Interactive Movie (1995)
The Discovery (1973)
The Annihilator Attacks (1972)
Also *Back to the Future* (1986) Writers Guild
    of America, nomination, Best Screenplay
    Written Directly for the Screen, shared
    with Robert Zemeckis; film nominated for
    Academy Award for Best Screenwriting;
    Golden Globes, nomination, Best
    Screenplay, Motion Picture.

MONTE HELLMAN (1932, New York, New York)

Silent Night, Deadly Night 3: Better Watch
    Out! (1989)
Iguana (1988)
Inside the Coppola Personality (1981)
Avalanche Express (1979)
China 9, Liberty 37 (1978)
The Greatest (1977)
Baretta (1975) (TV)
Shatter (1974) (uncredited)
Cockfighter/Born To Kill (1974) Venice
    International Film Festival, Film Award
Two-Lane Blacktop (1971)
The Shooting (1967)
Ride in the Whirlwind (1965)
Back Door to Hell (1964)
Flight to Fury (1964)
The Terror (1963) (uncredited)
Beast from Haunted Cave (1960)

GEORGE HICKENLOOPER (1965, St. Louis, Missouri)

Author *Reel Conversation: Candid Interviews with Film's Foremost Directors and Critics*, New York: Citadel Press, 1991

Mayor of Sunset Strip (2003) Independent Spirit Awards, nomination, Independent Spirit Award, Best Documentary.

The Man from Elysian Fields (2001)

The Big Brass Ring (1999) Edgar Allan Poe Awards, nomination, Edgar Award, Best Television Feature or Miniseries; Newport International Film Festival, nomination, Jury Award, Best Film

Dogtown (1997) Newport Beach Film Festival, Best Director; Hermosa Beach Film Festival, Best Director, Best Screenplay

Monte Hellman: America Auteur (1997)

Persons Unknown (1996)

The Low Life (1995)

Some Folks Call It a Slingblade (1994) Aspen Shortsfest, Best Short Film

The Killing Box (1993)

Picture This: The Times of Peter Bogdanovich in Archer City, Texas (1991)

Hearts of Darkness: A Filmmaker's Apocalypse (1991) DGA Award, nomination, Outstanding Directorial Achievement in Documentary; Emmy Award, Outstanding Individual Achievement—Informational Programming—Directing (also nomination, for writing)

Art, Acting, and the Suicide Chair: Dennis Hopper (1988) (TV)

WALTER HILL (1942, Long Beach, California)

The Prophecy (2002) (Video)

Undisputed (2002)

Supernova (2000) (as Thomas Lee)

Last Man Standing (1996)

Wild Bill (1995)

Geronimo: An American Legend (1993) Western Heritage Awards, Bronze Wrangler Award, Theatrical Motion Picture

Trespass (1992)

Another 48 Hrs. (1990)

Johnny Handsome (1989)

Red Heat (1988)

Extreme Prejudice (1987)

Crossroads (1986)

Brewster's Millions (1985)

Streets of Fire (1984)

48 Hrs. (1982) Edgar Allan Poe Awards, nomination, Edgar Award, Best Motion Picture; Cognac Festival du Film Policier, Grand Prix.

Southern Comfort (1981)

The Long Riders (1980) Cannes Film Festival, Golden Palm Award, nomination

The Warriors (1979)

The Driver (1978)

Hard Times (1975)

ARTHUR HILLER (1923, Edmonton, Alberta, Canada)

Jean Hersholt Humanitarian Award, Academy Award, 2002

Santa Clarita International Film Festival, Lifetime Achievement Award, 2001

DGA, Robert B. Aldrich Achievement Award, 1999

President, Academy of Motion Picture Arts and Sciences, 1996–1998

President, DGA, 1989–1993

DGA Honorary Life Member award, 1993

An Alan Smithee Film: Burn Hollywood Burn (1997) (as Alan Smithee)

Carpool (1996)

The Babe (1992)

Married to It (1991)

Taking Care of Business (1990)

See No Evil, Hear No Evil (1989)

Outrageous Fortune (1987)

Teachers (1984)

The Lonely Guy (1984)

Romantic Comedy (1983)

Author! Author! (1982)

Making Love (1982)

Nightwing (1979)

The In-Laws (1979)

Silver Streak (1976)

W.C. Fields and Me (1976)

The Man in the Glass Booth (1975)

The Crazy World of Julius Vrooder (1974)

Man of La Mancha (1972)

The Hospital (1971) Berlin International Film Festival, Special Jury Prize, OCIC Award, nomination, Golden Berlin Bear Award

Plaza Suite (1971)

Love Story (1970) Academy Award,
    nomination, Best Director; Golden
    Globes, Best Motion Picture Director
The Out-of-Towners (1970)
Popi (1969)
The Tiger Makes Out (1967)
Tobruk (1967)
Penelope (1966)
Promise Her Anything (1965)
The Americanization of Emily (1964)
The Wheeler Dealers (1963)
Miracle of the White Stallions (1963)
This Rugged Land (1962)
The Careless Years (1957)
Massacre at Sand Creek (1956)

TIM HUNTER
Control (2004)
The Failures (2003)
Video Voyeur: The Susan Wilson Story (2002)
    (TV)
Anatomy of a Hate Crime (2001) (TV)
Mean Streak (1999) (TV)
The Maker (1997)
The People Next Door (1996) (TV)
The Colony (1996) (TV)
The Saint of Fort Washington (1993)
Lies of the Twins (1991) (TV)
Beverly Hills 90210 (1990) (TV)
Paint It Black (1989)
River's Edge (1986) Sundance Film Festival,
    nomination, Grand Jury Prize, Dramatic;
    Independent Spirit Awards, nomination,
    Best Director
Sylvester (1985)
Tex (1982)

HENRY JAGLOM (1941, London, England)
Method Fest, Lifetime Achievement Award,
    1999
Going Shopping (2004)
Festival in Cannes (2001)
Déjà Vu (1997) AFI Fest, nomination, Grand
    Jury Prize
Last Summer in the Hamptons (1995)
Babyfever (1994)
Lucky Ducks (1993)
Venice/Venice (1992)
Eating (1990) Deauville Film Festival,
    nomination, Critics Award

New Year's Day (1989)
Someone to Love (1987)
Always (1985)
Can She Bake a Cherry Pie? (1983)
National Lampoon Goes to the Movies (1981)
Sitting Ducks (1980)
Tracks (1976)
A Safe Place (1971)

JONATHAN KAPLAN (1947, Paris, France)
Brokedown Palace (1999)
"ER" Emmy Award, nominations,
    Outstanding Directing for a Drama Series,
    1999, 2000, 2001
In Cold Blood (1996) (TV)
Reform School Girl (1994) (TV)
Bad Girls (1994)
Love Field (1992) Berlin International Film
    Festival, nomination, Golden Berlin Bear
Unlawful Entry (1992)
Immediate Family (1989)
The Accused (1988) Berlin International Film
    Festival, nomination, Golden Berlin Bear
Project X (1987)
Girls of the White Orchid (1983) (TV)
Heart Like a Wheel (1983)
The Gentleman Bandit (1981) (TV)
The Hustler of Muscle Beach (1980) (TV)
Over the Edge (1979)
11th Victim (1979) (TV)
Mr. Billion (1977)
White Line Fever (1975)
Truck Turner (1974)
The Slams (1973)
The Student Teachers (1973)
Night Call Nurses (1972)

IRVIN KERSHNER (1923, Philadelphia, Pennsylvania)
Ft. Lauderdale International Film Festival,
    President Award, Director of Distinction,
    2002
SeaQuest DSV (1993) (TV)
Robocop 2 (1990)
Traveling Man (1989) (TV)
Never Say Never Again (1983)
*Star Wars: Episode V—The Empire Strikes
    Back* (1980) Saturn Award, Best Director,
    Academy of Science Fiction, Fantasy, and
    Horror Films

Eyes of Laura Mars (1978)
Raid on Entebbe (1977) (TV) Emmy Award,
    nomination, Outstanding Directing in a
    Special Program—Drama or Comedy
The Return of a Man Called Horse (1976)
S*P*Y*S (1974)
Up the Sandbox (1972)
Loving (1970)
The Flim-Flam Man (1967)
A Fine Madness (1966)
The Luck of Ginger Coffey (1964)
Face in the Rain (1963)
Hoodlum Priest (1961) Cannes Film Festival,
    OCIC Award; Golden Palm Award,
    nomination
The Young Captives (1959)
Stakeout on Dope Street (1958)

**RANDAL KLEISER (1946, Philadelphia,
    Pennsylvania)**
Murder on the Hudson (2004)
The O.Z. (2002) (TV)
Royal Standard (1999) (TV)
Shadow of Doubt (1998)
It's My Party (1996)
Honey, I Shrunk the Audience (1995)
    (uncredited)
Honey, I Blew Up the Kid (1992)
White Fang (1991)
Getting It Right (1989)
Big Top Pee-wee (1988)
Flight of the Navigator (1986)
Grandview, U.S.A. (1984)
Summer Lovers (1982)
The Blue Lagoon (1980)
Grease (1978)
Portrait of Grandpa Doc (1977)
The Gathering (1977) (TV) Emmy,
    nomination, Outstanding Directing in a
    Special Program—Drama or Comedy
The Boy in the Plastic Bubble (1976) (TV)
Dawn: Portrait of a Teenage Runaway (1976)
    (TV)
All Together Now (1975) (TV)
Peege (1972)

JOHN LANDIS (1950, Chicago, Illinois)
Slasher (2004) (TV)
Susan's Plan (1998)
Blues Brothers 2000 (1998)
The Stupids (1996)

HIStory (1994) (Video)
Beverly Hills Cop III (1994)
Innocent Blood (1992)
Black or White (1991) (Video)
Oscar (1991)
Coming to America (1988)
Three Amigos (1986)
Spies Like Us (1985)
Disneyland's 30th Anniversary Celebration
    (1985) (TV)
Into the Night (1985) Cognac Festival du Film
    Policier, Special Jury Prize
*Michael Jackson: Making Michael Jackson's
    'Thriller'* (1983) (Video)
Thriller (1983) (Video)
Twilight Zone: The Movie (1983) Fantasporto,
    International Fantasy Film Award,
    nomination, Best Film
Trading Places (1983)
Coming Soon (1982) (Video)
An American Werewolf in London (1981)
The Blues Brothers (1980)
Animal House (1978)
The Kentucky Fried Movie (1977)
Schlock (1973) Fantafestival, Best Film

**DELBERT MANN (1920, Lawrence,
    Kansas)**
President, DGA, 1967–1971
DGA Honorary Life Member Award, 2002
DGA Robert B. Aldridge Achievement
    Award, 1997
Lily in Winter (1994) (TV)
Incident in a Small Town (1994) (TV)
Against Her Will: An Incident in Baltimore
    (1992) (TV)
Ironclads (1991) (TV)
April Morning (1988) (TV)
The Last Days of Patton (1986) (TV)
The Ted Kennedy, Jr. Story (1986) (TV)
A Death in California (1985) (TV)
Love Leads the Way (1984) (TV)
Brontë (1983)
The Gift of Love: A Christmas Story (1983)
    (TV)
The Member of the Wedding (1982) (TV)
    DGA Award, nomination, Outstanding
    Directorial Achievement in Dramatic
    Specials
Night Crossing (1981)
All the Way Home (1981) (TV)

To Find My Son (1980) (TV)
All Quiet on the Western Front (1979) (TV)
  Emmy Award, nomination, Outstanding
  Directing in a Limited Series or Special
Torn Between Two Lovers (1979) (TV)
Thou Shalt Not Commit Adultery (1978)
  (TV)
Tom and Joann (1978) (TV)
Home to Stay (1978) (TV)
Love's Dark Ride (1978)
Breaking Up (1978) (TV) Emmy Award,
  nomination, Outstanding Directing in a
  Special Program—Drama or Comedy
Birch Interval (1977)
Tell Me My Name (1977) (TV)
*Francis Gary Powers: The True Story of the U-
  2 Spy Incident* (1976) (TV)
A Girl Named Sooner (1975) (TV)
The Man Without a Country (1973) (TV)
No Place to Run (1972) (TV)
She Waits (1972) (TV)
Kidnapped (1971)
Jane Eyre (1970) DGA Award, nomination,
  Outstanding Directorial Achievement in
  Specials
David Copperfield (1969) (TV)
Heidi (1968) (TV)
The Pink Jungle (1968)
Fitzwilly (1967)
Mister Buddwing (1966)
Dear Heart (1964)
Quick Before It Melts (1964)
A Gathering of Eagles (1963)
That Touch of Mink (1962)
The Outsider (1962)
Lover Come Back (1961)
The Dark at the Top of the Stairs (1960) DGA
  Award, nomination, Outstanding
  Directorial Achievement in Motion
  Pictures
Middle of the Night (1959)
Separate Tables (1958)
Desire Under the Elms (1958)
The Bachelor Party (1957)
Marty (1955) Academy Award; DGA Award,
  Outstanding Directorial Achievement in
  Motion Pictures; Cannes Film Festival,
  Golden Palm Award, OCIC Award
Marty (1953) (TV)
Also *Goodyear Television Playhouse* and *Philco
  Television Playhouse* (multiple episodes)

NANCY MEYERS (1949, Pennsylvania)
Something's Gotta Give (2003)
What Women Want (2000)
The Parent Trap (1998)
Also *Private Benjamin* (1980) Academy
  Award, nomination, Best Writing,
  Screenplay Written Directly for the
  Screen; Writers Guild of America, Best
  Comedy Written Directly for the Screen

**ROBERT ELLIS MILLER (1932, New
  York, New York)**
Angel of Pennsylvania Avenue (1996)
A Walton Wedding (1995) (TV)
Pointman (1994) (TV)
Killer Rules (1993) (TV)
Bed and Breakfast (1992)
Brenda Starr (1989)
Hawks (1988)
Intimate Strangers (1986) (TV)
The Other Lover (1985) (TV)
Her Life as a Man (1984) (TV)
Reuben, Reuben (1983)
Madame X (1981) (TV)
Rough Cut (1980) (uncredited)
The Baltimore Bullet (1980)
Ishi: The Last of His Tribe (1978) (TV)
Just an Old Sweet Song (1976) (TV)
The Girl from Petrovka (1974)
The Buttercup Chain (1970) Cannes Film
  Festival, nomination, Golden Palm Award
The Heart is a Lonely Hunter (1968)
Sweet November (1968)
Any Wednesday (1966)

SYLVIA MORALES (Phoenix, Arizona)
Resurrection Blvd. (1999–2001) (TV)
La Limpia (1995) (TV)
A Century of Women (1994) (TV)

**DANIEL PETRIE (1920, Glace Bay, Nova
  Scotia, Canada)**
DGA Robert B. Aldridge Achievement
  Award, 1996
Wild Iris (2001) (TV)
Walter and Henry (2001) (TV) DGA Award,
  nomination, Outstanding Directorial
  Achievement in Children's Programs
Inherit the Wind (1999) (TV) DGA Award,
  nomination, Outstanding Directorial
  Achievement in Movies for Television

Monday After the Miracle (1998) (TV)
The Assistant (1997)
Calm at Sunset (1996) (TV)
Kissinger and Nixon (1995) (TV) DGA
    Award, nomination, Outstanding
    Directorial Achievement in Dramatic
    Specials
Lassie (1994)
A Town Torn Apart (1992) (TV) Emmy
    Award, nomination, Outstanding
    Individual Achievement in Directing for a
    Miniseries or a Special
Mark Twain and Me (1991) (TV) Emmy
    Award, Outstanding Children's Program
My Name is Bill W. (1989) (TV) DGA
    Award, nomination, Outstanding
    Directorial Achievement in Dramatic
    Specials; Emmy Award, nomination,
    Outstanding Drama/Comedy Special
Cocoon: The Return (1988)
Rocket Gibraltar (1988)
Square Dance (1987)
Half a Lifetime (1986) (TV)
The Execution of Raymond Graham (1985)
    (TV)
The Bad Boy (1984)
The Dollmaker (1984) (TV) DGA Award,
    Outstanding Directorial Achievement in
    Dramatic Specials
Six Pack (1982)
Fort Apache the Bronx (1981)
Resurrection (1980)
The Betsy (1978)
The Quinns (1977) (TV)
Eleanor and Franklin: The White House Years
    (1977) (TV) DGA Award, Outstanding
    Directorial Achievement in Specials;
    Emmy Award, Outstanding Direction in a
    Special Program—Drama or Comedy
Lifeguard (1976)
Sybil (1976) (TV)
Harry S. Truman: Plain Speaking (1976) (TV)
Eleanor and Franklin (1976) (TV) DGA
    Award, Outstanding Directorial
    Achievement in Specials; Emmy Award,
    Outstanding Directing in a Special
    Program—Drama or Comedy
Returning Home (1975) (TV)
Buster and Billie (1974)
The Gun and the Pulpit (1974) (TV)
Mousey (1974) (TV)

The Neptune Factor (1973)
Trouble Comes to Town (1973) (TV)
Hec Ramsey (1972) (TV)
Moon of the Wolf (1972) (TV)
Big Fish, Little Fish (1971) (TV)
A Howling in the Woods (1971) (TV)
The Man and the City (1971) (TV), DGA
    Award, Outstanding Directorial
    Achievement in Dramatic Series
Silent Night, Lonely Night (1969) (TV)
The Spy With a Cold Nose (1966)
The Idol (1966)
Stolen Hours (1963)
The Main Attraction (1962)
A Raisin in the Sun (1961) Cannes Film
    Festival, nomination, Golden Palm
    Award, Gary Cooper Award; DGA
    Award, nomination, Outstanding
    Directorial Achievement in Motion
    Pictures
The Bramble Bush (1960)
The Cherry Orchard (1959) (TV)
Also Studio One (TV) (multiple episodes)

MYRL A. SCHREIBMAN (1945, Cleveland, Ohio)

Liberty and Bash (1990)
Hunters' Blood (1987) (Producer)
Angel of H.E.A.T. (1982)

MICHAEL SCHULTZ (1938, Milwaukee, Wisconsin)

L.A. Law: The Movie (2002)
The Adventures of Young Indiana Jones: Tales
    of Innocence (1999) (Video)
My Last Love (1999) (TV)
Killers in the House (1998) (TV)
Young Indiana Jones: Travels with Father
    (1996) (TV)
Shock Treatment (1995) (TV)
Young Indiana Jones and the Hollywood Follies
    (1994) (TV)
Livin' Large! (1991)
Hammer, Slammer, & Slade (1990) (TV)
Jury Duty: The Comedy (1990) (TV)
Tarzan in Manhattan (1989) (TV)
Rock 'n' Roll Mom (1988) (TV)
Disorderlies (1987)
The Spirit (1987) (TV)
Timestalkers (1987) (TV)
Krush Grove (1985)

The Last Dragon (1985)
The Jerk, Too (1984) (TV)
For Us the Living: The Medgar Evers Story (1983) (TV)
Benny's Place (1982) (TV)
Carbon Copy (1981)
Bustin' Loose (1981) (uncredited)
Scavenger Hunt (1979)
Sgt. Pepper's Lonely Hearts Club Band (1978)
Which Way Is Up? (1977)
Greased Lightning (1977)
Car Wash (1976) Cannes Film Festival, Golden Palm Award, nomination; Technical Grand Prize
Cooley High (1975)
Honeybaby, Honeybaby (1974)
To Be Young, Gifted, and Black (1972) (TV)
Together for Days (1972)
Also Tony Award, nomination for directing, *Does a Tiger Wear a Necktie?* (1969)

KRISHNA SHAH

American Drive-In (1985)
Hard Rock Zombies (1984)
Cinema Cinema (1979)
Shalimar (1978)
The River Niger (1976)
Rivals (1972)
Also, *The Prince of Light* (2000) Santa Clarita International Film Festival, Best Animation, Writing

CHARLES SHYER (1941, Los Angeles, California)

What's It All About Alfie (2004)
The Affair of the Necklace (2001)
Father of the Bride Part II (1995)
I Love Trouble (1994)
Father of the Bride (1991)
Baby Boom (1987)

Irreconcilable Differences (1984)
Also *Private Benjamin* (1980), Academy Award, nomination, Best Writing, Screen Play Written Directly for the Screen; Writers Guild of America, Best Comedy Written Directly for the Screen; *House Calls* (1978) Writers Guild of America, nomination, Best Comedy Written Directly for the Screen

ELLIOT SILVERSTEIN (1927, Boston, Massachusetts)

DGA Honorary Life Member Award, 1990
DGA Robert B. Aldridge Achievement Award, 1985
Flashfire (1993)
Rich Men, Single Women (1990) (TV)
Fight for Life (1987) (TV)
Night of Courage (1987) (TV)
Betrayed by Innocence (1986) (TV)
The Car (1977)
Nightmare Honeymoon (1973)
A Man Called Horse (1970)
The Happening (1967)
Cat Ballou (1965) DGA Award, nomination, Outstanding Directorial Achievement in Motion Pictures
Belle Sommers (1962) (TV)

SANDY TUNG (1950, Staten Island, New York)

Soccer Dog: European Cup (2004)
Shiloh 2: Shiloh Season (1999)
Confessions of a Sexist Pig (1998) New Orleans Film Festival, Judge's Award; International Filmfest Mannheim-Heidelberg, Special Prize in Memoriam—R.W. Fassbinder
Across the Tracks (1991)
A Marriage (1983)

~

Appendix B: Supplementary Interviews and Information

Actors—Robin Bartlett, Frances Bay, Alan Blumenfeld, Tom Bosley, Tom Bower, Judy Brown, Charles Durning, Raymond Forchion, Joanna Gleason, Ann-Marie Johnson, Val Lopez, Richard Masur, George McDaniel, Leonard Nimoy, Edward James Olmos, Suzanne Pleshette, Valerie Red-Horse, Edger Small, Rod Steiger, George Takei, Barbara Whinnery.

UCLA Faculty and Staff—Nicholas Browne, Jeffrey Cole, Lewis Hunter, Denise Mann, Teri Bond Michael, Chon Noriega, Howard Suber.

Directors Guild of America—Gina Blumenfeld, Ted Elrich, Allison Holmes, Andy Levy, Charles Warn.

Screen Actors Guild—Rudy Lopez, Patricia Metoyer, Marcia Smith, Bart Story, Valerie Yaros.

Film Industry Professionals—Sandy Bresler (agent), Debbie Klein (agent), Gershom Clark Morningstar (film newsletter editor and producer), Judith Moss (agent), Howard Parad (psychotherapist to the industry), Jordan Roberts (screenwriter), Fred Roos (producer).

I also received valuable assistance from librarians at the Academy of Motion Picture Arts and Science, the film library at the University of Southern California, and the Arts (and Film) Library at the University of California, Los Angeles—especially from Head Reference Librarian Lisa D. Kernan.

For consultation and editorial assistance on the manuscript I am indebted to R. Scott Penza (Creative Hive), Barbara Marinacci (The Bookmill), Gersh Morningstar (*Florida Blue Sheet*), Ted Elrich (*DSA Magazine*), and my wife, Judith Rothman.

My fervent thanks to these wonderful, helpful people and to all of my other many encouragers and collaborators, in larger and lesser capacities, who make a work such as this possible.

~

Notes

Preview

1. David Shaw, "Lights, Camera, Action—How the News Media Cover Hollywood," *Los Angeles Times*, Four-Part Series, 12–15 February 2001.

2. Peter Bart admitted in a magazine interview to hawking his script. See Amy Wallace, "Is This the Most Hated Man in Hollywood?" *Los Angeles Magazine* (September 2001): 98–107, 177–83. Some books portraying mendacity in filmland include Lynda Rosen Obst, *Hello, He Lied: And Other Truths From the Hollywood Trenches* (Boston: Little, Brown, 1996); William Goldman, *Which Lie Did I Tell?: More Adventures in the Screen Trade* (New York: Pantheon Books, 2000); Julia Phillips, *You'll Never Eat Lunch in This Town Again* (New York: Random House, 1991); and Peter Bart, *The Gross: The Summer That Ate Hollywood* (New York: St. Martin's Press, 1999) and *Dangerous Company: Dark Tales From Tinseltown* (New York: Hyperion/Miramax Books, 2003).

3. Specifics of these substantial treatments of filmmaking are as follows: Robert Sklar, *Movie-Made America: A Cultural History of American Movies* (New York: Vintage Books, 1994); Neal Gabler, *An Empire of Their Own: How the Jews Invented Hollywood* (New York: Doubleday, 1989); Emanuel Levy, *Small-town America in Film: The Decline and Fall of Community* (New York: Continuum, 1991); Andrew Sarris, *You Ain't Heard Nothin' Yet: The American Talking Film, History and Memory, 1927–1949* (New York: Oxford University Press, 1998); Richard Schickel, *Matinee Idylls: Reflections on the Movies* (Chicago: Ivan R. Dee, 1999); J. Hoberman, *The Dream Life: Movies, Media, and the Mythology of the Sixties* (New York: New Press, 2003).

4. Hortense Powdermaker, *Hollywood: The Dream Factory: An Anthropologist Looks at the Movie-Makers* (Boston: Little, Brown, 1950).

5. This study is exploratory and in the mode of what typically is called qualitative or ethnographic research. See Norman K. Denzin and Yvonna S. Lincoln, eds., *Handbook of Qualitative Research* (Thousand Oaks, CA: Sage, 2000); Scott Grills, ed., *Doing Ethnographic Research: Fieldwork Settings* (Thousand Oaks, CA: Sage, 1998).

6. The Projections series of interviews of filmmakers has some twelve volumes. See, for example, John Boorman and Walter Donohue, *Film-makers on Film-making* (London: Boston: Faber and Faber, 1995).

7. C. Wright Mills, *The Sociological Imagination* (New York: Grove Press, 1959).

Chapter 1

1. Elia Kazan, "On What Makes a Director," in *Directors Close Up: Interviews With Directors Nominated for Best Film by the Directors Guild of America*, ed. Jeremy Kagan (Boston: Focal Press, 2000), 241–53. (Quote is on page 252).

2. Robert King Merton, *Social Theory and Social Structure* (New York: Free Press, 1968). Talcott Parsons is another major contributor to functional/structural theory. See his book, *Sociological Theory and Modern Society* (New York: Free Press, 1967).

3. Philosopher/social scientist Theodor Adorno locates the machinery of Hollywood within the "culture industry," an instrumentality used by capitalist elites to keep the citizenry sedated and politically passive. Accordingly, the popular culture is inundated with status-quo-supporting pap, rather than "true art." Theodor W. Adorno, *The Culture Industry: Selected Essays on Mass Culture* (London: Routledge, 1991). A revisionist Marxist, Adorno sees the critical levers of control over society shifting from the economic to the cultural realm.

4. In his book *Reel Power: The Struggle for Influence and Success in the New Hollywood* (New York: Plume, 1986), Mark Litwak endorses these comments about the slippery character of test marketing, quoting director George Roy Hill (*Butch Cassidy and the Sundance Kid*) telling how he stuffed a lobby polling box with preview cards he himself filled out to win a dispute with his producer over a sequence in a film (page 235). The mainstream business world is not exempt from erroneous test marketing and strategic planning methods. A classic statement on this is in Thomas L. Berg, "Autopsies of Marketing Failures," in Taylor W. Meloan and Charles M. Whitlo, eds., *Competition in Marketing* (Los Angeles: University of Southern California School of Business Administration, 1964), 180–203. Also see Kevin J. Clancy, *Marketing Myths That Are Killing Business: The Cure for Death Wish Marketing* (New York: McGraw-Hill, 1994).

5. Thomas Schatz, *The Genius of the System: Hollywood Filmmaking in the Studio Era* (New York: Henry Holt, 1996), 491–92.

6. Peter Biskind, *Easy Riders, Raging Bulls: How the Sex-Drugs-And-Rock 'N' Roll Generation Saved Hollywood* (New York: Touchstone Books, 1998).

7. The U.S. Commerce Department documents that the negative impact of runaway productions on the economy was 10.3 billion in 1998, a five-fold increase over runaway effects in 1990. *The Migration of U.S. Film and Television Production: Impact of "Runaways" on Workers and Small Business in the U.S. Film Industry* (Washington, DC: U.S. Department of Commerce, 2001). In a poll of members, sponsored by the Directors Guild of America and Screen Actors Guild and conducted by the Monitor Company, runaway production was named by members of both guilds as the most serious problem facing the entertainment industry. *The Economic Impact of U.S. Film and Television Runaway Production* (Santa Monica: Monitor, June 1999).

8. Nathanael West, *The Day of the Locust* (New York: New American Library, 1983); Carey McWilliams, *Southern California: An Island on the Land* (Salt Lake City: Perigrine Smith, 1946); Hortense Powdermaker, *Hollywood: The Dream Factory*.

9. Kenneth Turan writes of the declining commitment of directors to the art in his column "Frailty, Thy Name Is Director," *Los Angeles Times*, 9 April 2000, Section 7, 33–35. The salary levels of directors are specified in the *Basic Agreement*, published by the Directors Guild of America.

10. William Goldman, *The Big Picture: Who Killed Hollywood? And Other Essays* (New York: Applause, 2000); *The End of Cinema as We Know It: American Film in the Nineties*, ed. Jon Lewis (New York: New York University Press, 2001); "The Monster That Ate Hollywood," *Frontline*, PBS, 2001.

Chapter 2

1. Erikson linked the origin of an individual's identity crisis to the adolescent years and posited that those who are not able to resolve the crisis then would be faced with recurring personal conflicts in later stages of life. Erik H. Erikson, *Identity: Youth and Crisis* (New York: Norton, 1968).

2. A few such relevant books on directing include Steven D. Katz, *Film Directing Shot by Shot: Visualizing From Concept to Screen* (Studio City, CA: Michael Wiese Productions, 1991); Michael Rabiger, *Directing: Film Techniques and Aesthetics* (Boston: Focal Press, 1996); and Sidney Lumet, *Making Movies* (New York: Vintage Books, 1995).

3. The jazz band reference is in Eric Sherman (for the American Film Institute), *Directing the Film: Film Directors on the Art* (Los Angeles: Acrobat Books, 1976). The artist/politico notion is in Mark Litwak, *Reel Power*.

4. The classic discussion of this two-dimensional concept of task-oriented and people-oriented leadership is by Robert Freed Bales, *Interaction Process Analysis: A Method for the Study of Small Groups* (Cambridge, MA: Addison Wesley, 1950). For an update see Robert Freed Bales, *Social Interaction Systems: Theory and Measurement* (New Brunswick, NJ: Transaction, 1999). There is a detailed discussion of the contradictory demands on leaders in R&D centers in Donald Pelz, "Creative Tensions in the Research and Development Climate," *Science* 157, no. 3785 (July 1967): 160–65. Some pertinent studies of leadership include Daniel Goleman, *Leadership That Gets Results* (Cambridge, MA: Harvard Business School Press, 2001), 53–85. The leadership grid is shown in Robert R. Blake and Anne Adams McCanse, *Leadership Dilemmas—Grid Solutions* (Houston: Gulf Publishing, 1991).

5. Creative aspects of leadership are discussed in Warren G. Bennis, *On Becoming a Leader* (Reading, MA: Addison Wesley, 1989), 194. A discussion of new ways of working productively with highly creative employees is in Subir Chowdhury, *The Talent Era* (Upper Saddle River, NJ: Prentice Hall, 2002).

Chapter 3

1. The classic love-hate relationship between directors and actors is highlighted in Delia Salvi, *Friendly Enemies: Maximizing the Director-Actor Relationship* (New York: Watson-Guptill, 2003).

2. Judith Weston's remarks are in her book *Directing Actors: Creating Memorable Performances for Film and Television* (Studio City, CA: Michael Wiese Productions, 1996), Sidney Lumet's observations, which follow, are in *Making Movies* (New York: Vintage, 1996).

3. Hackman made these comments to reporter Robert W. Welkos, "Cover Story," *Los Angeles Times*, Calendar Section, 16 December 2001, 9, 94–96.

4. The statistic on actors in Los Angeles was given by Kit Rochlis, Editor-in-Chief of *Los Angeles Magazine*, together with the observation that there are more actors in the movie capital than anyplace else in the world. Kit Rochlis, "What Lies Between," *Los Angeles Magazine* (March 2001): 18. Actors are the messengers of the screenwriter, but they also find ways to embellish the message. Harold Pinter, a writer and actor, believes the actor enters into the character through another door that fleshes out the character in ways the writer never imagined. Mel Gussow, "Pinter Gives Notes on Pinter," *New York Times*, 16 June 2001, 5, 8.

5. Olivier's reflection on acting is in *Merriam-Webster's Dictionary of Quotations* (Springfield, MA: Merriam-Webster, 1992), 413.

6. Brando's quote is in *Merriam-Webster's Dictionary of Quotations*, 412.

7. Weston, *Directing Actors*.

8. Wyler's stand-back technique is described by Susan King, "William Wyler: The Invisible Hand," *Los Angeles Times*, 17 July 2002, 10–11. Despite his seeming passivity, some industry people considered Wyler an extreme perfectionist because of his endless retakes. Paul A. Helmick, *Cut, Print and That's a Wrap: A Hollywood Memoir* (Jefferson, NC: McFarland, 2001).

9. Richard L. Bare, *The Film Director*, 2nd ed. (Foster City, CA: IDG Books Worldwide, 2000).

10. The pioneering work on creativity theory was by Joy Paul Guilford in writings such as *The Nature of Human Intelligence* (New York: McGraw-Hill, 1967) and "Frames of Reference for Creative Behavior in the Arts," in *Creativity: Its Educational Implications*, ed. John Curtis Cowan et al. (Debuque, IA: Kendall/Hunt, 1981).

11. The theoretical underpinnings of the process of creativity are captured in Graham Wallas, *The Art of Thought* (New York: Brace and World, 1926).

Chapter 4

1. Some writings that present intellectual or historical background on the evolving digital era include Thomas Elsaesser and Kay Hoffmann, eds., *Cinema Futures: The Screen Arts in the Digital Age* (Amsterdam: Amsterdam University Press, 1998), and Paolo Cherchi Usai, *The Death of Cinema: History, Cultural Memory and the Digital Dark Age* (London: British Film Institute, 2001). But practical and technical treatments that provide how-to-do-it information on craft aspects are more prevalent. The best of these is probably Thomas A. Ohanian and Michael E. Phillips, *Digital Filmmaking: The Changing Art and Craft of Making Motion Pictures*, 2nd ed. (Oxford: Focal, 2000). Along similar lines are Ben Long and Sonja Schenk, *The Digital Filmmaking Handbook* (Hingham, MA: Charles River Media, 2002); Dale Newton, *Digital Filmmaking 101* (Studio City, CA: Michael Wiese Productions, 2000); Eileen Elsey and Andrew Kelly, *In Short: A Guide to Short Film-making in the Digital Age* (London: BFI Publications, 2002).

2. Coppola's quote is in Stuart Klawans, "Films," *Nation* (29 September 2003): 34–37 (the quote is on page 36).

3. Godfrey Cheshire stated his views in two articles he authored, "The Death of Film" and "The Decay of Cinema," *New York Press*, 30, 31 January 2001, www.nypress.com/12/30/film/film2.cfm; www.newyorkpressess.com12/31/film/film4.cfm (20 November 2003). Paolo Cherchi Usai, *The Death of Cinema*, makes some of the same points about what he sees as deleterious effects of digital on cinema.

4. George Spiro Dibie, "An Art Form With Unlimited Possibilities," *Filmmakers of the Future, Supplement to the International Cinematographers Guild Magazine* (September 2000): 3.

5. The contributions of Cassavetes are documented in Tom Charity, *John Cassavetes: Lifeworks* (London: BFI Publishing, 2001), and Ray Carney, *The Films of John Cassavetes: Pragmatism, Modernism, and the Movies* (New York: Cambridge University Press, 1994).

6. There is a good overview of the Indie movement in Emanuel Levy, *Cinema of Outsiders: The Rise of American Independent Film* (New York: New York University Press, 1999); Greg Merritt, *Celluloid Mavericks: A History of Independent Film* (New York: Thunder's Mouth Press, 2000); Gladstone L. Yearwood, ed., *Black Cinema Esthetics: Issues in Independent Black Filmmaking* (Athens: Center for Afro-American Studies, Ohio University, 1982); and Vincent LoBrutto, *The Encyclopedia of American Independent Filmmaking* (Westport, CT: Greenwood Press, 2002).

7. For further background on early film-on-the-margins, see A. L. Rees, *A History of Experimental Film and Video* (London: British Film Institute, 1999), and P. Adams Sitney, *Visionary Film: The American Avant-Garde 1943–1978*, 2nd ed. (New York: Oxford University Press, 1979).

8. Problems in independent film distribution are detailed in Jon M. Garon, *The Independent Filmmaker's Law and Business Guide: Shooting and Distributing Independent and Digital Films* (Chicago: A Cappella Books, 2002).

9. Mounting submissions at Sundance are outlined by Geoffrey Gilmore in his article "Long Live Indie Film: Reports of Its Demise Have Been Exaggerated," *Nation* (2 April 2001): 17–20.

10. Gilmore discusses pitfalls and confusions in defining the Indies in "Long Live Indie Film."

11. Expansion in art-house venues is reported by Mindy Sink, "Arts in America," *New York Times*, Arts Section, 4 July 2002, 2.

12. The growing use of previsualization is detailed in P. J. Huffstutter, "What's a Movie Before It's a Movie?" *Los Angeles Times*, Section C, 16 July 2003, 1, 12.

13. Michael Allen, *Contemporary US Cinema* (New York: Longman, 2003).

14. Everett M. Rogers, *Diffusion of Innovations*, 5th ed. (New York: Free Press, 2003), is the lead book on innovation and change. Related books on technological change include Rosalind Williams, *Retooling: A Historian Confronts Technological Change* (Cambridge: MIT Press, 2002); Vijay Mahajan and Robert A. Peterson, *Models for Innovation Diffusion* (Beverly Hills: Sage, 1985); and Malcolm Gladwell, *The Tipping Point: How Little Things Can Make a Big Difference* (Boston: Little, Brown, 2002). My own research in this field is in Jack Rothman et al., *Marketing Human Service Innovations* (Beverly Hills: Sage, 1983).

15. The Allison Anders quote is from an interview—David Geffner, "Collaborations: Directors and Cinematographers Go Digital," *DGA Magazine*, January 2003, www.dga.org/news/v27_5/indie_collaborations.php3 (16 November 2003).

16. Thomas Elsaesser, "Cinema Futures: Convergence, Divergence, Difference," in *Cinema Futures: Cain, Abel or Cable?*, ed. Thomas Elsaesser and Kay Hoffmann (Amsterdam: Amsterdam University Press, 1998), 9–26 (quote is on page 26).

Chapter 5

1. There is a brief history of the Directors Guild drive to win creative rights— including the director's cut—in Kristine Andersen, "The Rights of Spring," *DGA Magazine* 21, no. 1 (March/April 1996): 20. Also see *DGA Creative Rights Handbook, 2000–2002* (Los Angeles: Directors Guild of America, 2000).

2. An elaborated history of relevant developments in filmmaking is in Bruce T. Torrence, *Hollywood: The First Hundred Years* (New York: New York Zoetrope, 1982); Douglas Gomery, *Movie History: A Survey* (Belmont, CA: Wadsworth, 1991); Lary May, *Screening Out the Past: The Birth of Mass Culture and the Motion Picture Industry* (Chicago: University of Chicago Press, 1980); Karl Brown, *Adventures with D. W. Griffith* (New York: Farrar, Straus & Giroux, 1973).

3. Contractual specifications on cutting allowance time and other provisions regarding filmmakers' prerogatives for a "director's cut" are in *DGA 2002 Basic Agreement* (Los Angeles: Directors Guild of America, 2002), Section 3, 104, and Section 7, 504–5. The Berne Convention began its work in September 1886 and completed its first draft of principles on May 4, 1896. There was a series of continuing revisions in 1908, 1914, 1928, 1948, 1967, 1971, and

an amendment in 1979. For the basic document, see *Intellectual Property Conference of Stockholm, 1967. International Convention for the Protection of Literary and Artistic Works; Proposals for Revising the Substantive Copyright Provisions (Articles 1 to 20) Prepared by the Government of Sweden with the Assistance of BIRPI* (Geneva: United International Bureaux for the Protection of Intellectual Property, 1966).

4. Robert Altman speaks of his script ruses in Alain Silver and Gary Walkow, "Indie Films—Robert Altman," *DGA Magazine* 25, no. 5 (January 2001): 63–67.

5. Moral rights are embedded in the Berne Convention for the Protection of Literary and Artistic Works.

6. This quote is in "Remarks From Elliot Silverstein at the 2000 John Huston Award Dinner," www. artistsrights.org/cf/news/detail.cfm?QID=641 (25 March 2002).

7. The books on directing I reviewed, written by working directors and academics, and giving sparse coverage to organizational politics in the director's role repertoire, include: Harold Clurman, *On Directing* (New York: Fireside, 1997); Renée Harmon, *Film Directing: Killer Style and Cutting Edge Technique* (Los Angeles: Lone Eagle, 1998); Steven D. Katz, *Film Directing Shot by Shot: Visualizing From Concept to Screen* (Studio City: Michael Wiese Productions, 1991); Carl Linder, *Filmmaking: A Practical Guide* (Englewood Cliffs, NJ: Prentice-Hall, 1976); Sidney Lumet, *Making Movies* (New York: Vintage Books, 1995); David Mamet, *On Directing Film* (New York: Penguin Books, 1992); Michael Rabinger, *Directing: Film Techniques and Aesthetics*, 3rd ed. (Boston: Focal Press, 2003); Ken Russell, *Directing Film: The Director's Art From Script to Cutting Room* (Washington, DC: Brassey's, 2001); John Sayles, *Thinking in Pictures: The Making of the Movie "Matewan"* (Cambridge, MA: Da Capo, 2003); Judith Weston, *The Film Director's Intuition* (Studio City, CA: Michael Wiese Productions, 2003).

8. Ground-breaking research on interpersonal influence was conducted by John R. P. French and Bertram Raven and reported by them in "The Bases of Social Power," in *Studies in Social Power*, ed. Dorwin Cartwright (Ann Arbor: University of Michigan, 1959), 150–67. Elaboration on the theory is in Paul Hersey et al., *Management of Organizational Behavior: Leading Human Resources*, 8th ed. (Upper Saddle River, NJ: Prentice-Hall, 2001); Jeffrey Pfeffer, *Managing With Power: Politics and Influence in Organizations* (Boston: Harvard Business School Press, 1992); and William L. Gardner and Bruce J. Alovio, "The Charismatic Relationship: A Dramaturgical Perspective," *Academy of Management Journal* 23, no.1 (1998): 32–58.

9. These data and other information on DVD developments are reported by Richard Natale, "Press Play to Access the Future," *Los Angeles Times*, Calendar Section, 7 April 2002, 4, 80.

Chapter 6

1. An overall review of the place of ethnic groups in filmmaking is in James Robert Parish, *Encyclopedia of Ethnic Groups in Hollywood* (New York: Facts on File, 2003).

2. There's further information on the historically changing role of women filmmakers in Ally Acker, *Reel Women: Pioneers of the Cinema* (New York: Continuum, 1991), and Susan Brownmiller, *In Our Time: Memoir of a Revolution* (New York: Dial Press, Random, 1999).

3. Mollie Gregory, *Women Who Run the Show* (New York: St. Martin's Press, 2002).

4. "DGA Annual Report on Women and Minority Hiring Reveals Bleak Industry Record for 1999," Directors Guild of America Release, Office of Charles Warn, Los Angeles, January 2001. Updated data were furnished through a personal communication to the author from the DGA Department of Communications and Media Relations, April 2003.

5. Martha M. Lauzen, "The Celluloid Ceiling: Behind-the-Scenes Employment of Women in the Top 250 Films of 2001," Statistics on Women Directors, www. moviesbywomen.com/ Stats2001.html (29 June 2003).

6. Further discussion of Latinos in the film industry is in Harry P. Pachon et al., *Missing in Action: Latinos in and out of Hollywood* (Los Angeles: Thomas Rivera Center, Screen Actors Guild, 1999); Gary D. Keller, *Hispanics and United States Film: An Overview and Handbook* (Tempe, AZ: Bilingual Press/Editorial Bilingue, 1994). For Asian Americans, see Roger Garcia, ed., *Out of the Shadows: Asians in American Cinema* (New York: Asian CineVision, 2001); Peter X. Feng, ed., *Screening Asian Americans* (New Brunswick: Rutgers University Press, 2002). For African Americans, see Mark Reid, *Redefining Black Film* (Berkeley: University of California Press, 1993), and Jesse Algeron Rhines, *Black Film/White Money* (New Brunswick: Rutgers University Press, 1996).

7. Patrick Goldstein makes this observation on women executives not supporting other women in his column "The Big Picture," *Los Angeles Times*, 8 April 2003, E1, E6.

8. These estimates on women and minority decision makers in green-lighting films are given by Lorenz Muñoz in her article "Diversity in Oscars Still Elusive," *Los Angeles Times*, 24 March 2001, 1, 17. The subject is discussed more broadly by Edith Folb, "Who's Got the Room at the Top? Issues of Dominance and Nondominance in Intracultural Communication," in Larry A. Samover and Richard E. Porter, eds., *Intercultural Communication: A Reader* (Belmont, CA: Wadsworth, 1985), 119–27.

9. Tell-all reporter/voyeur Paul Rosenfield dissects the "Old Boys" social network in *The Club Rules: Power, Money, Sex and Fear—How It Works in Hollywood* (Los Angeles: Warner Books, 1992).

10. Further discussion of the breakthrough in black filmmaking is in Thomas Cripps, "*Sweet Sweetback's Baad Asssss Song* and the Changing Politics of Genre Film," in *Close Viewings: An Anthology of New Film Criticism*, ed. Peter Lehman (Tallahassee: Florida State University Press, 1990), 238–61. Also Gerald Martinez et al., *What It Is, What It Was!: The Black Film Explosion of the 70s in Words and Pictures* (New York: Hyperion/Miramax Books, 1998).

11. Lynda Obst writes of the retreat by women filmmakers in "Calling Susan Faludi," *Los Angeles Times Book Review*, 17 November 2002, 16.

Chapter 7

1. The often tumultuous history of writers in Hollywood is recounted in Tom Stempel, *Framework: A History of Screenwriting in the American Film* (New York: Continuum, 1991).

2. Hortense Powdermaker, *Hollywood: The Dream Factory* (Boston: Little, Brown, 1950).

3. Background on the guild is in "History of the Writers Guild of America," Writers Guild of America, http//www.essortment.com/historywriters_rjuh.htm (2 October 2002).

4. Glimmerings of "development hell" are in Peter Lefcourt and Laura J. Shapiro, eds., *The First Time I Got Paid for It: Writers' Tales From the Hollywood Trenches* (New York: Public Affairs, 2000).

5. A good summary of conflicts and contentions between writers and directors is spelled out in Michael Cieply, "Creative Tensions: The WGA-DGA Divide," *Los Angeles Times*, Section M, 22 July 2001, 3.

6. Frances Marion is quoted in Marsha McCreadie, *The Women Who Write the Movies: From Frances Marion to Nora Ephron* (Secaucus, NJ: Carol Publishing, 1994), 34. Jorja Prover's

book is *No One Knows Their Names: Screenwriters in Hollywood* (Bowling Green, OH: Bowling Green State University Popular Press, 1994).

7. The writers' income data is from Writers Guild of America, *2002 WGA Annual Report to Writers*, "The Marketplace for Film, Television and Other Audio-Visual Writers," www.wga.org/annual/2002/market.html (5 November 2003).

8. David Lean's cable is reproduced in Ted Elrick, "A Film By," *DGA Magazine* (June/July 1998): 39–43 (quote is on page 42).

9. The Directors Guild analyzed and responded to John Wells's statement in Ted Elrick, "Here They Go Again," *DGA Magazine*, November 1999, www.dga.org/thedga/cr_here_they_go.php3 (21 November 2003).

10. Phil Alden Robinson and Tom Schulman, Writers Guild of America, "Dear DGA: Thy Name Is," www.wga.org/WrittenBy/0400/dga.html (19 November 2003).

11. The relevant theories are articulated in Andrew Abbott, *The System of Professions: An Essay on the Division of Expert Labor* (Chicago: University of Chicago Press, 1988).

12. This analysis of conflict in organizational and professional contexts draws on John R. Schermerhorn et al., *Organizational Behavior*, 8th ed., especially the chapter on "Conflict and Negotiation" (New York: John Wiley, 2000), and Jennifer M. George and Gareth R. Jones, *Essentials of Managing Organizational Behavior*, especially the chapter on "Managing Power, Politics, Conflict, and Negotiation" (San Francisco: Jossey-Bass, 1997).

13. Lewis A. Coser, *The Functions of Social Conflict* (Glencoe, IL: Free Press, 1956).

14. An informed review of power dynamics and creative relationships in the writer-director duality is in Sean Mitchell, "Lip Service," *Los Angeles Times Magazine*, 25 March 2001, 16–19. Also see Brian Lowry, "Power Play: Credit the Writer or the Director?" *Los Angeles Times*, Section F, 28 February 2001, 1, 11.

Chapter 8

1. D. W. Griffith, "The Movies 100 Years From Now," quoted in *Film Makers on Film Making: Statements on Their Art by Thirty Directors*, ed. Harry M. Geduld (Bloomington: Indiana University Press, 1967), 49–55.

2. Arthur De Vany, *Hollywood Economics: How Extreme Uncertainty Shapes the Film Industry* (New York: Routledge, 2004).

3. Mark Litwak, *Reel Power: The Struggle for Influence and Success in the New Hollywood* (New York: Plume, 1986).

4. Puttnam's observations on these matters are in David Puttnam, with Neil Watson, *Movies and Money* (New York: Knopf, 1998).

5. Attendance data is in Motion Picture Association, Worldwide Market Research, "2002 U.S. Movie Attendance Study," www.mpaa.org/useconomicreview/ 2002_2002_Review. pdf (10 November 2003).

6. Dwight Macdonald's statement is in his article, "A Theory of Mass Culture," in *Mass Culture: The Popular Arts in America*, ed. Bernard Rosenberg and David Manning White (Glencoe, IL: Free Press, 1957), 59–73 (quote is on page 61).

7. These data are in the cited Motion Picture Association study. Patrick Goldstein makes the same observation about the emergence of a mature and stable audience, "A Graying, Older Audience," *Los Angeles Times*, Section F, 4 September 2002, 1, 5.

8. Jonathan Rosenbaum, *Movie Wars: How Hollywood and the Media Conspire to Limit What Films We Can See* (Chicago: A Cappella, 2000).

9. Chandler's musings were in an article about the 1946 Oscar ceremony written for *The Atlantic Monthly* and excerpted from "The Raymond Chandler papers: Selected Letters and Non-Fiction, 1909–1959" in Stephen Schwartz, "Hollywood's Big Sleep," *Nation* (2 April 2001): 50.

10. Stephen Lowenstein, *My First Movie: Twenty Celebrated Directors Talk About Their First Film* (New York: Pantheon Books, 2001).

11. Max Weber analyzes bureaucracies in *The Theory of Social and Economic Organization*, translated by A. M. Henderson and T. Parsons (New York: Free Press, 1947).

12. The potential for adaptability in organizations is discussed in Edward E. Lawler III, et al., *Creating a Strategic Human Resources Organization: An Assessment of Trends and New Directions* (Stanford, CA: Stanford University Press, 2003). Also see Arnold S. Judson, *Changing Behavior in Organizations: Minimizing Resistance to Change* (Cambridge, MA: B. Blackwell, 1991).

13. There is good information on procedures and their problems—how to set them up and how to change them—in the literature of policy implementation. Michael Hill and Peter Hupe, *Implementing Public Policy: Governance in Theory and Practice* (Thousand Oaks, CA: Sage, 2002). Also see Robert E. Lane, "Why Businessmen Violate the Law," *Journal of Criminal Law, Criminology and Police Science* 44 (1953): 151, 154–60.

14. Directors Guild of America, *DGA Creative Rights Handbook, 2000–2002* (Los Angeles: Directors Guild of America, no date).

15. William Fadiman's comments are in his book *Hollywood Now* (New York: Liveright, 1972), 155–56.

16. Martin Dale, *The Movie Game: The Film Business in Britain, Europe and America* (London: Cassell, Wellington House, 1997).

17. The market share statistics are in "Moreover: Culture Wars," *Economist*, 12–18 September 1998, www.marshallinside.usc.edu/mweinstein/teaching/fbe552secure/notes/economist.html (20 November 2003).

18. The early history of the French film industry is covered in Sir Austen Chamberlain, *Twenty-Five Years A King: The Book of the Pathé Film* (London: Black, 1935).

19. U.S. cinema's economic and cultural hegemony is analyzed in Kerry Segrave, *American Films Abroad: Hollywood's Domination of the World's Movie Screens From the 1890s to the Present* (Jefferson, NC: McFarland, 1997), and John Tomlinson, *Cultural Imperialism: A Critical Introduction* (Baltimore: Johns Hopkins University Press, 1991). Other countries have a national "film policy" that drives their cinematic activities; the U.S. functions as though it has none of that, although the MPAA serves as an informal proxy for government in this connection. For a review of the film policy concept, see Albert Moran, ed., *Film Policy: International, National, and Regional Perspectives* (London: Routledge, 1996).

20. I develop these concepts of planned change more fully in Jack Rothman, "Approaches to Community Intervention," in Jack Rothman et al., *Strategies of Community Intervention* (Itasca, IL: F. E. Peacock, 2001), 27–64. A somewhat similar formulation, but geared to urban planning issues, is in John Friedman, *Planning in the Public Domain: From Knowledge to Action* (Princeton, NJ: Princeton University Press, 1987).

Chapter 9

1. The "New Hollywood" is a somewhat imprecise term for a complex phenomenon. Efforts aimed at definition are by Jim Hillier, *The New Hollywood* (New York: Continuum, 1992), and

James Bernardoni, *The New Hollywood: What the Movies Did With the New Freedoms of the Seventies* (Jefferson, NC: McFarland, 1991).

2. The studio system is described, from a positive point of view, in Thomas Schatz, *The Genius of the System: Hollywood Filmmaking in the Studio Era* (New York: Henry Holt, 1996). Some of the early Hollywood history is captured concisely in Louis Giannetti and Scott Eyman, *Flashback: A Brief History of Film*, 4th ed. (Upper Saddle River, NJ: Prentice Hall, 2001).

3. A broad analysis of the Paramount case is in Ralph Cassidy, *Impact of the Paramount Decision on Motion Picture Distribution and Price Making* (Los Angeles: University of Southern California, 1958).

4. U.S. Department of Commerce, *The Migration of U.S. Film and Television Production: Impact of "Runaways" on Workers and Small Business in the U.S. Film Industry* (Washington, DC: U.S. Department of Commerce, 2001). Monitor Company, *The Economic Impact of U.S. Film and Television Runaway Production* (Santa Monica: Monitor, June 1999).

5. The work of Storper and his associates is reported in Michael Storper, *The Regional World* (New York: Guilford Press, 1997), and Michael Storper and Susan Christopherson, *The Changing Organization and Location of the Motion Picture Industry: Interregional Shifts in the United States* (Los Angeles: University of California, Los Angeles, Graduate School of Architecture and Urban Planning, 1985).

6. David F. Prindle, *Risky Business: The Political Economy of Hollywood* (Boulder, CO: Westview, 1993). Arthur De Vany, *Hollywood Economics: How Extreme Uncertainty Shapes the Film Industry* (New York: Routledge, 2004).

7. An example of the use of turbulent environment analysis is in Gabriel Goren, "The Management of Computing in a Turbulent Environment: Organizational Responses to the Advent of Personal Computing," Dissertation, University of California, Irvine, 1986.

8. The "Big Opening–Fast Fade" mania is documented in Rick Lyman, "Even Blockbusters Find Fame Fleeting in a Multiplex Age," *New York Times*, Section A, 13 August 2001, 1, 12.

9. Verlyn Klinkenborg, "The Blockbuster Culture of Summer," *New York Times*, 19 August 2001, 12.

10. Cassavetes's contributions are chronicled in Tom Charity, *John Cassavetes: Lifeworks* (London: Omnibus, 2001).

11. Donald Barthelme, *Snow White* (New York: Atheneum, 1967); cited by John Powers, "It Ain't Cool," *LA Weekly*, 29 March–4 April 2002, 16.

Index

~

About the Author

Jack Rothman, author and researcher, has been a professor at the distinguished level at UCLA and currently holds emeritus status. He also has taught at the University of Michigan and the University of Pittsburgh. He has a Ph.D. from Columbia University, where he organized his studies around social psychology, with a focus on sociological analysis. He also hold a master's degree in social work from Ohio State University.

Rothman's research has centered on community and organizational analysis, including planned change in social institutions. This covers ethnic neighborhoods in Pittsburgh, the automotive industry in Detroit, local social service departments in Great Britain, and mental health agencies in Los Angeles.

Professor Rothman has had some twenty-five books published by leading companies (Wiley, Allyn and Bacon, Longman, Columbia University Press, Prentice-Hall, and others). He has also published in the *Nation*, the *Los Angeles Times* Op-Ed pages, *Social Policy*, and the *Humanist*.

After moving to Los Angeles, he turned his attention to the film industry, the dominant social institution in the region. The UCLA Faculty Senate sponsored his study of social science research findings on filmmaking.

Rothman received the Gunner Myrdal award of the Evaluation Research Society, and the Outstanding Lifetime Achievement Award of the Society for Community Organization and Social Administration. He has received Fulbright Senior Research Fellowships for studies in Great Britain and Israel. Jack Rothman has been a lifelong member of the American Sociological Association and the National Association of Social Workers.

For diversions, he can be seen surfing the Santa Monica beach *bike* path or doing off-hours stand-up comedy performances at clubs around Los Angeles such as the Comedy Store, the Improv, and the Ice House.